Warbird Pinup Girls

A TRIBUTE TO THE 1940'S NOSE ART PINUP GIRLS

PHOTOGRAPHS BY CHRISTIAN KIEFFER

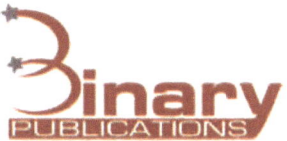

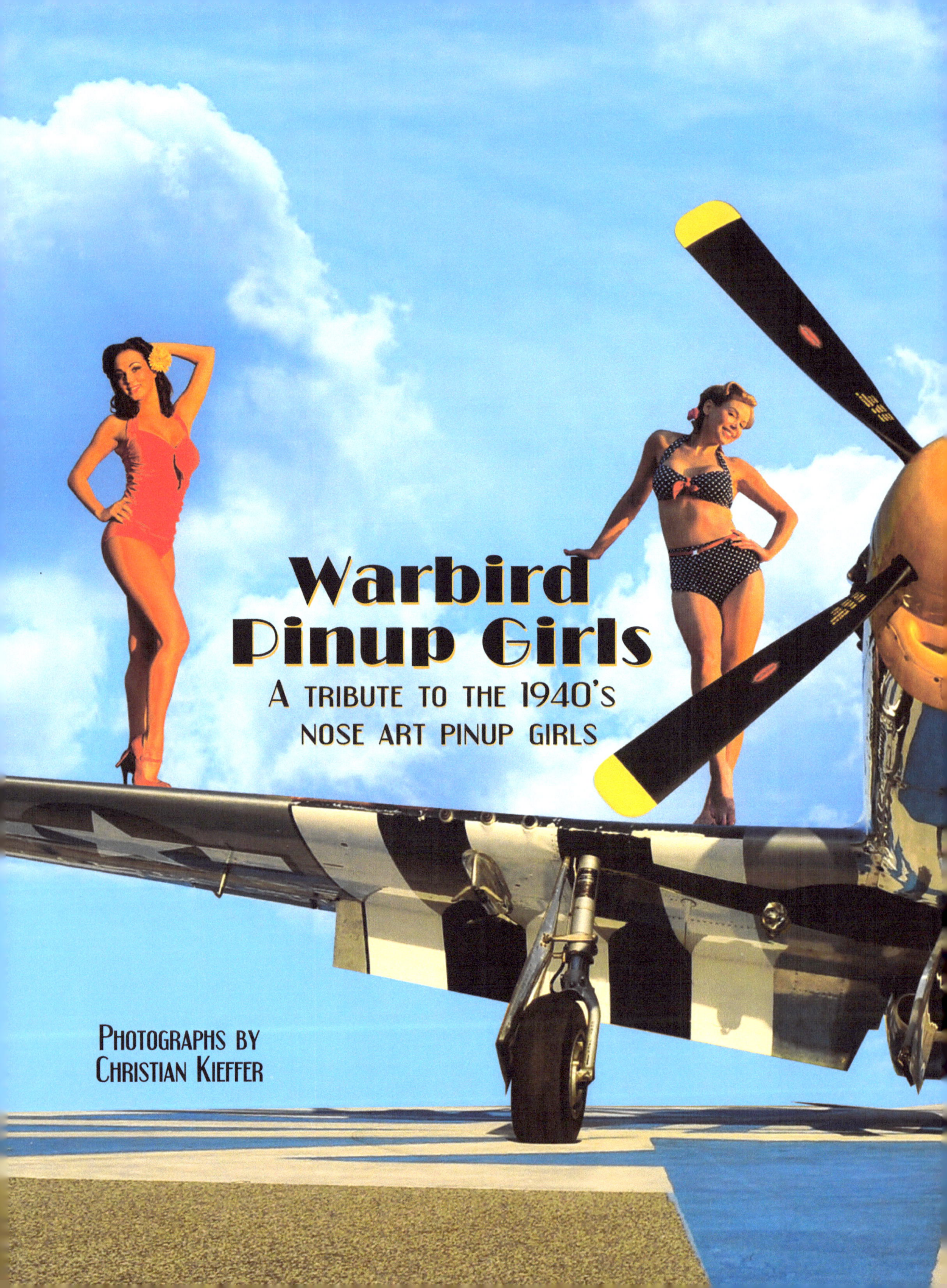

Warbird Pinup Girls

A TRIBUTE TO THE 1940's NOSE ART PINUP GIRLS

PHOTOGRAPHS BY
CHRISTIAN KIEFFER

INTRODUCTION

I don't think there has ever been anything more romantic than a pilot who honors his heart's desire by painting her on the side of his fighter plane. Nose art, that's what they call it. In WWII the command structure allowed this American folk art to be procured as a way to keep morale high and also as a way to bring a sense of individuality to the cold mechanized way of life that the pilots and crews endured in the days of war. I have always been a huge enthusiast of warbirds and the life of a WWII fighter pilot. As a child I had reoccurring dreams of flying with the famous AVG "Flying Tigers".

I often wonder if I wasn't reincarnated from this historic time. The nose art was hard to ignore, as they were often the beautiful starlets of 1940's Hollywood. Many of them were nude yet were never too reveling and had nicknames that often only the crew understood. Nose art came in many forms not just beautiful women but cartoon characters and other designs and names, but it was the ladies that caught my eye. Many of these images and names became undeniably famous, like the "Enola Gay" which adorned the B-29 that dropped the nuclear bomb on Japan or the B-17 "Memphis Belle" which was brought to greater fame in the 1990 Hollywood picture of the same name. These icons were one of a kind and showed the real character of a great nation that went to war and did its duty. My book is a tribute to the warriors who rode the wind and the ladies that brought them home.

When WWII ended, tens of thousands of airplanes were returning from overseas to be flown directly to the junkyard and chopped up for scrap. Many of these beautiful works of art went right with them and were lost forever. There have been a few of these panels preserved just before being destroyed but the lions share are lost forever only to be remembered in photographs.

Years later I remember reading that shortly after the first Gulf war the armed forces decided that nose art was no longer a proper discipline and pulled all forms of it from military aircraft. I thought this was a sad day and the true end to a golden age. Long live the Pinup Girl.

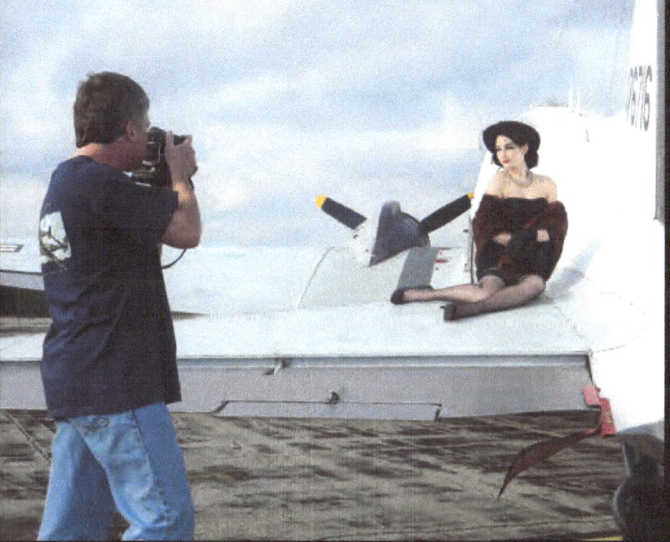

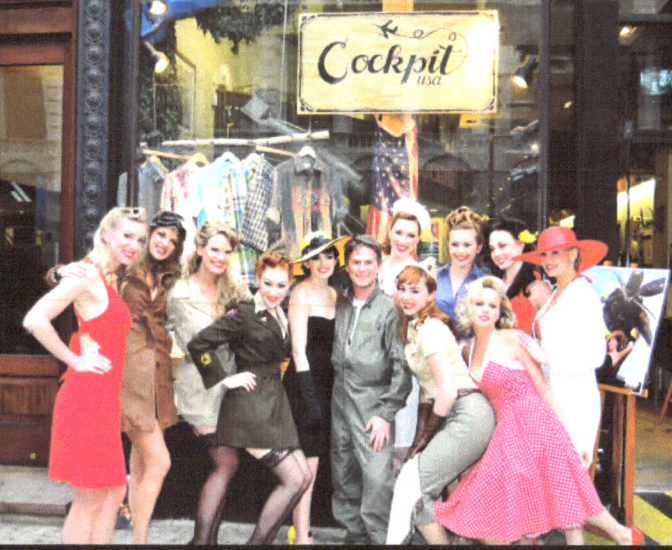

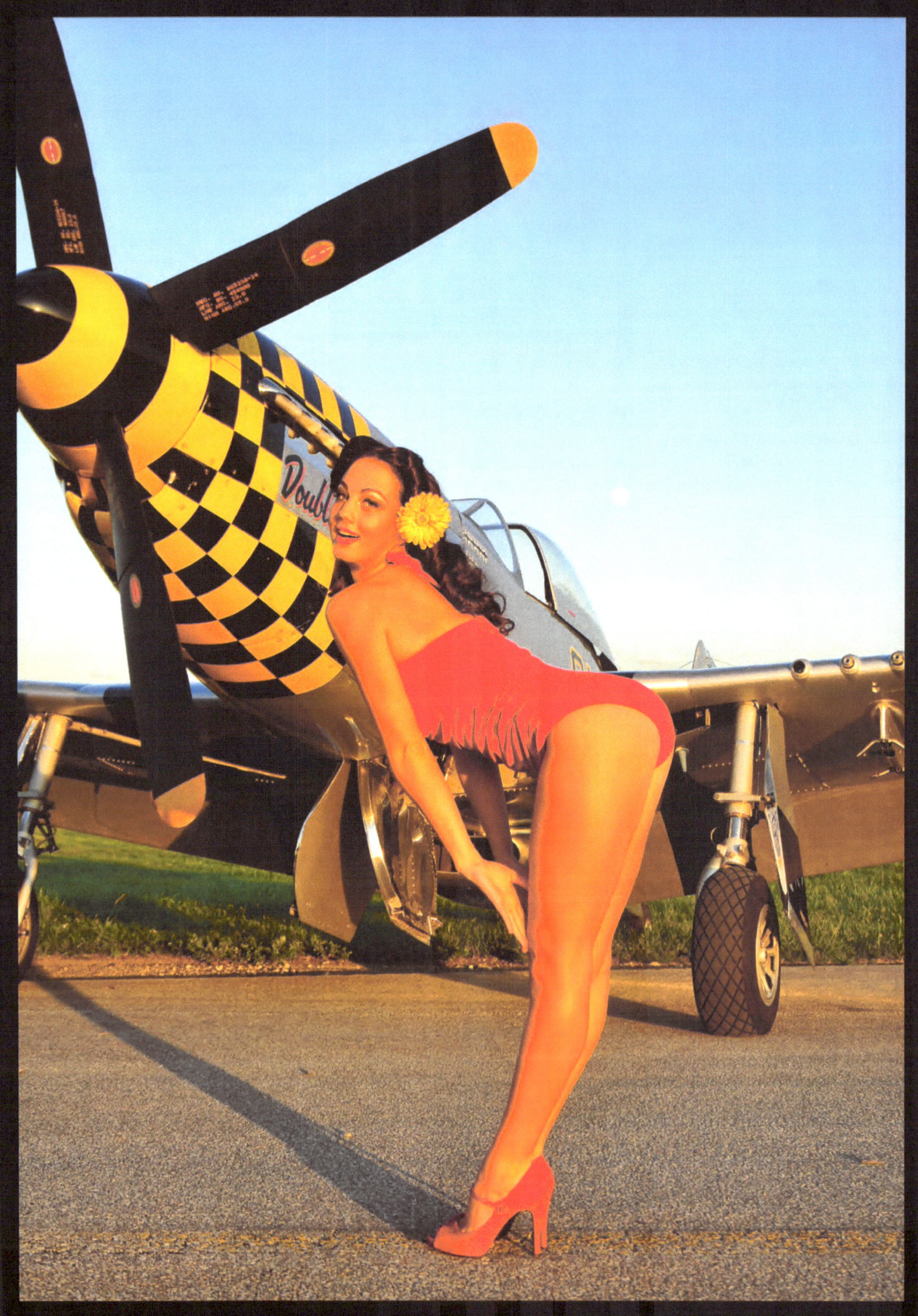

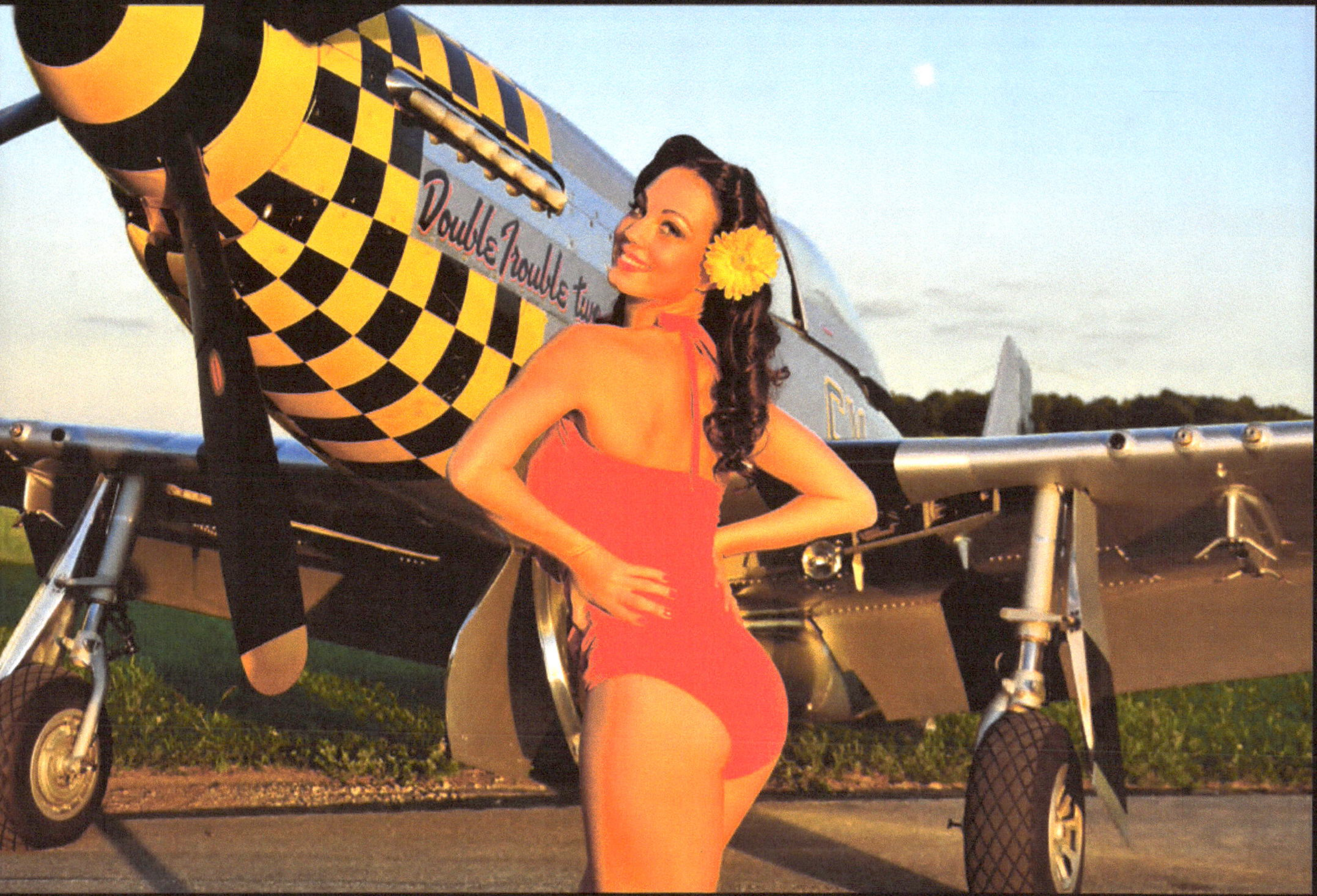

JESSICA

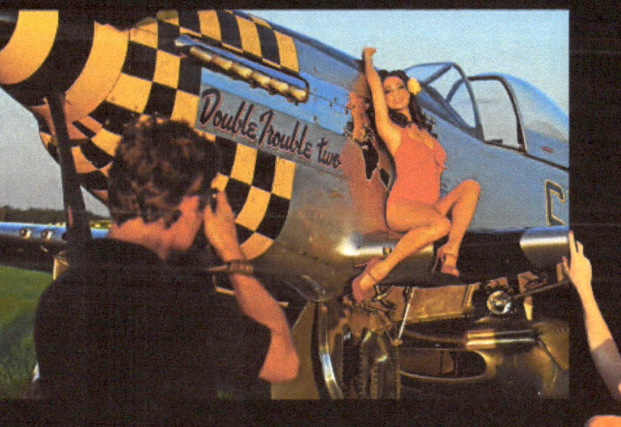

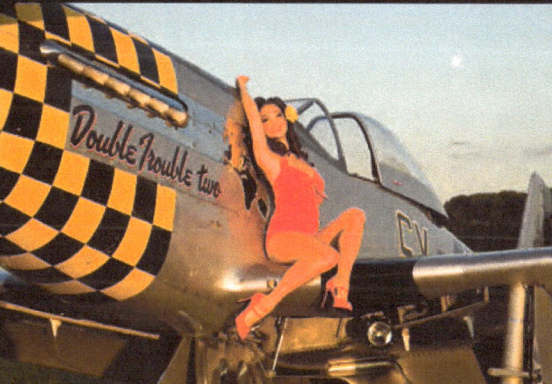

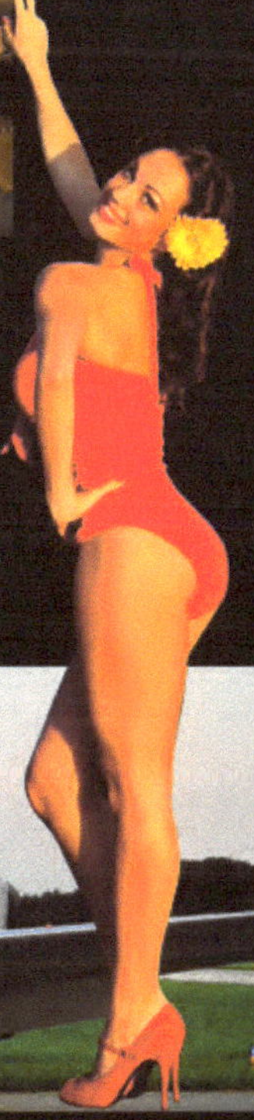

The P-51D "Double Trouble II" was part of the famed "Horsemen" trio, an acrobatic Mustang team.
The Horsemen team was traveling through my area and I managed to catch all three which are featured in our 2011 Warbird Pinup Girls calendar.

August 2011 pinup girl Jessica or as she is affectionately known as "Jessica Rabbit", Jessica is a professional dancer now working in Hollywood.
She represents one of my all time favorite looks of all the Warbird Pinup Girls.

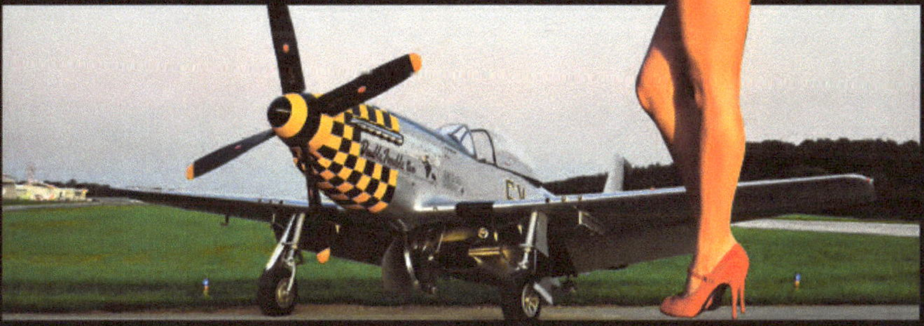

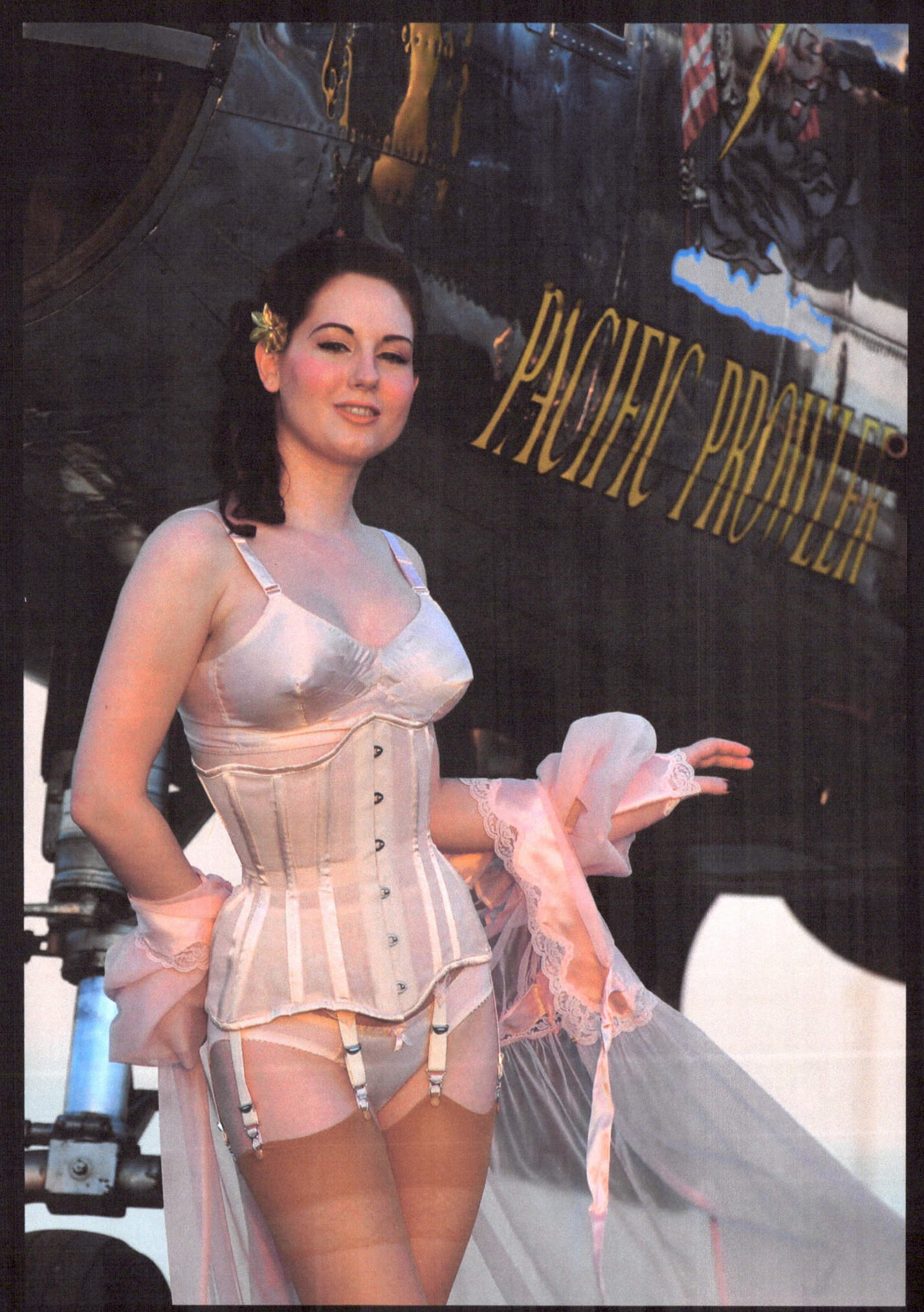

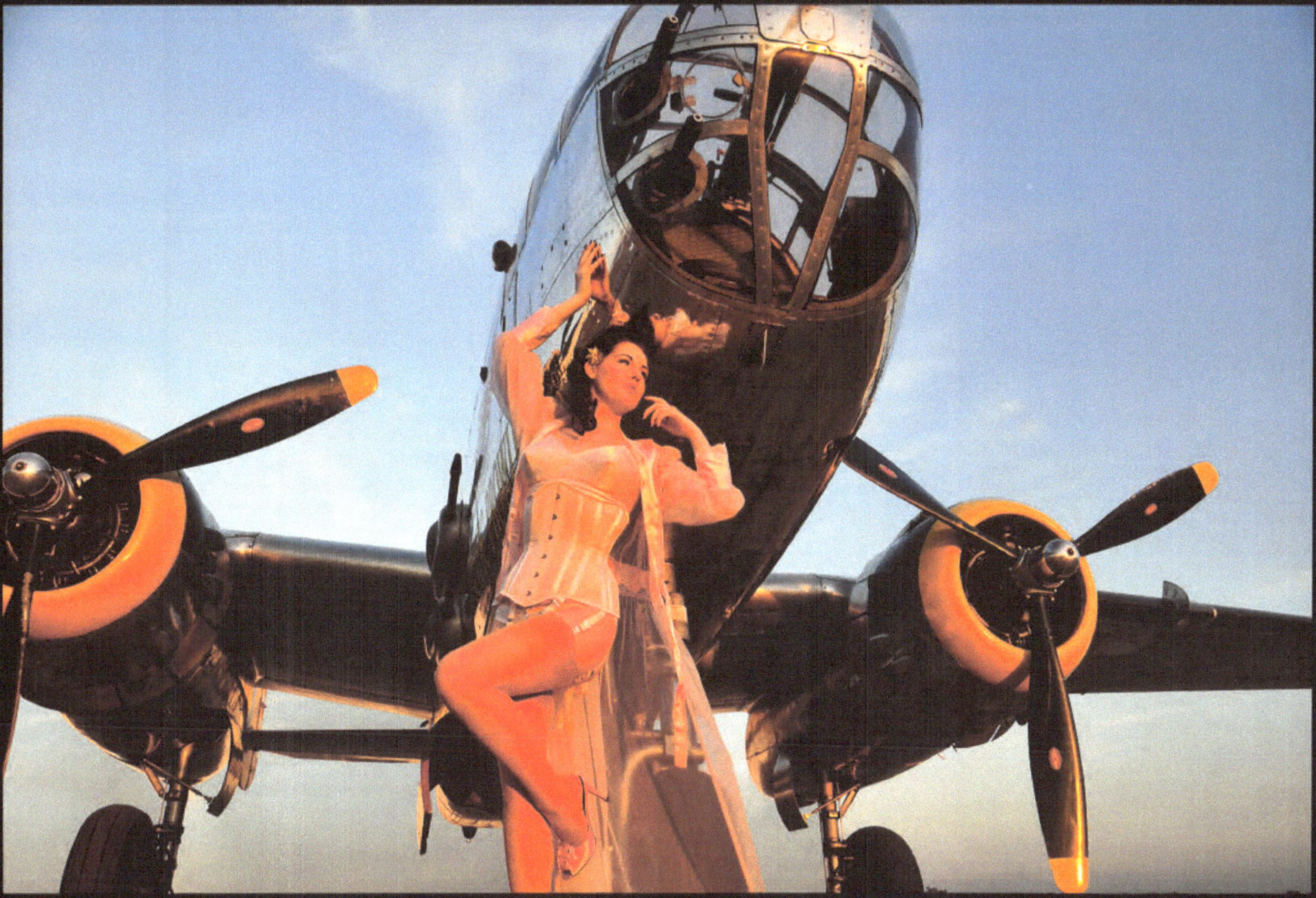

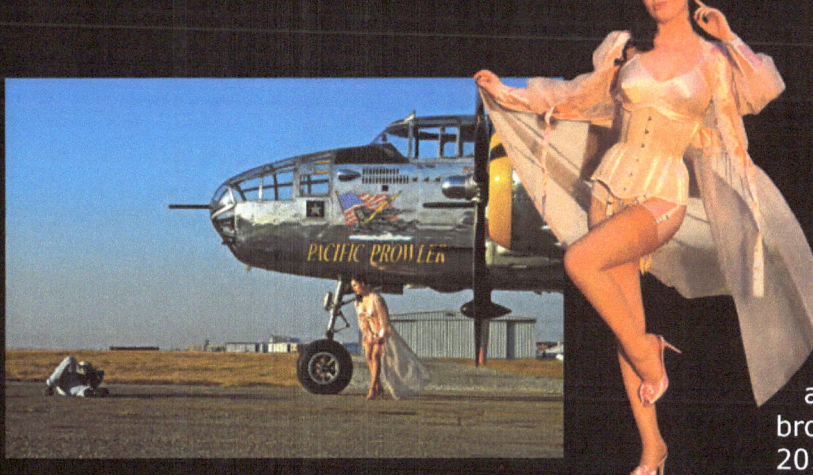

Angela

The Pacific Prowler is a "J" Model North American B-25 Mitchell. The original Prowler was deployed to the Pacific Theater and flew over 120 missions before returning home after the war.

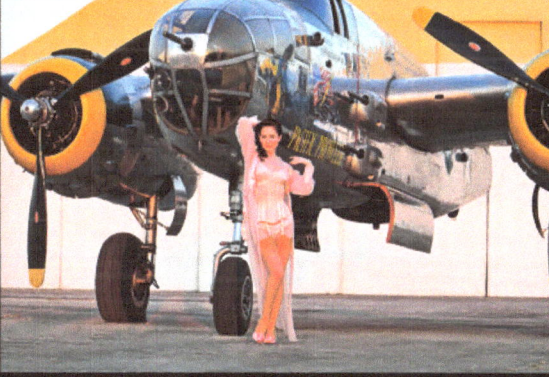

Angela is one of the country's premier pinup and burlesque artists. She travels nation-wide performing at many of the top venues. Angela is pure pleasure to work with as she is a true pinup girl and is so versatile we brought her back to reappear in the 2014 Warbird Pinup Girls calendar.

The "Pacific Prowler" resides in Dallas Texas at the Vintage Flying Museum where she serves as a training plane for those who want to learn to fly this legendary WWII airplane.

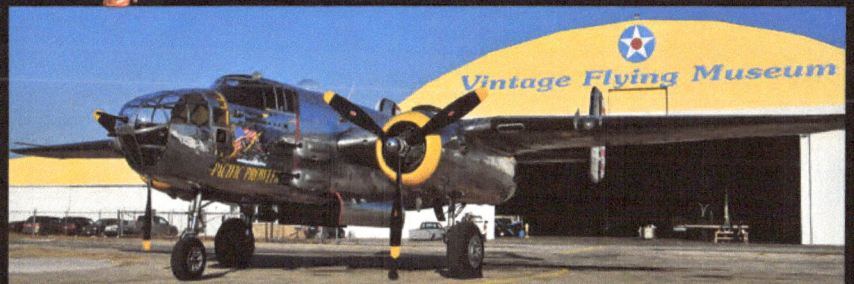

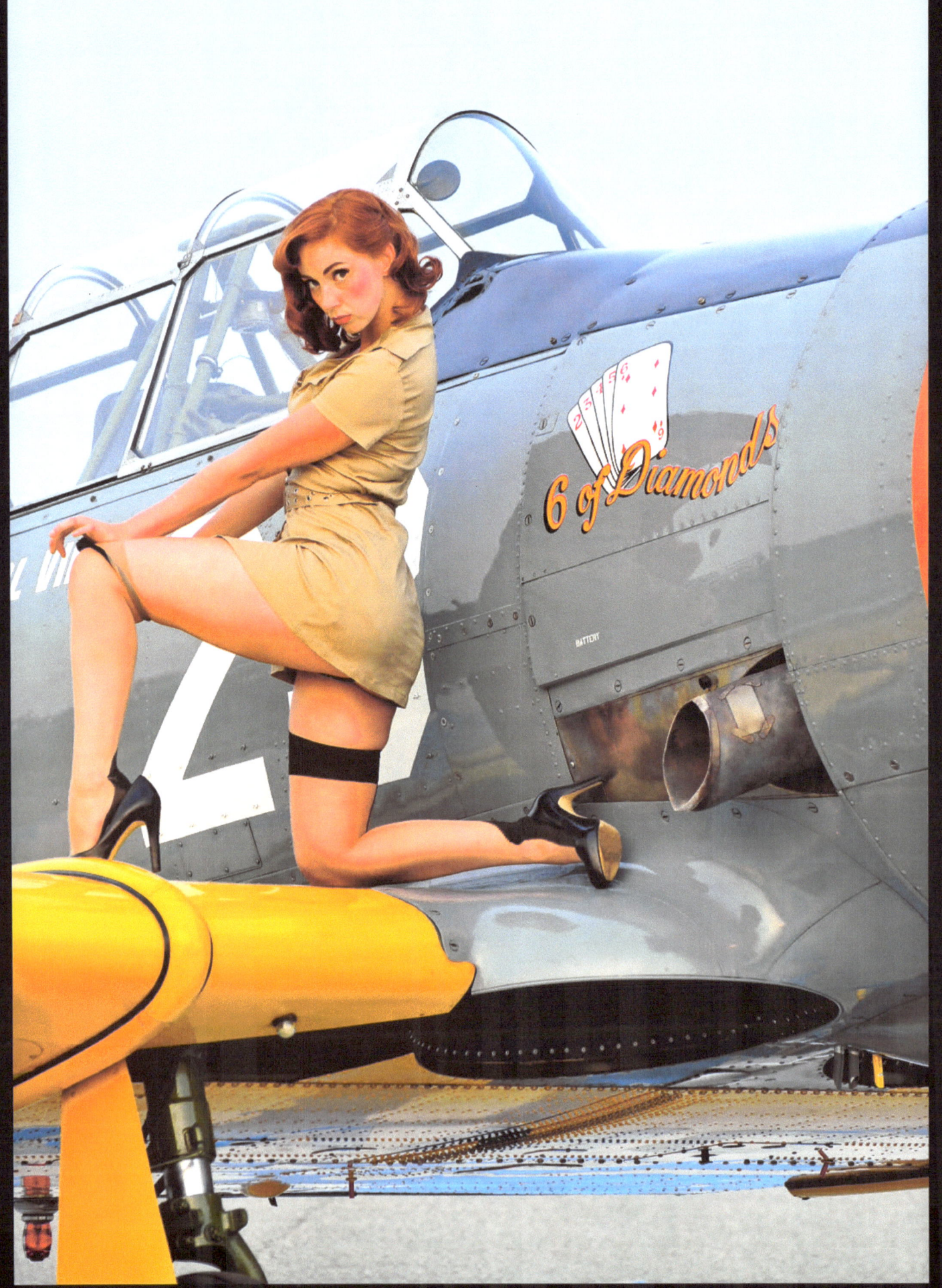

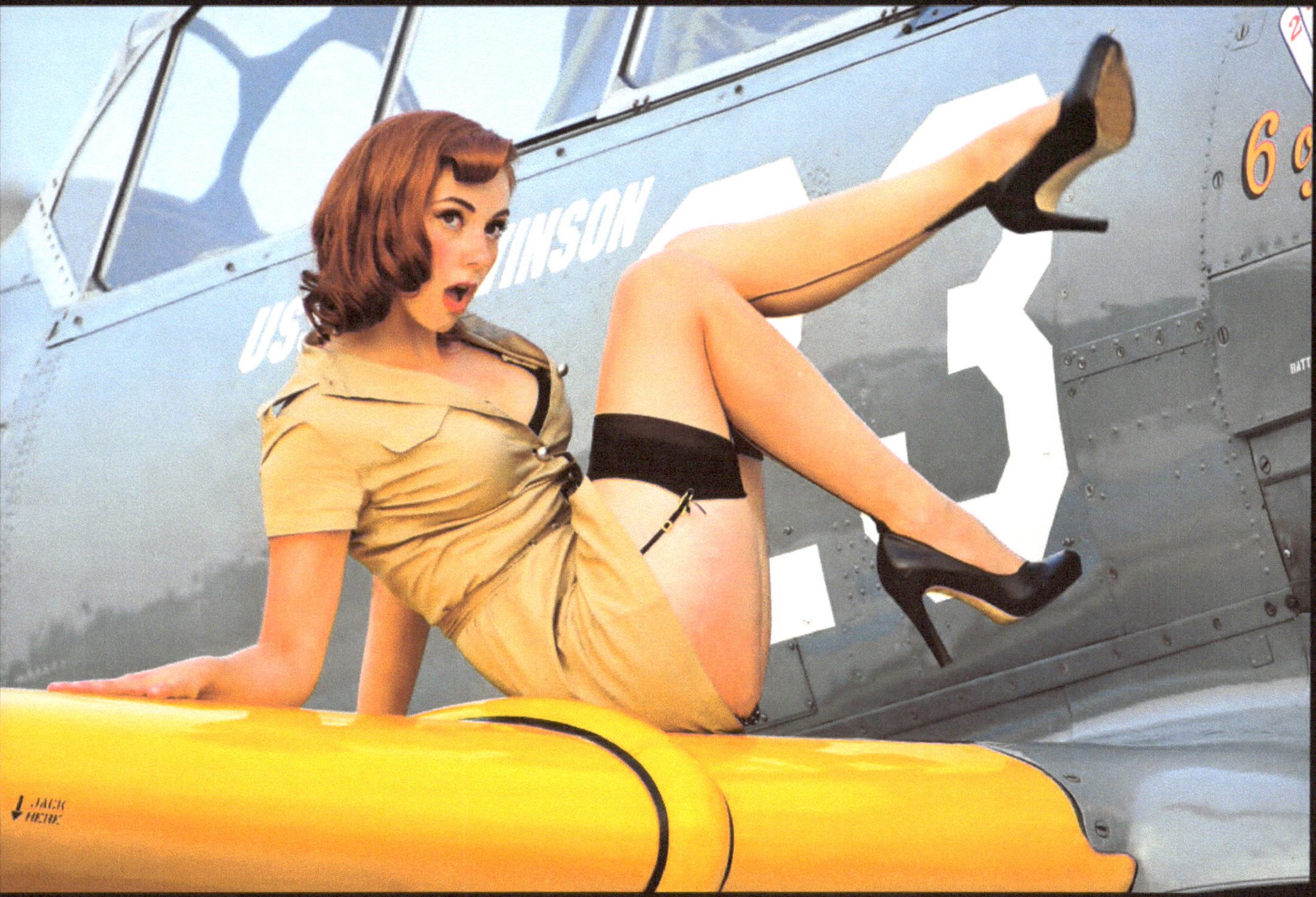

KACIE

The T-6 Texan was a single-engine advanced trainer aircraft used to train pilots. The T-6 Texan has a reputation as a rugged and trustworthy WWII trainer. The T-6 did see combat in many theaters and many wars. This beautiful example lives in Coatesville Pennsylvania.

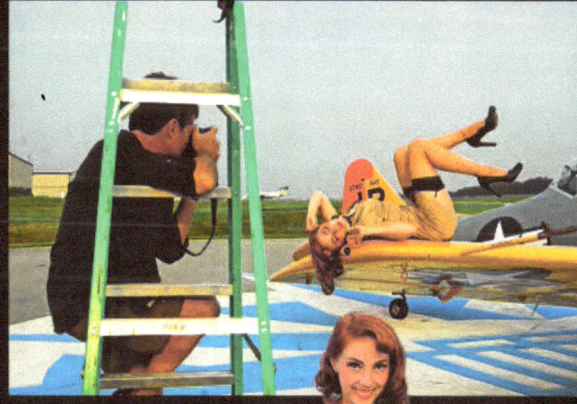

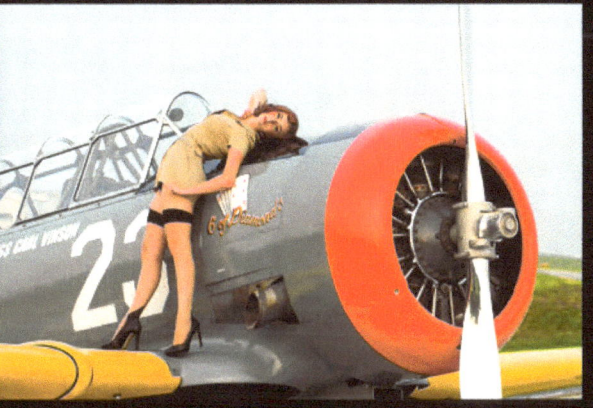

One of our most popular redheads, 2011 October pinup model Kacie stormed across the air show circuit making the most appearances with the Warbird Pinup Girls. Guys from across the globe continue to ask about her.

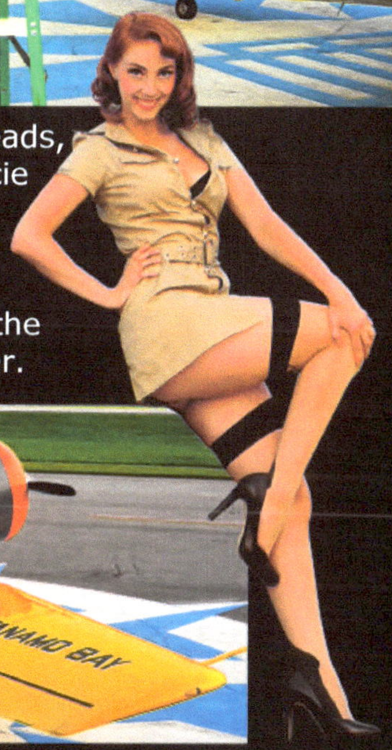

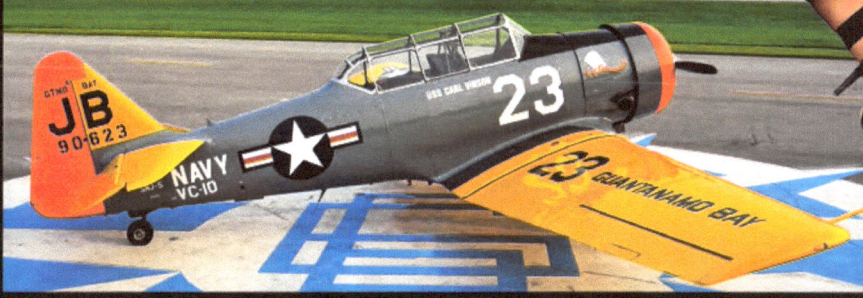

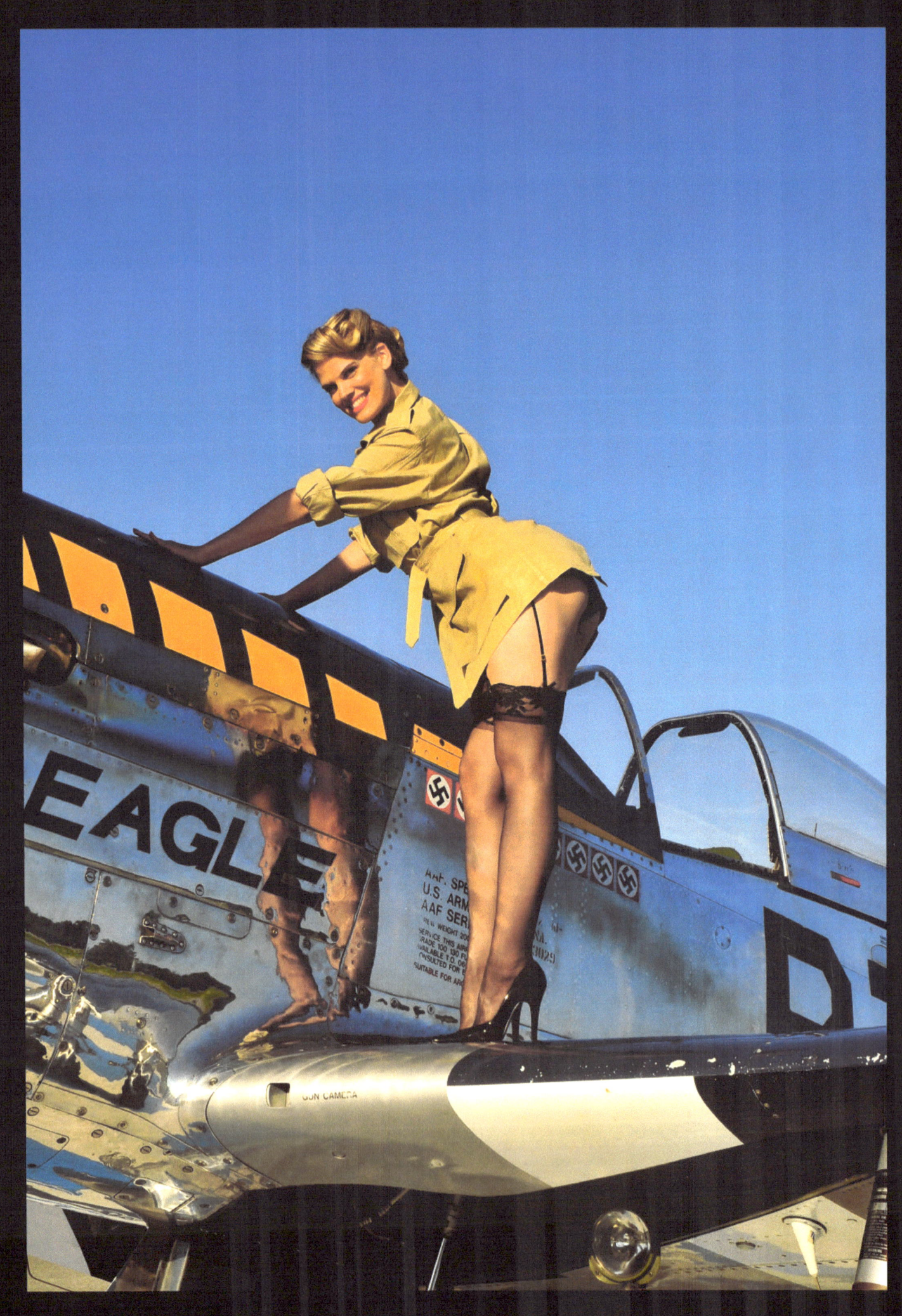

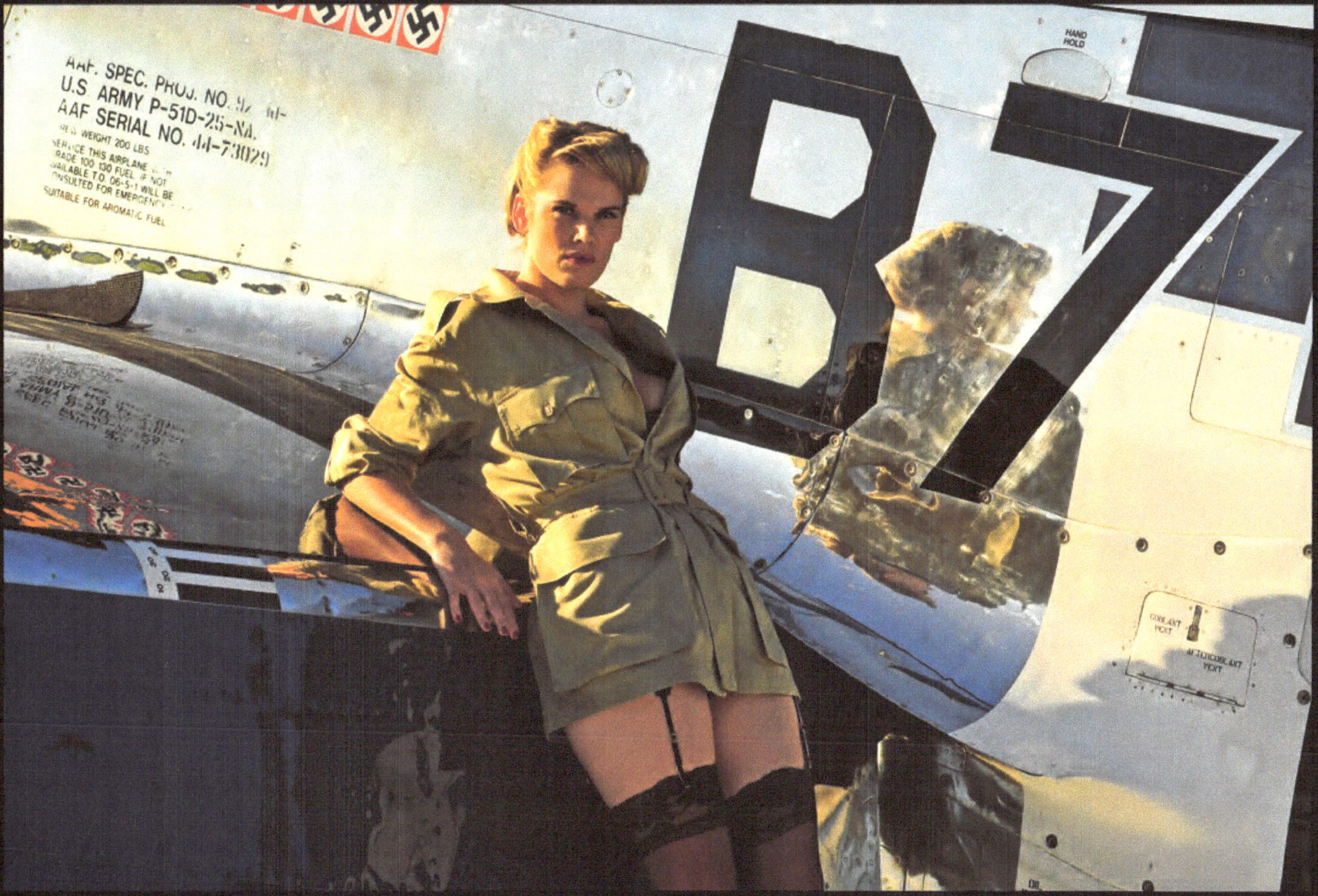

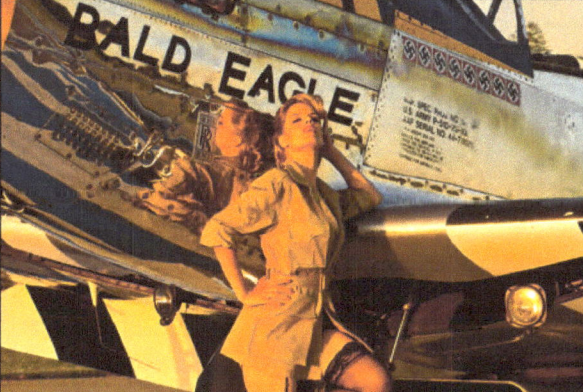

LINDSAY

The P-51D "Bald Eagle" was the first warbird I had ever worked with. She served as the inspiration for the Warbird Pinup Girls concept. A veteran friend of mine led me to her. You may recognize the "Bald Eagle" as one of the original members of the "Horsemen" acrobatic team of which all three appear in my 2011 calendar. The "Bald Eagle" is one of those Mustangs that has a great deal of character and history to it. The story has it she was pulled out of a dusty hanger in the Banana Republic and restored to flying condition.

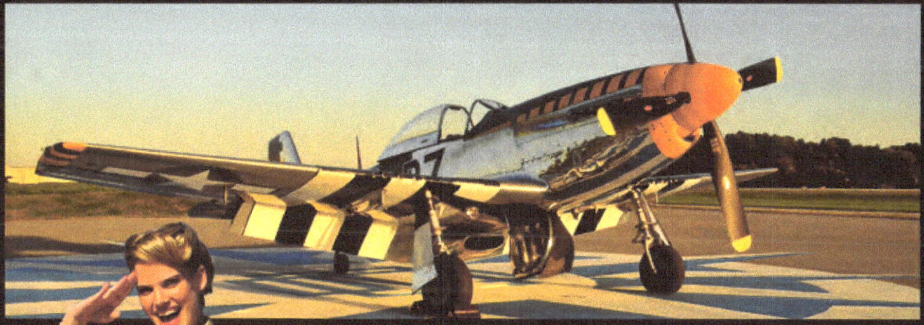

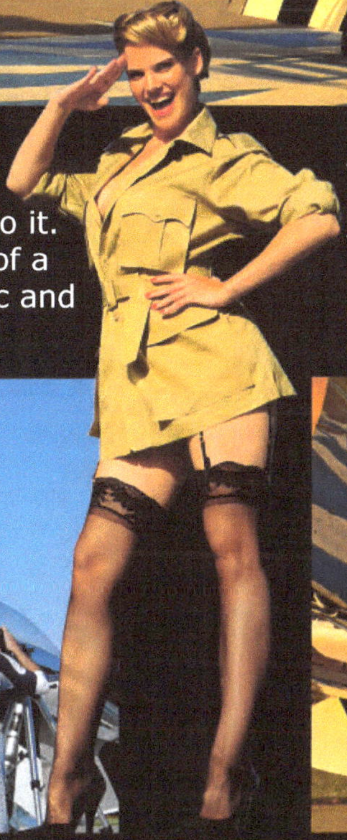

November 2011 pinup girl Lindsay is truly the girl next door. We found her right here in Lancaster, our home base and she turned out to be a real knockout. Lindsay's image is one of my favorites as it is a perfect combination of sexy, saultry and romantic lighting. A true classic.

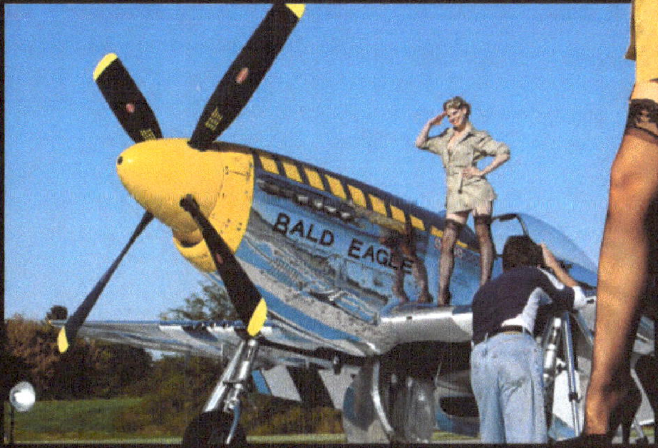

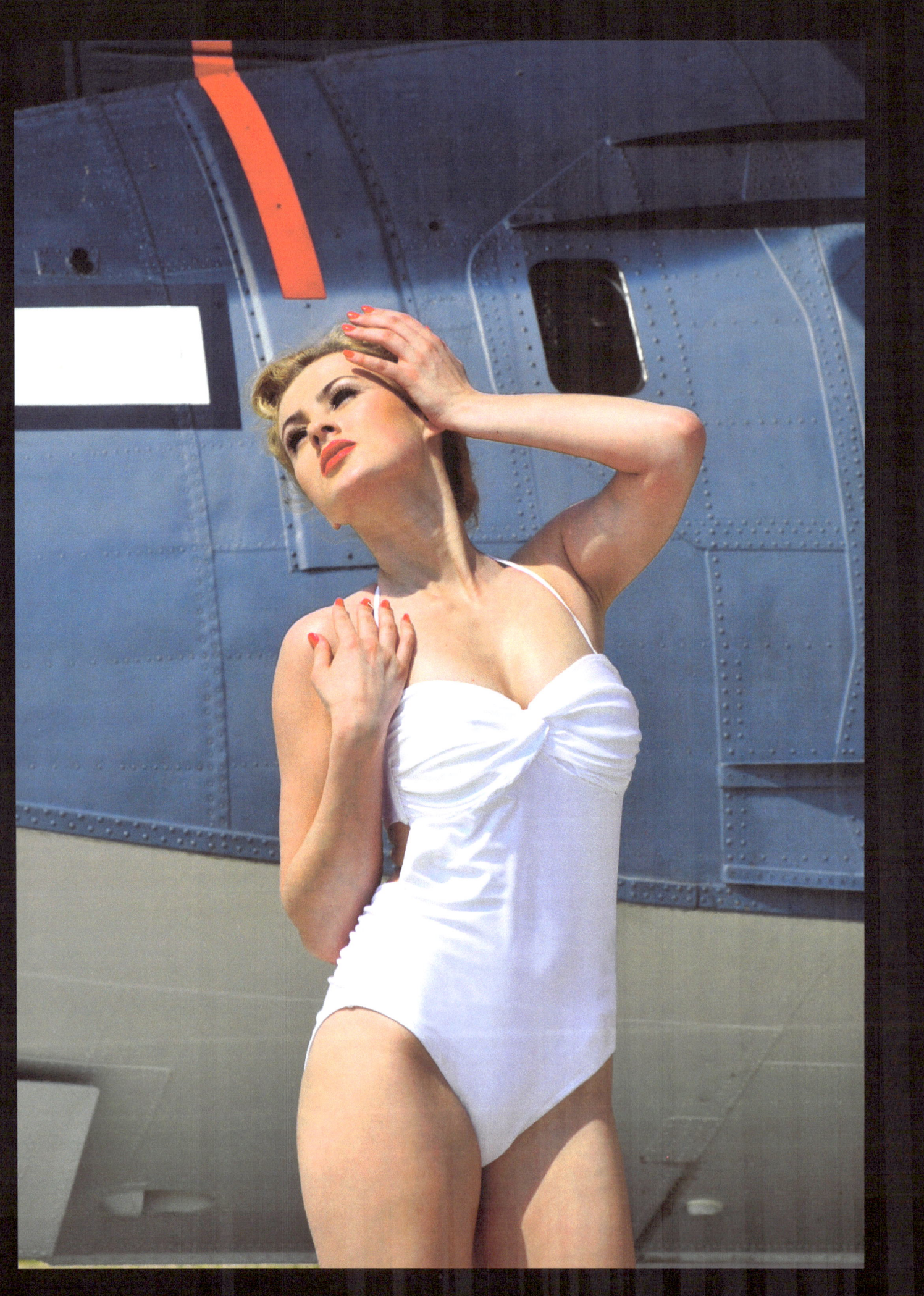

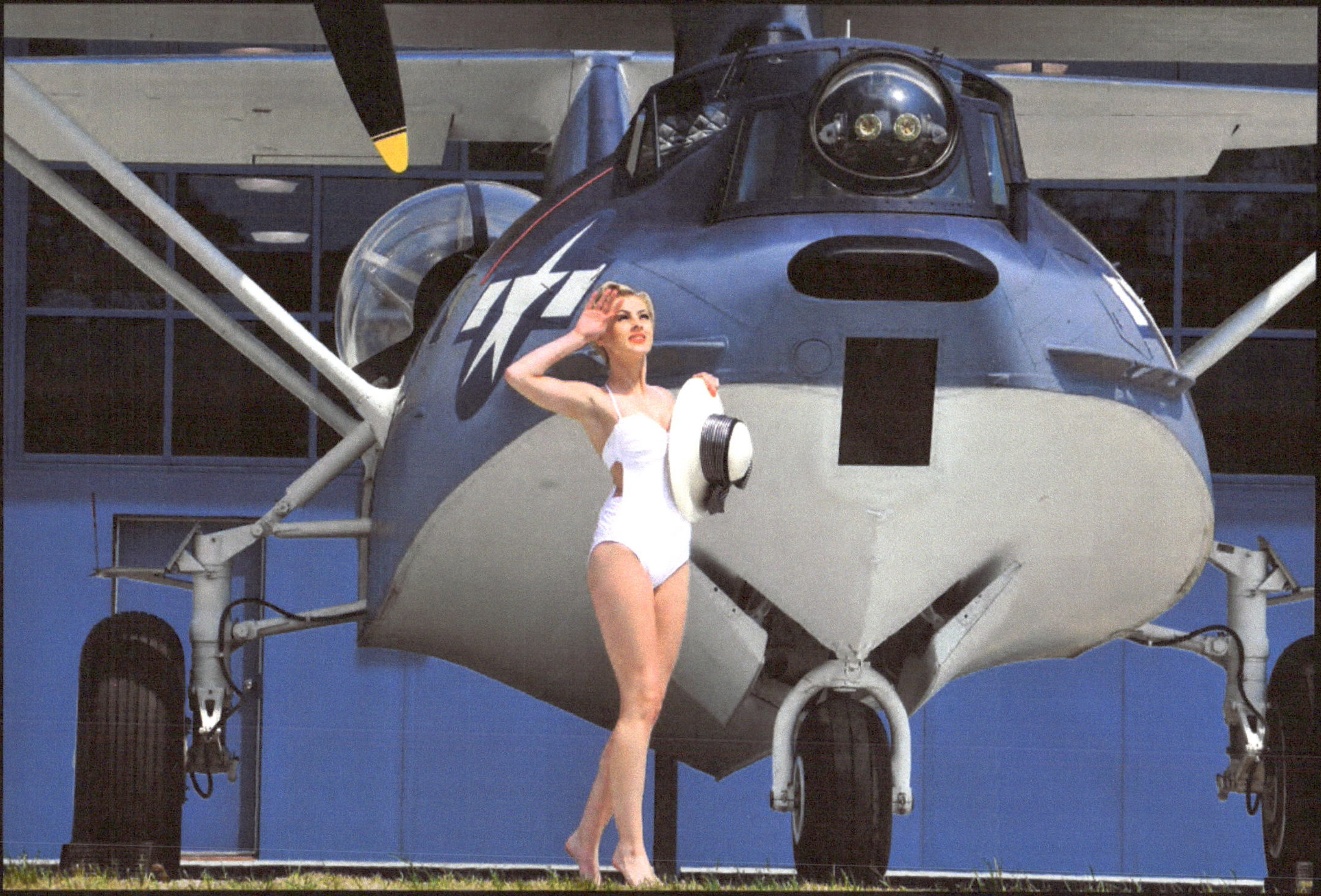

KAROLINA

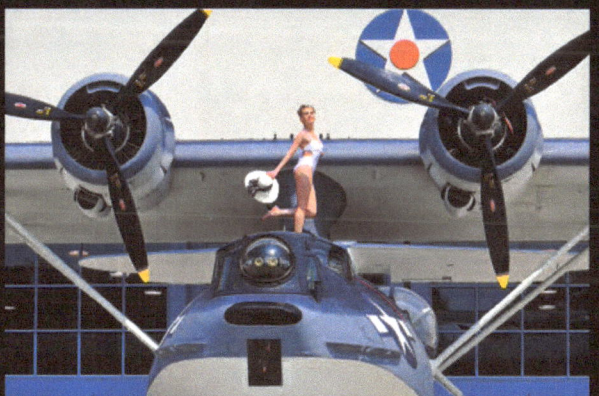

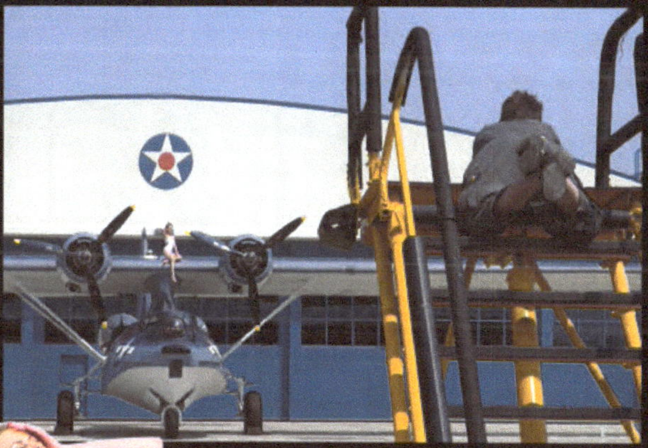

The PBY Catalina was an underrated workhorse of WWII. Serving roles as far ranging as search and rescue, cargo delivery and even combat roles as a torpedo bomber. Our Catalina is by far one of the finest examples remaining in the air. She is well kept and serviced by the Fighter Factory in Virginia Beach.

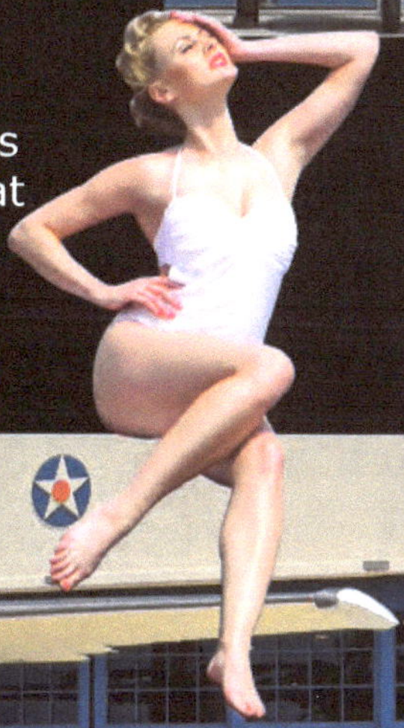

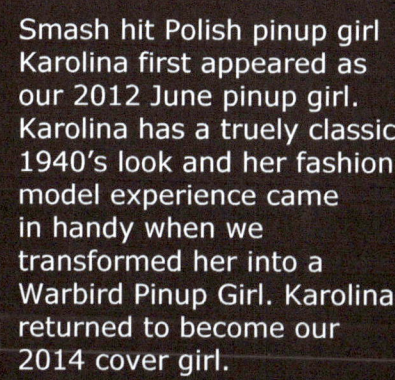

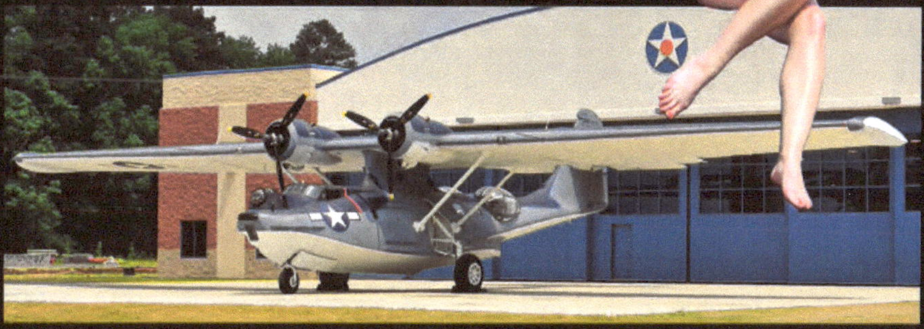

Smash hit Polish pinup girl Karolina first appeared as our 2012 June pinup girl. Karolina has a truely classic 1940's look and her fashion model experience came in handy when we transformed her into a Warbird Pinup Girl. Karolina returned to become our 2014 cover girl.

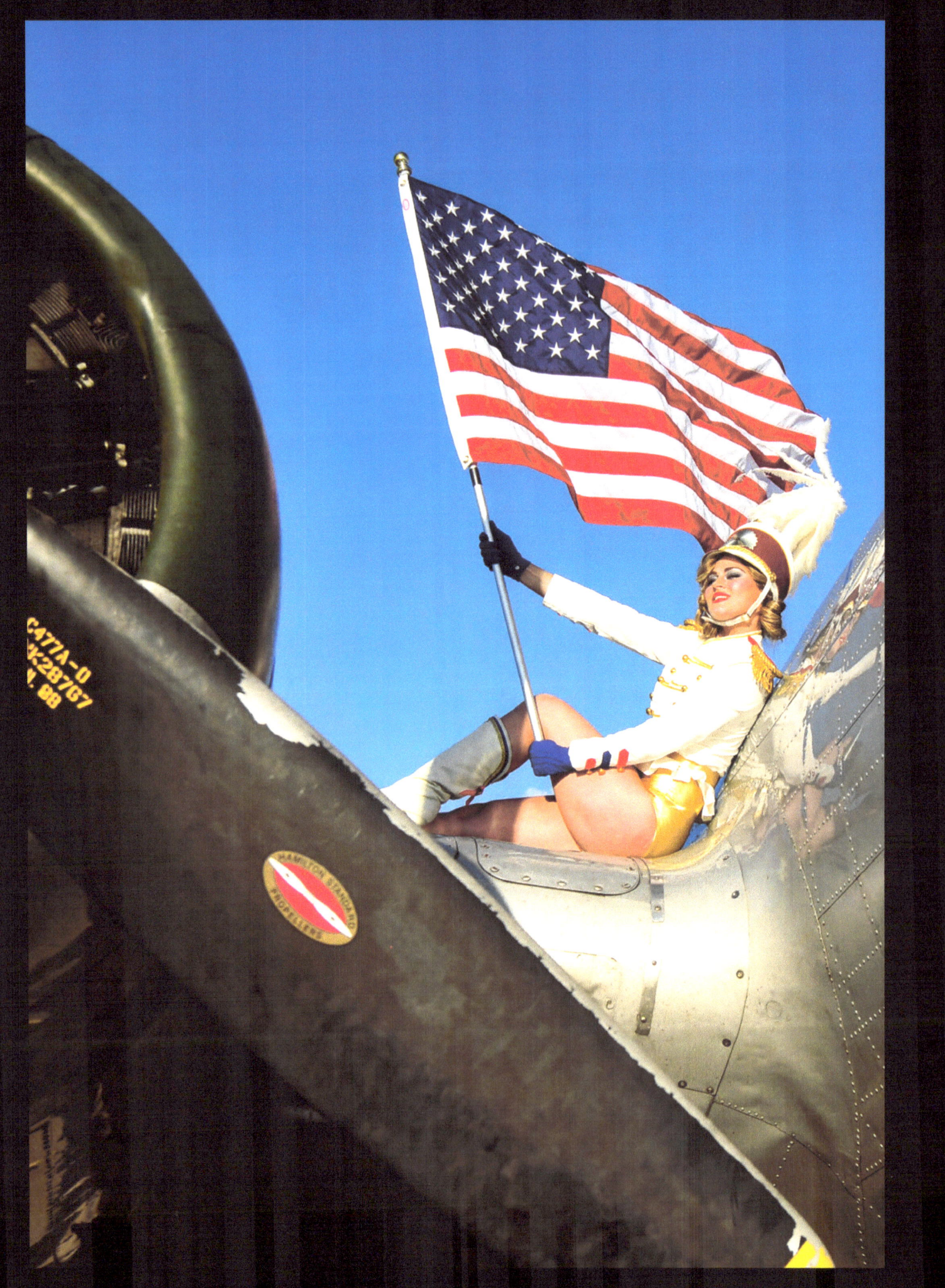

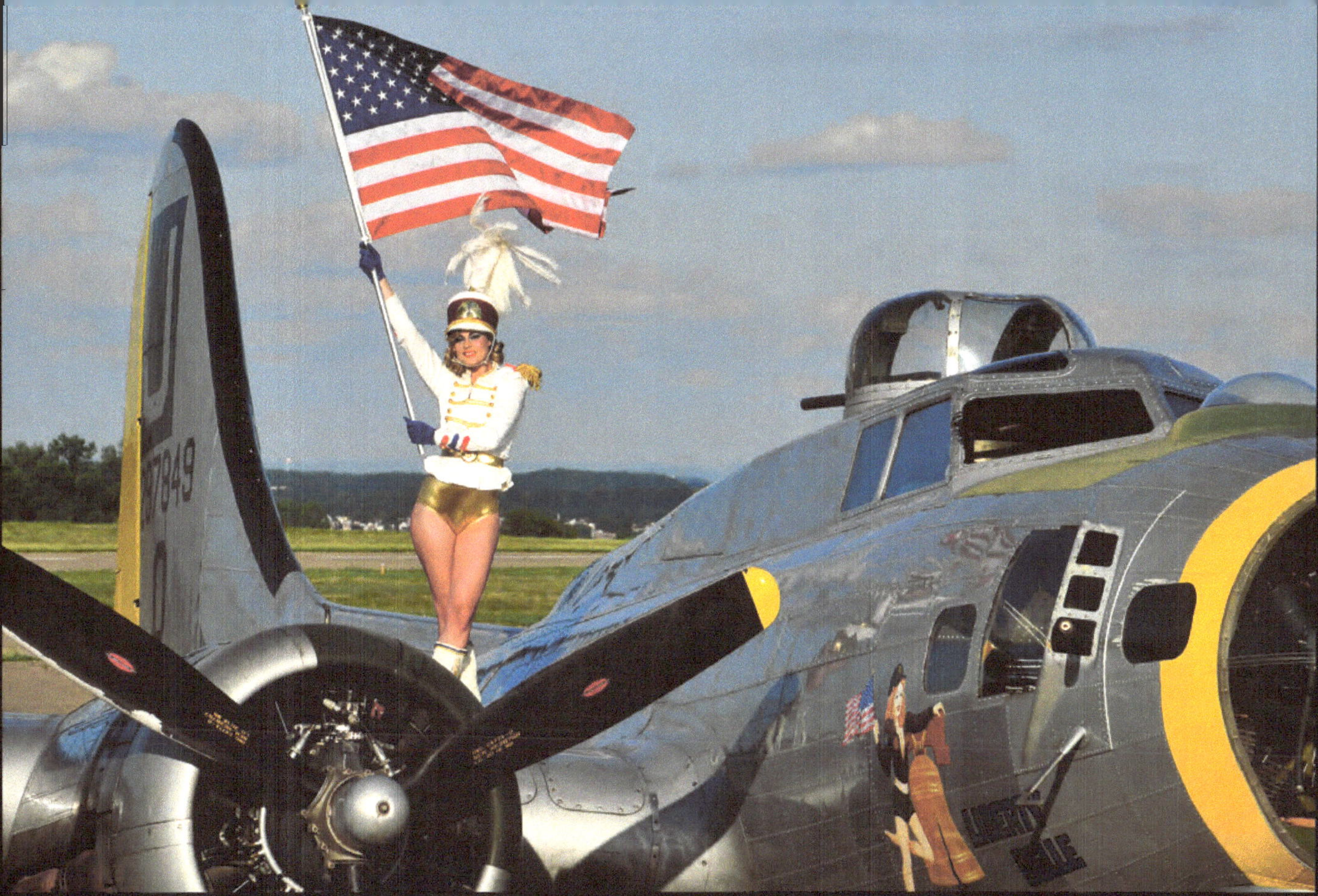

Heather

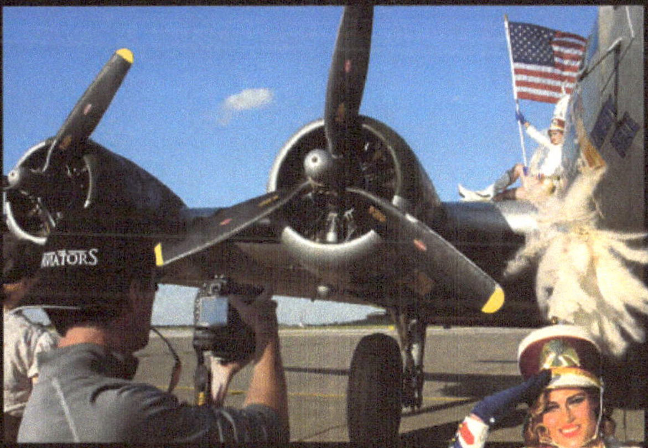

We were truly blessed to have the opportunity to work with the B-17 "The Liberty Belle". One of the few remaining B-17 Flying Fortresses in the world, became a tragic loss on June 13th 2011, as she had to make a forced landing outside of Chicago. All crew members escaped safely, however the aircraft was a total loss. We feel honored to have been the last professional crew to work with her before her loss.

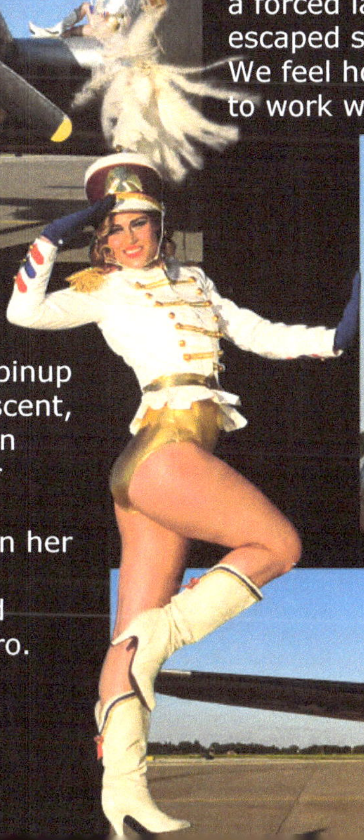

Pinup girl Heather had the distinguished honor of becoming our patriotic July pinup girl. Heather, of Russian descent, couldn't be more American in this classic and patriotic war time pinup girl.
Heather was a real trooper in her high heel boots and custom made Majorette uniform and waved the old glory like a pro. God Bless America.

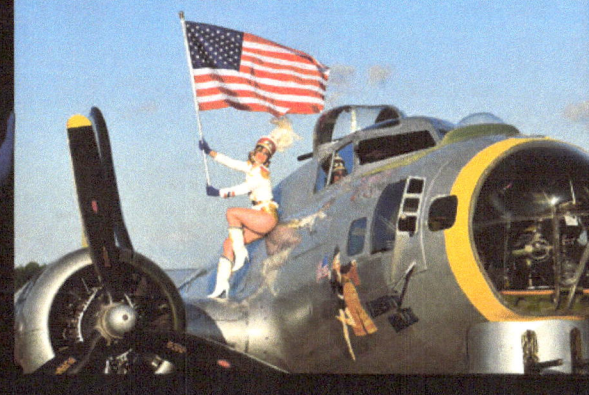

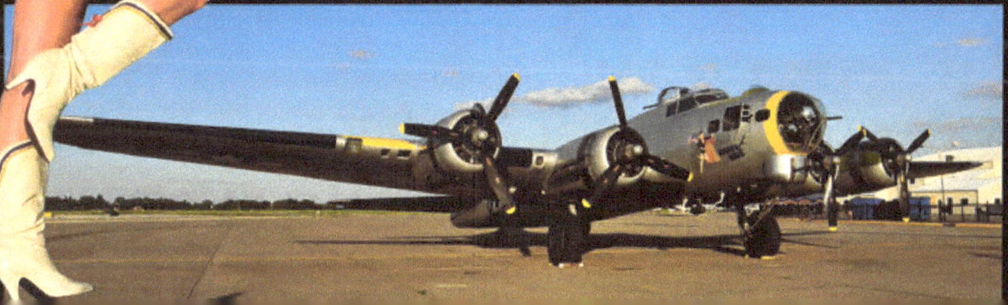

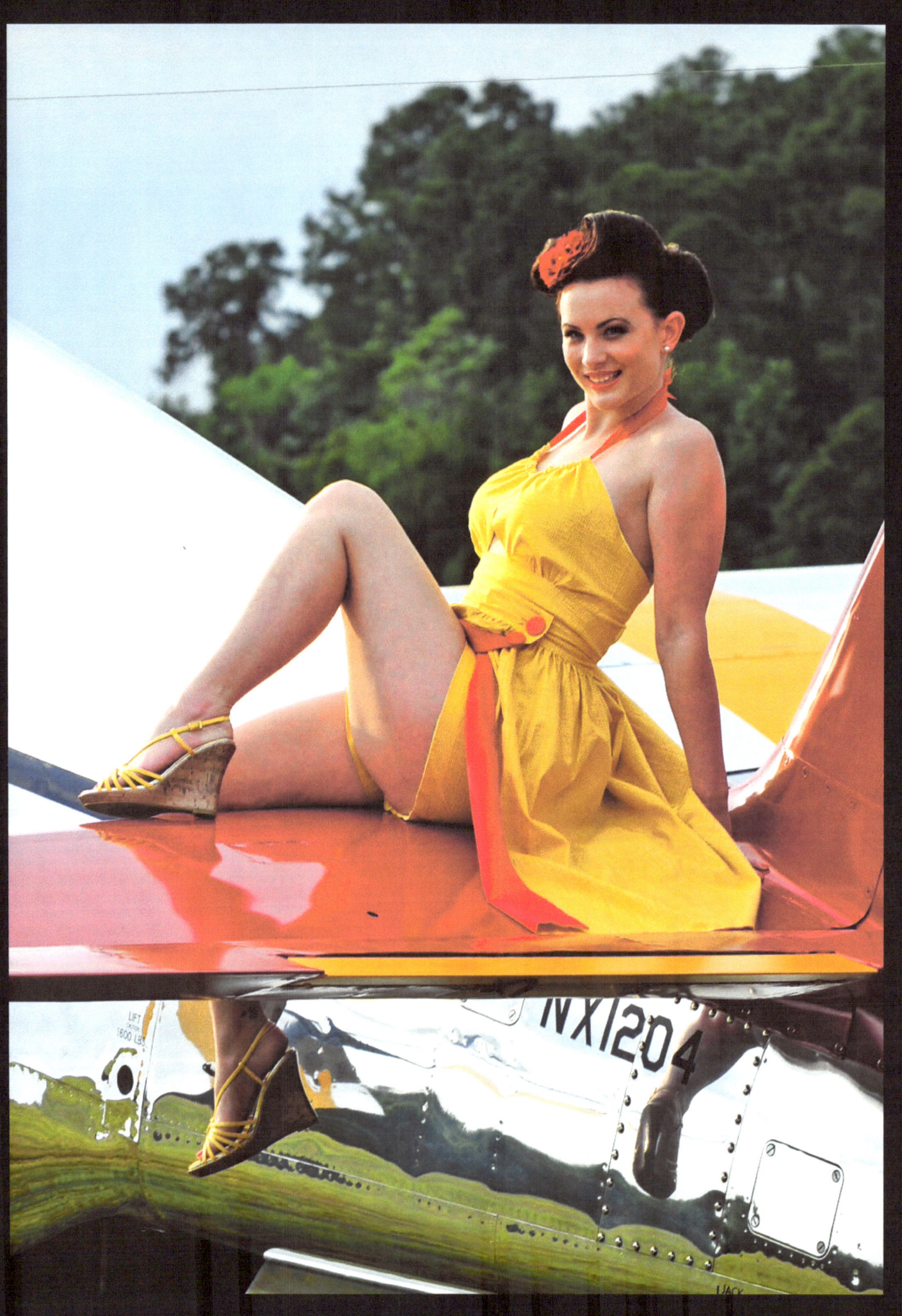

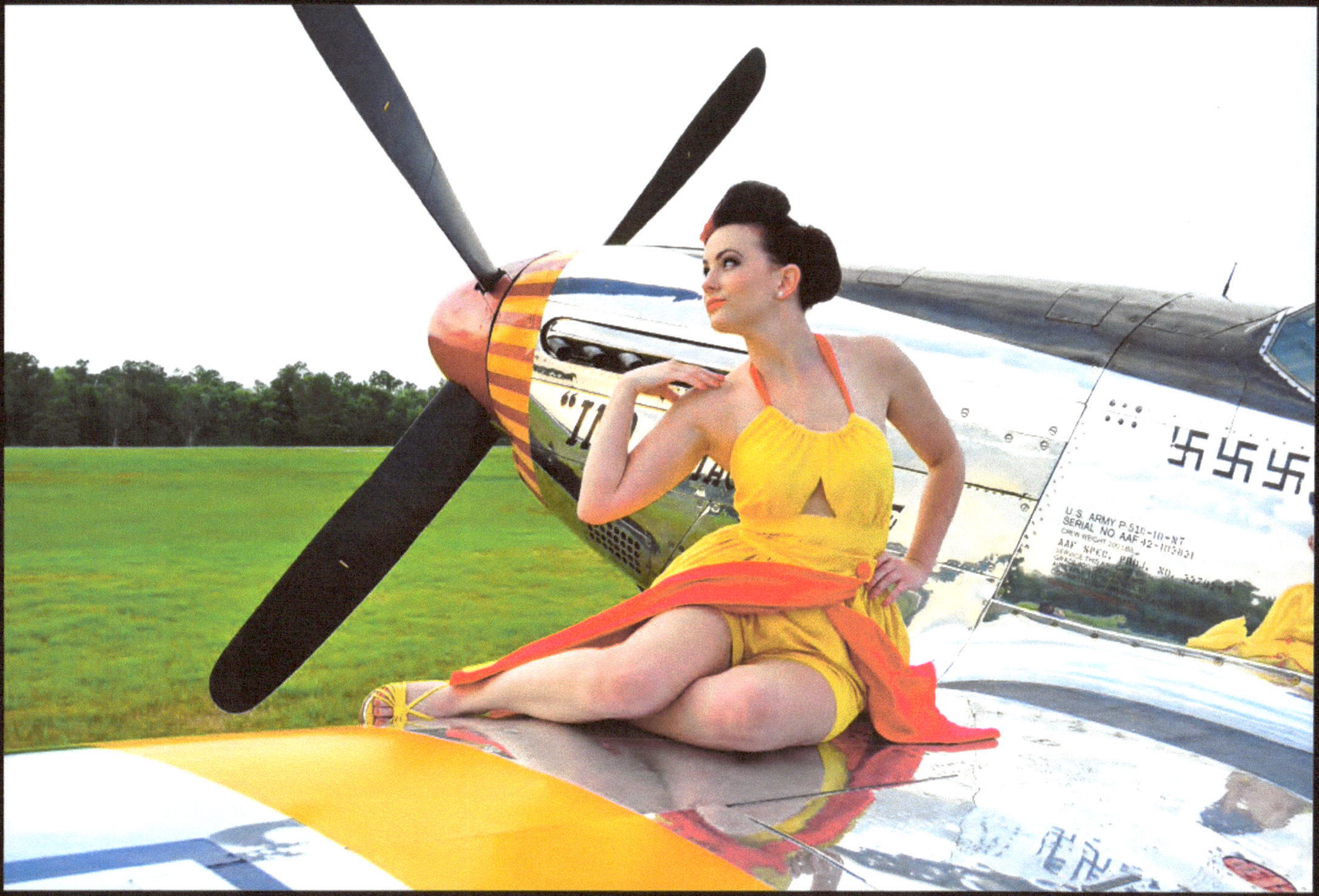

HALIE

This P-51 C Model has been painted to represent Lee Archer's "Ina the Macon Belle". Lee was a courageous member of the Tuskegee Airmen. Lee was the only black U.S. pilot to earn an "ace" designation.

September/October pinup girl Halie is a fresh talent we pulled out of central Florida. With little pinup experience she managed to pull off one of my favorite images of 2013's all Mustangs edition.

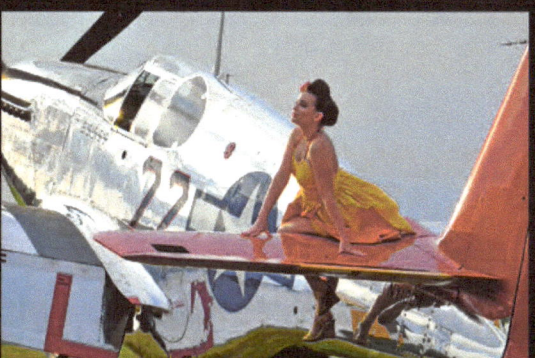

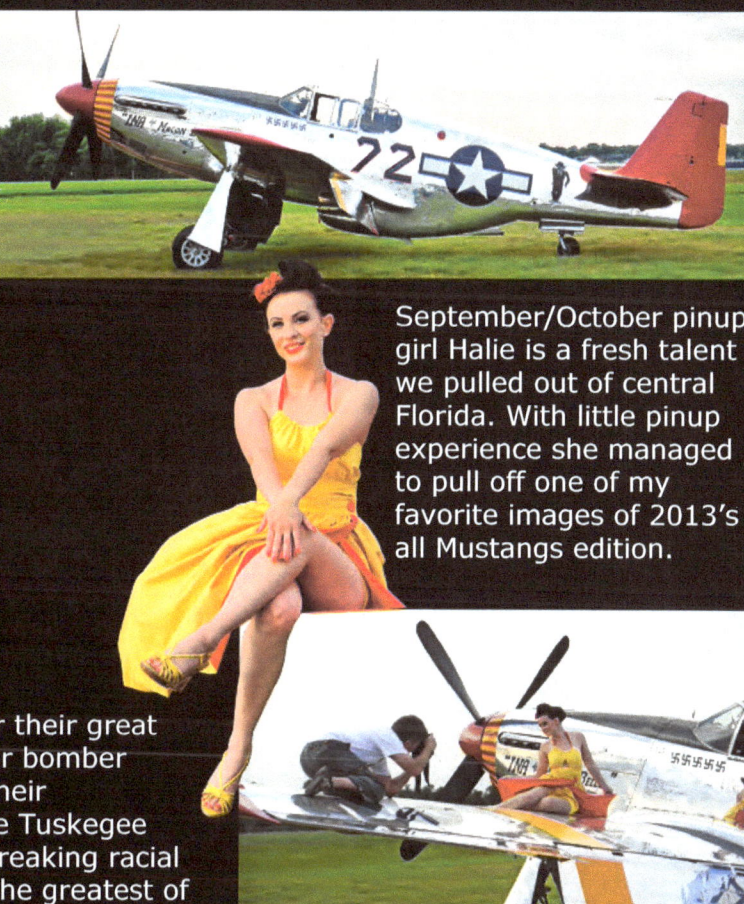

The famous Tuskegee Airmen were noted for their great skill over Europe. Towards the end of the war bomber groups were requesting their escort due to their outstanding performance and patriotism. The Tuskegee will forever go down in history for not only breaking racial barriers but proving their advantage in this the greatest of all wars.

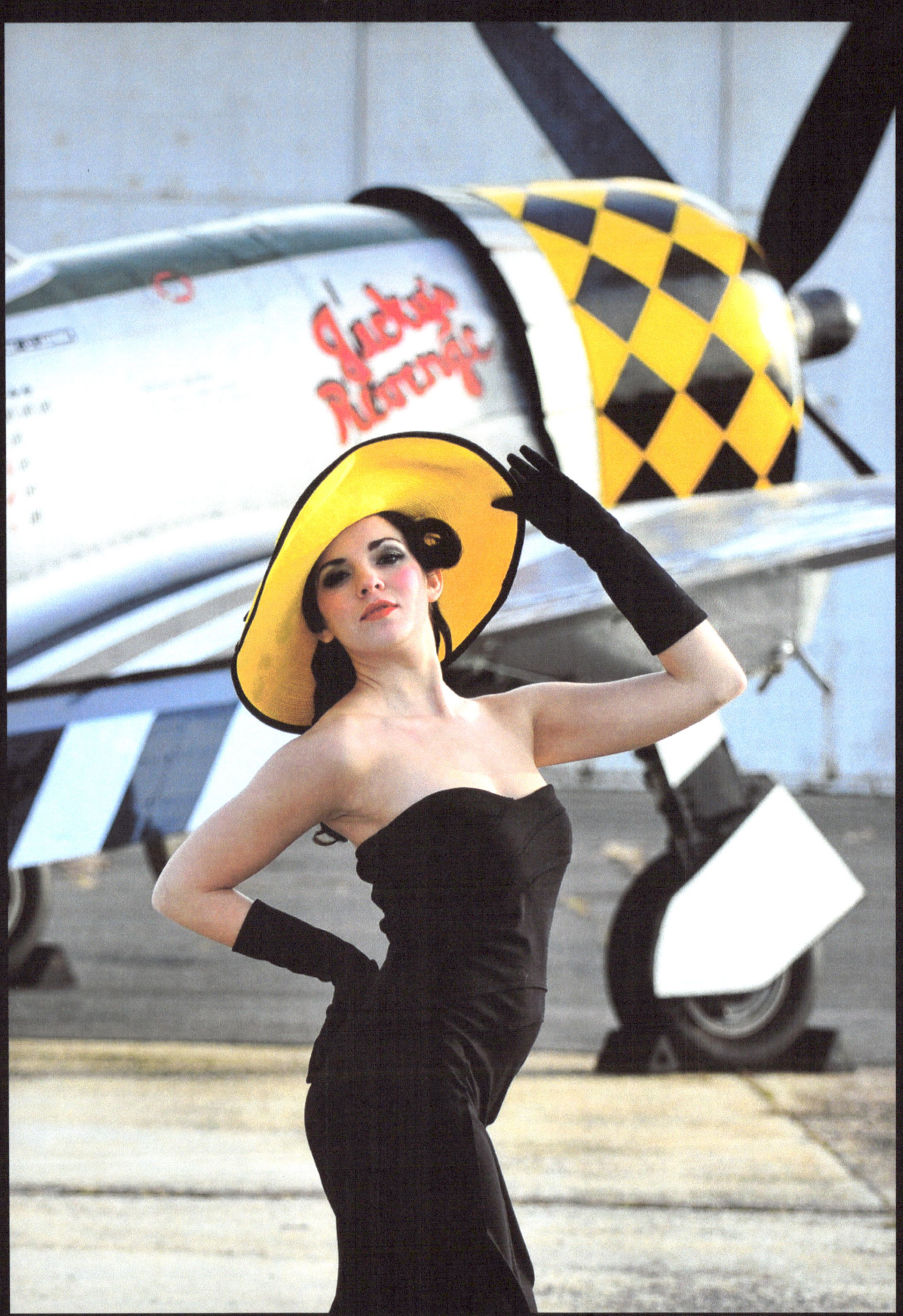

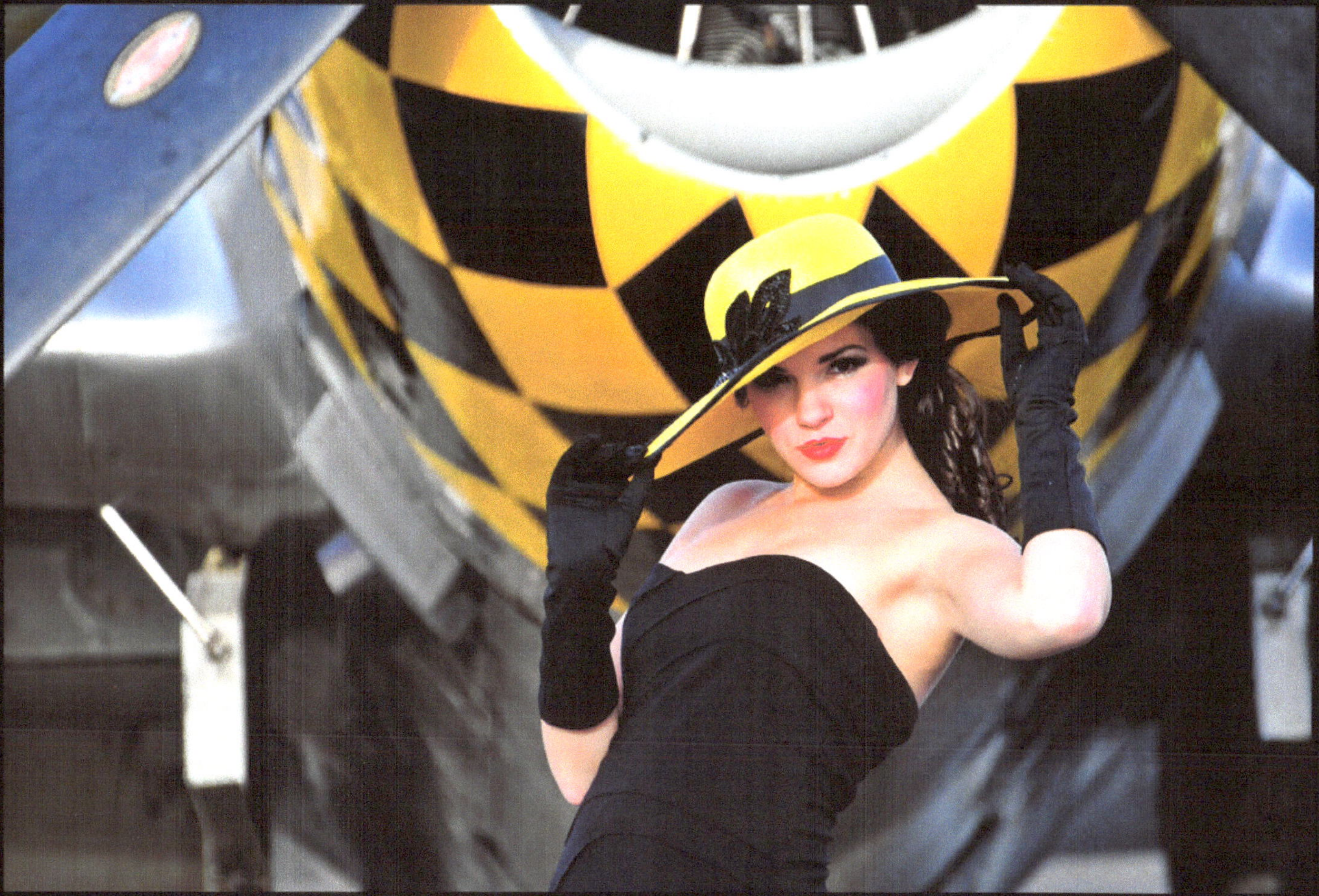

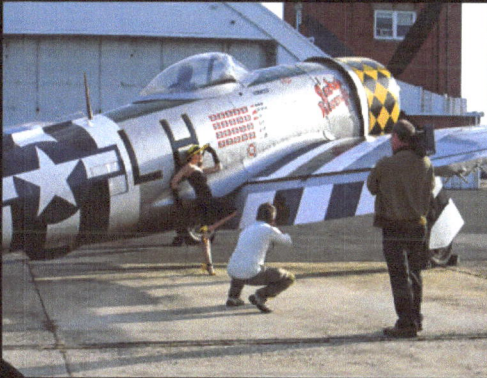

JENNA

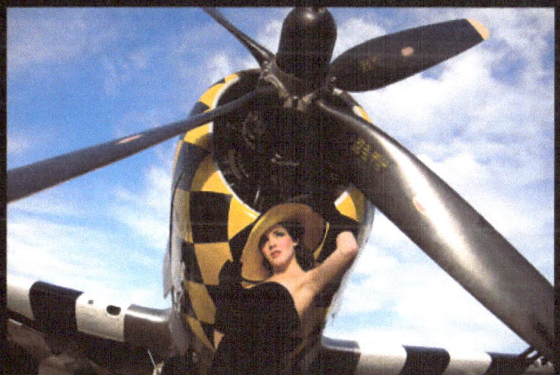

"The Jug", yes that's what they call her. One of WWII's most successful fighter planes, the P-47 Thunderbolt had the largest engine of any fighter in WWII. One of the few flight worthy P-47's remaining, the "Jacky's Revenge" was the perfect backdrop for my first release of the Warbird Pinup Girls calendar in 2011. The "Jacky's Revenge" flies regularly out of the American Airpower Museum on long Island.

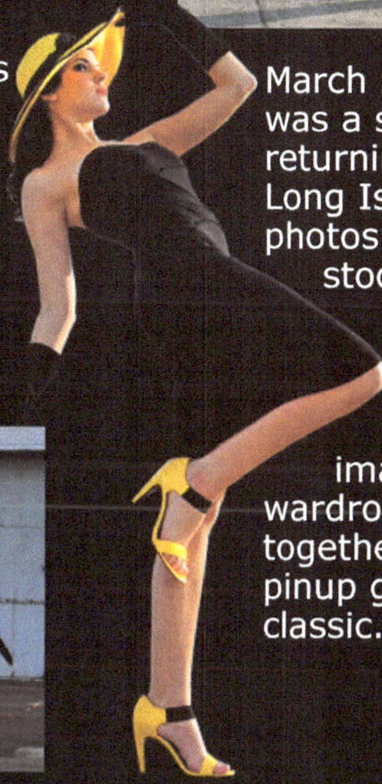

March 2011 pinup girl Jenna was a sleeper hit. After returning from our shoot on Long Island I reviewed the photos and the cover shot stood out immediately. This image still stands out as one of my most successful retro images to date. With light, wardrobe and aircraft coming together with our beautiful pinup girl to create a true classic.

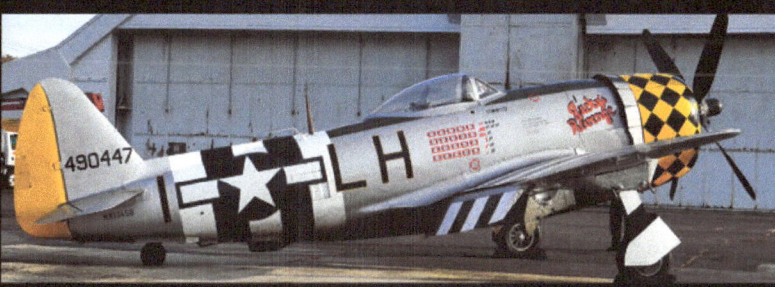

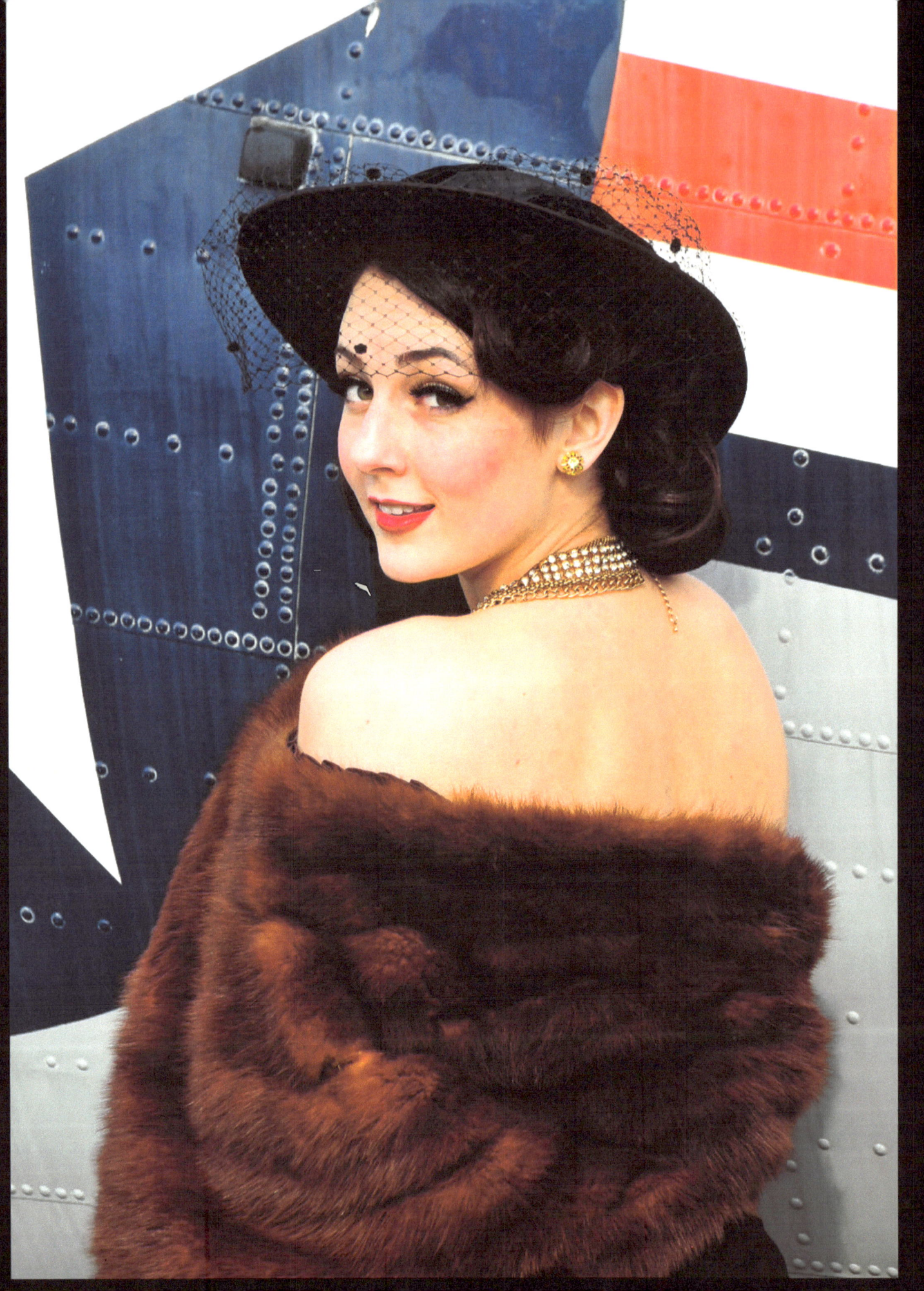

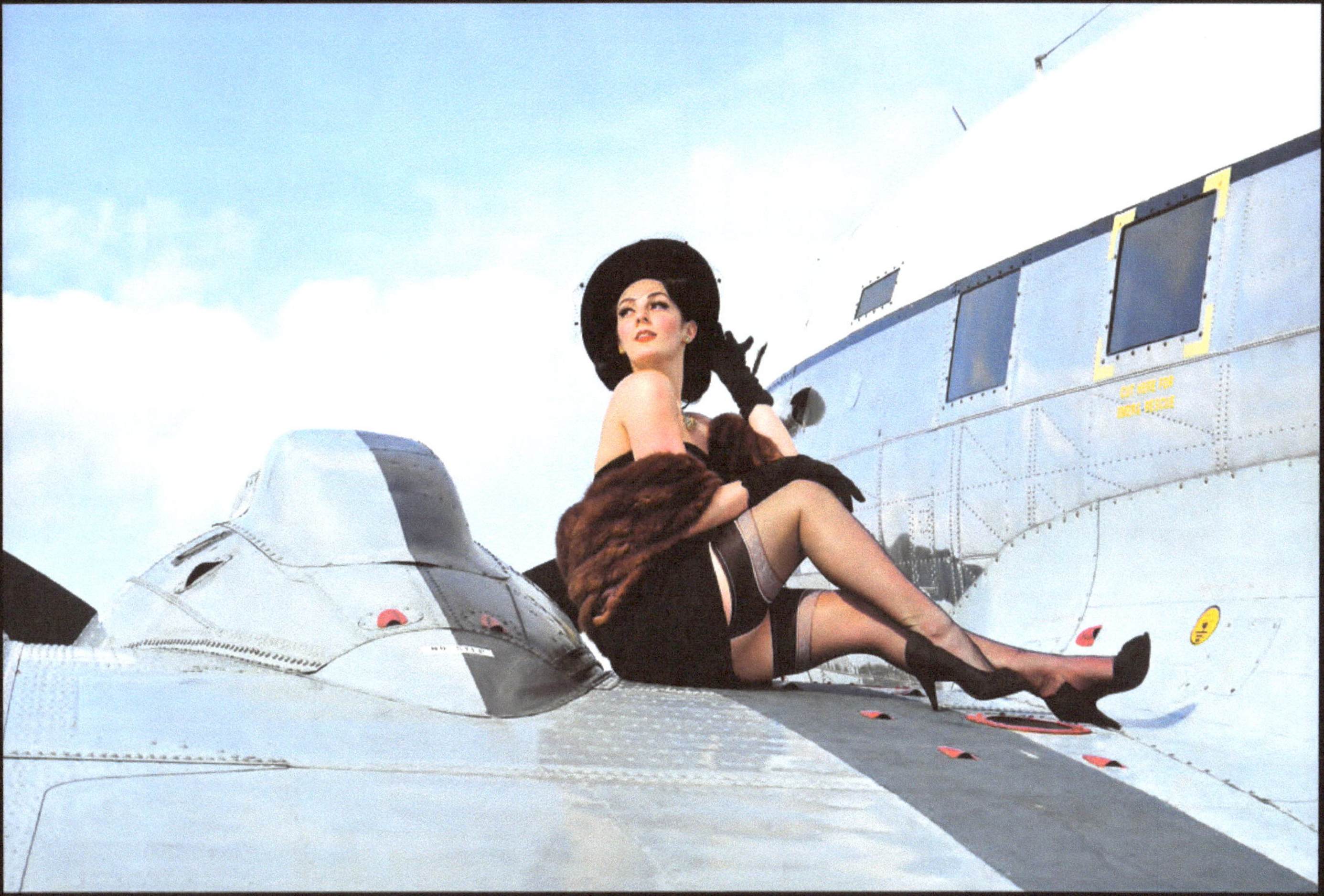

Victoria

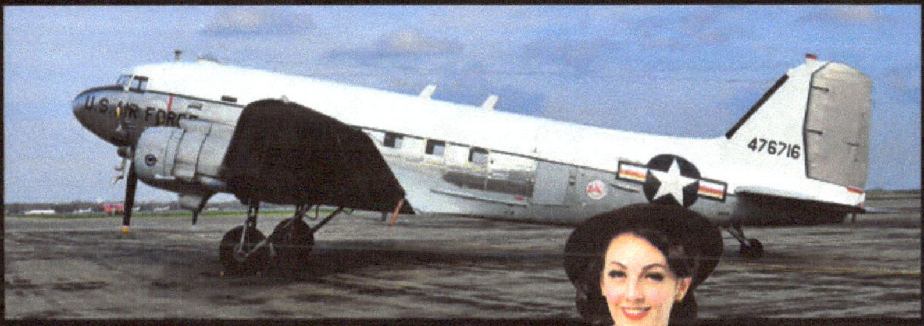

January 2014 pinup girl Victoria is a real classic "girl next door" from Michigan. Victoria contacted us about modeling shortly before our trip to Michigan and it seemed like it was meant to be. Victoria had little pinup modeling experience but she was easily transformed into a real classic 1940's lady right in front of our eyes.

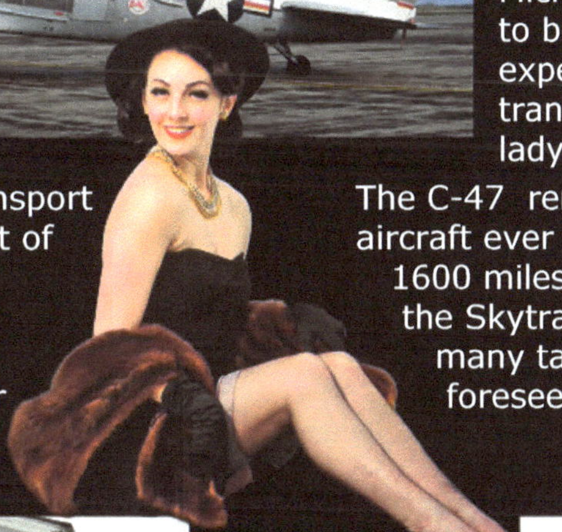

The C-47 Skytrain was a transport plane that was developed out of the civilian airliner DC-3. Serving many roles from transporting troops and equipment, to the famous air drops of the 101st Airborne troops.

The C-47 remains one of the most reliable aircraft ever designed. With a range of over 1600 miles and a top speed of 224 MPH, the Skytrain has been used globally for many tasks and will remain in use for the foreseeable future.

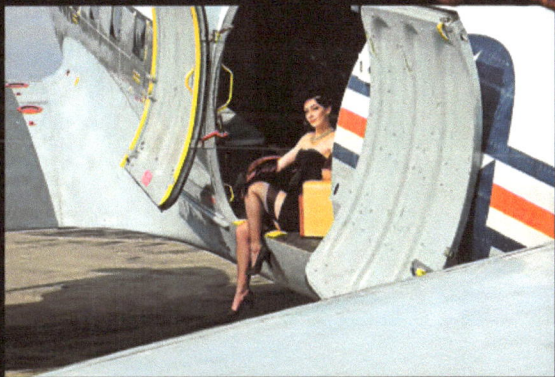

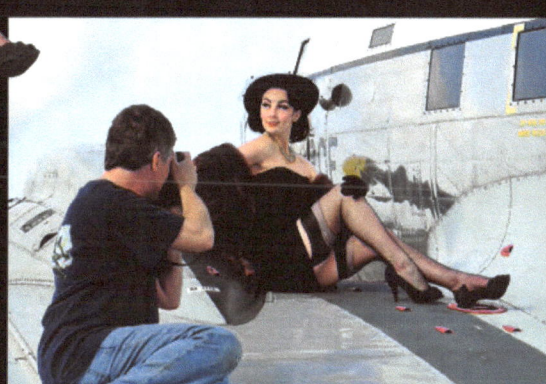

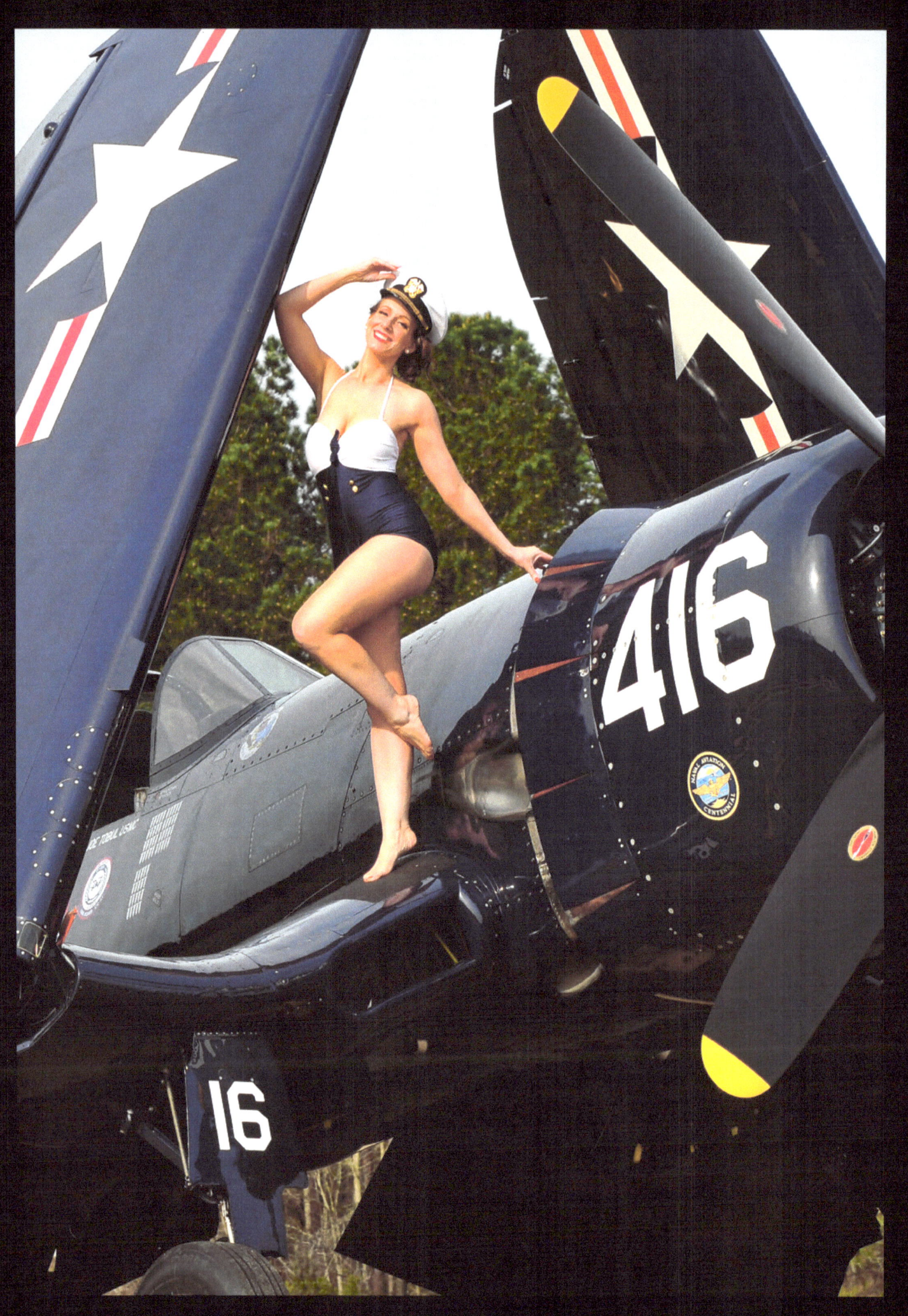

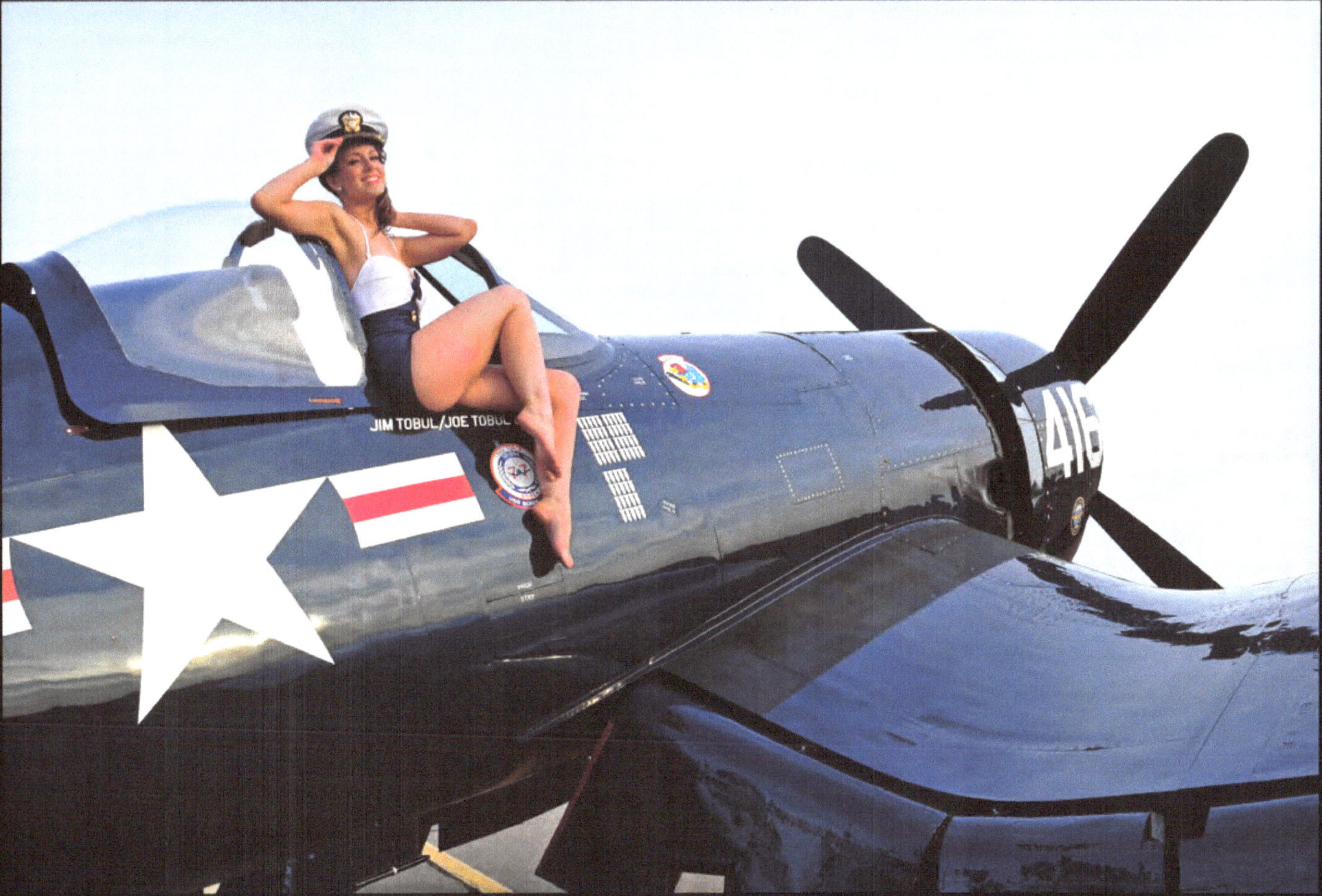

Kelly

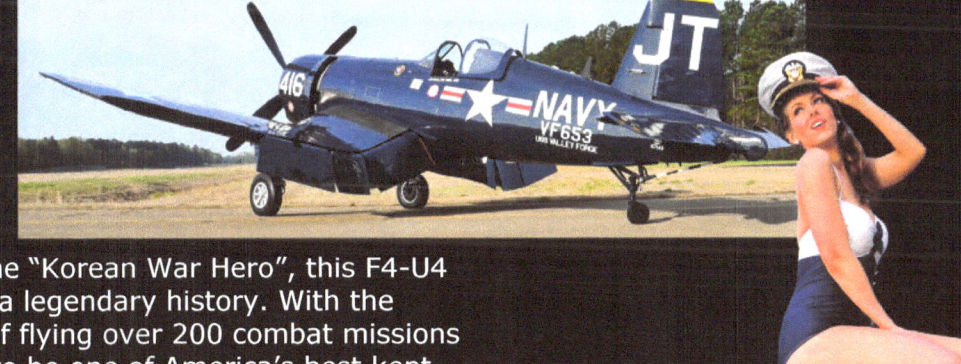

Known as the "Korean War Hero", this F4-U4 Corsair has a legendary history. With the distinction of flying over 200 combat missions she stands to be one of America's best kept and most actively flown fighters of that time. This exquisite Corsair lives in Bamberg, South Carolina and is owned and operated by Jim Tobul Air shows.

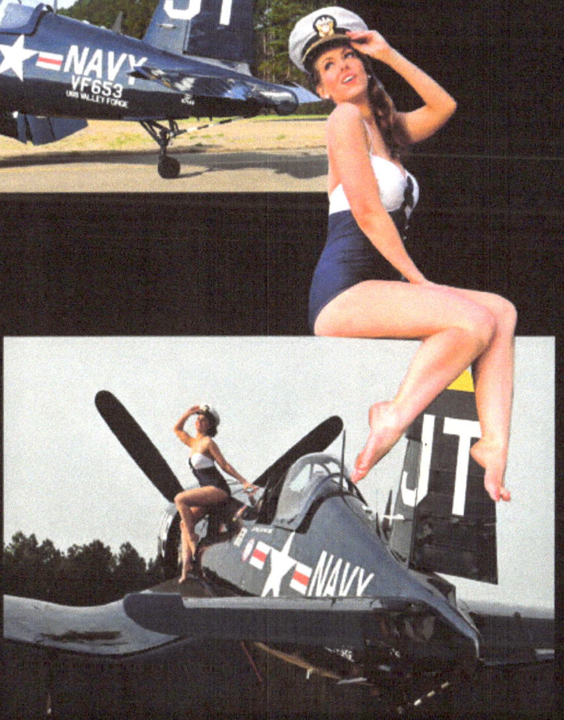

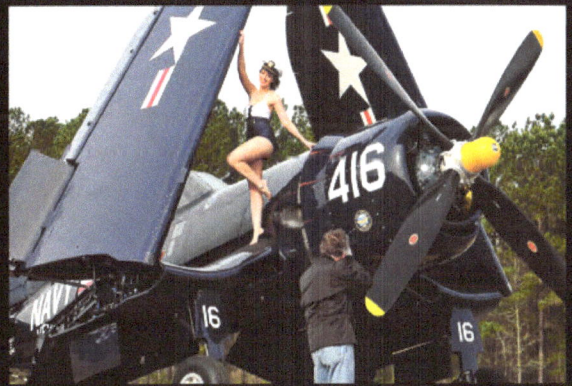

Returning 2011 pinup girl Kelly did a great job posing with the Corsair in a classic bathing suit despite the chilly April morning in South Carolina.

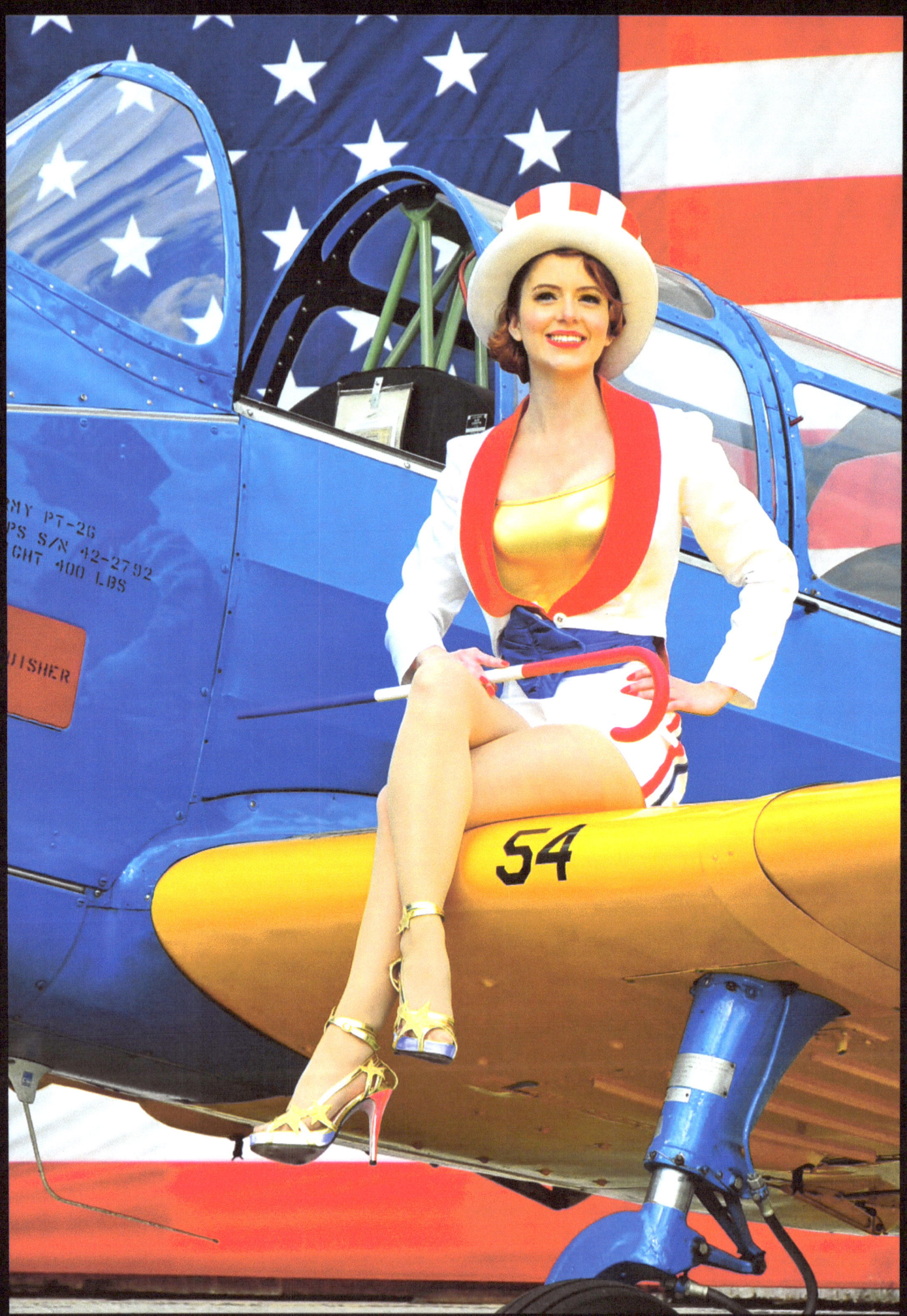

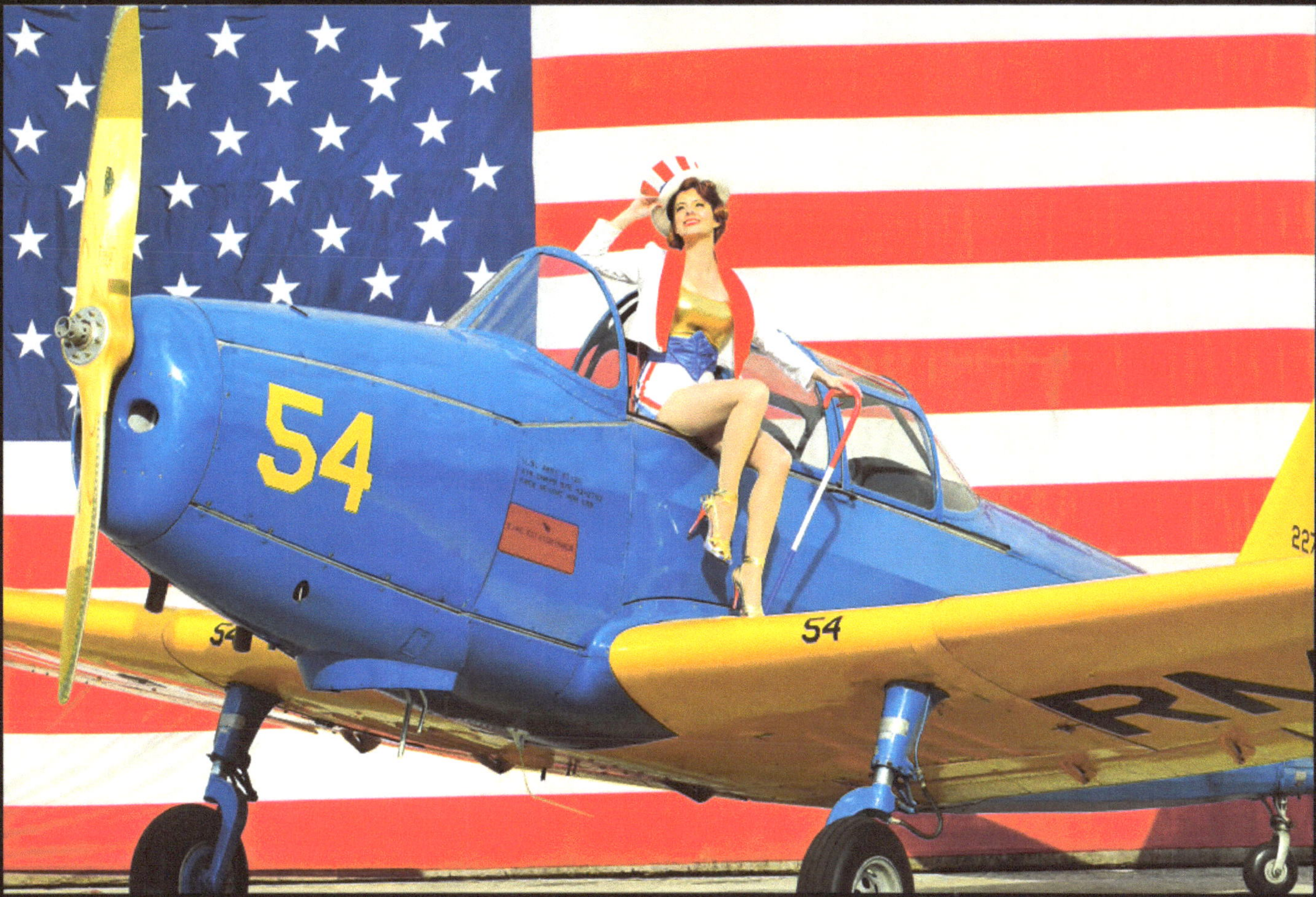

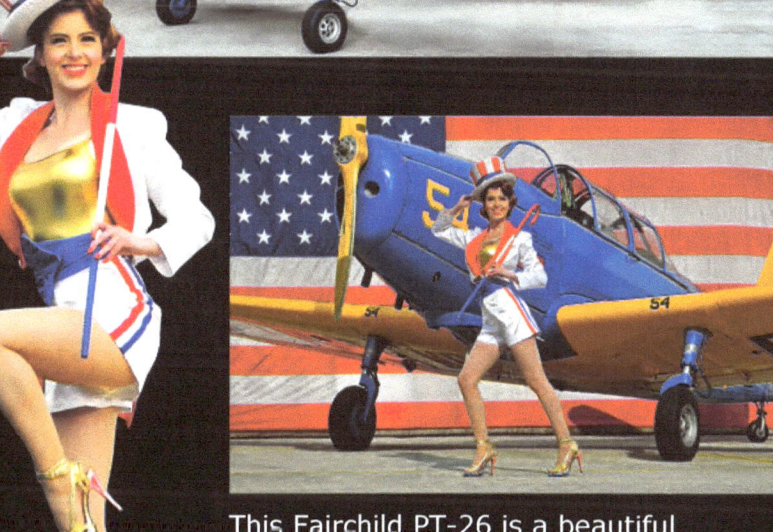

SHANNON

Shannon came to us through the enthusiasm of one of our fans at a local air show. Actually, it was Shannon's mom that suggested we take a look at her to be one of our pinup girls.

We don't normally take these kind of references too seriously but in the case of Shannon we're glad we did. We ended up giving Shannon an opportunity to test shoot with us and she turned out one of our favorite patriotic July pinup girls for the upcoming 2015 Warbird Pinup Girls calendar. Shannon's wardrobe was custom made for us based on an original 1940's pinup painting.

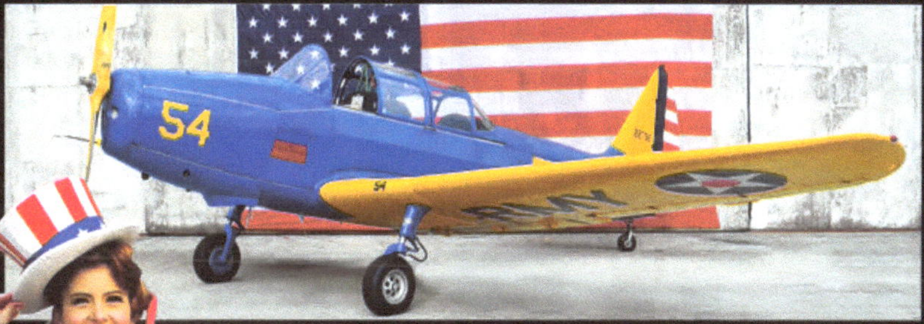

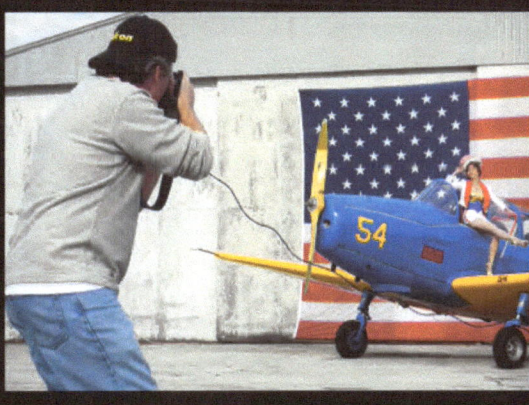

This Fairchild PT-26 is a beautiful example of the restoration work done by MD Aero in Smoketown Pennsylvania. We wanted to feature this often over-looked plane as they served as an entry level trainer for many of the legendary fighter pilots from WWII.

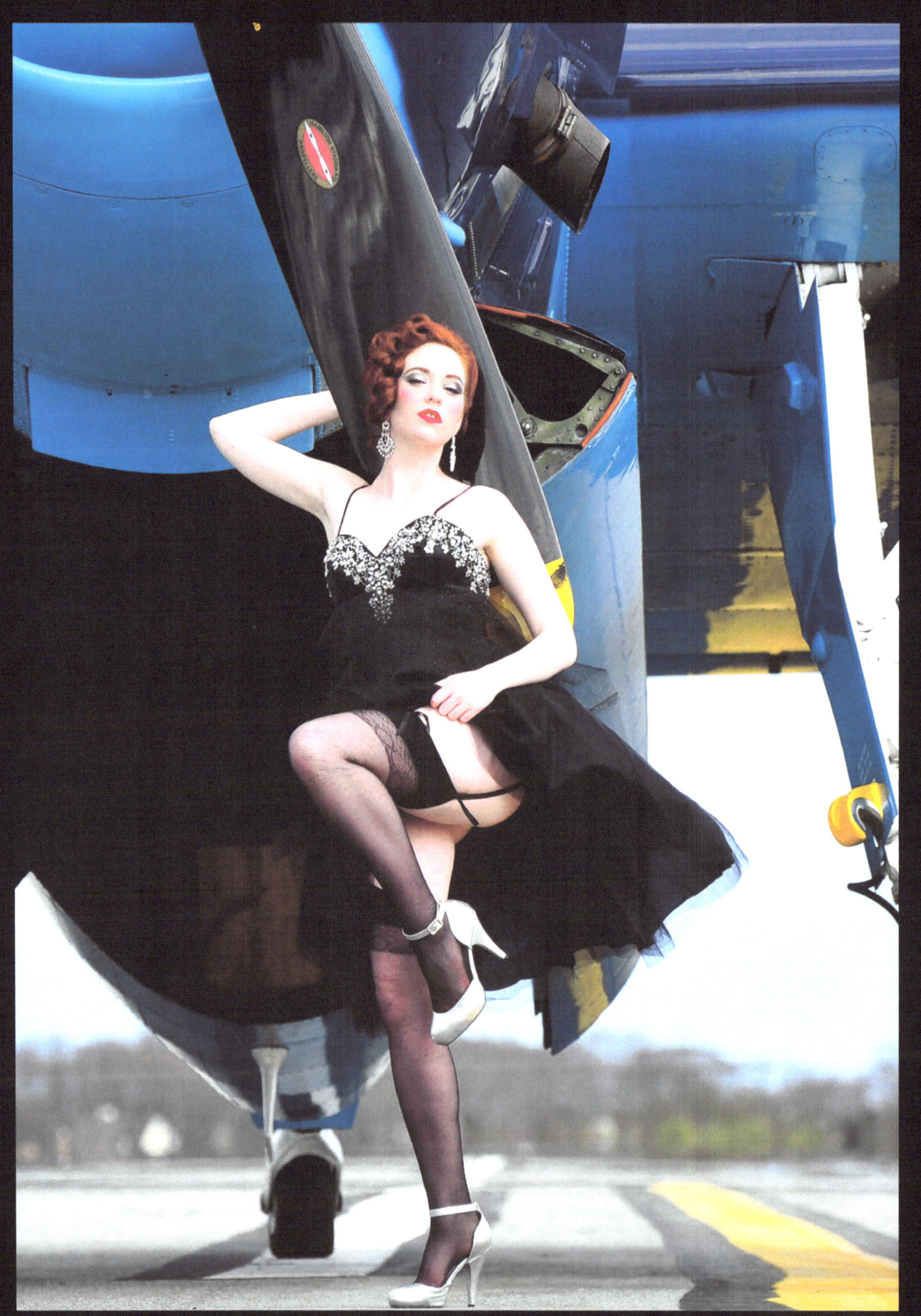

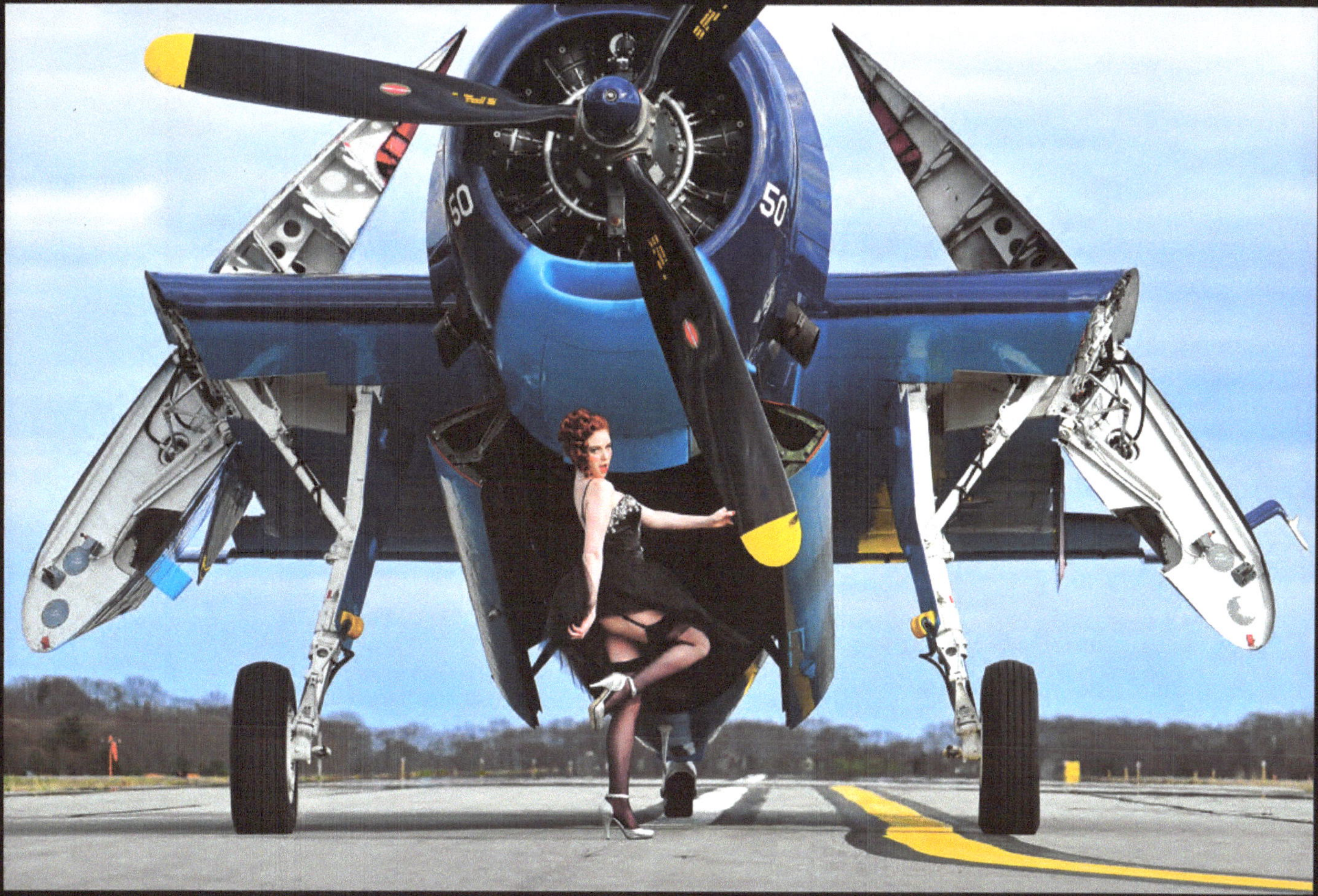

BARBIE

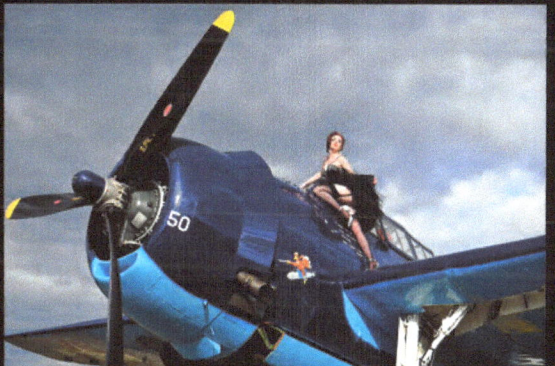

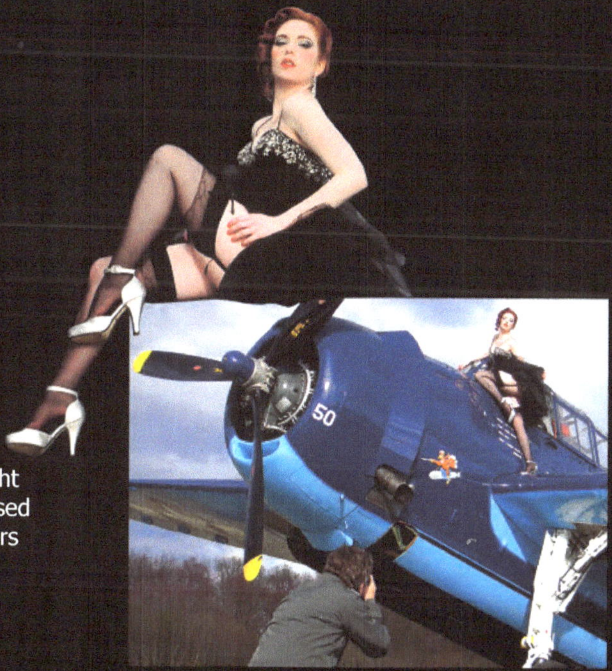

This old "Turkey Bird" is a beautiful example of the remaining TBM Avengers left in flying condition. We were blessed to have Simmons Aviation in Connecticut open the hangar doors for us to highlight this rare aircraft. The TBM was instrumental in naval warfare as it was used to drop torpedoes on enemy vessels. Notice the extended bomb bay doors for the use of torpedoes. A true work horse of WWII aviation.

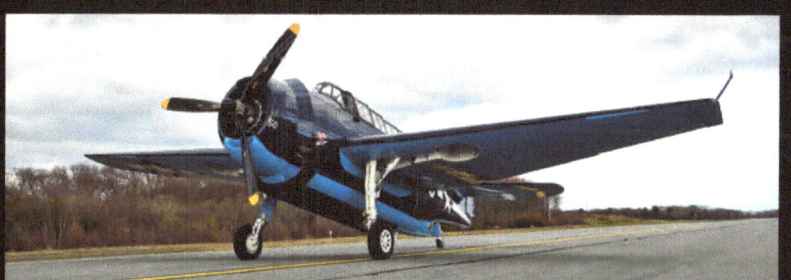

Barbie, a city girl from New York without much pinup experience, shined brightly when the sun finally came out. Barbie is one of those girls you can just see her potential from a mile away. She brought a sense of grace and class to her pinup image you don't see every day.

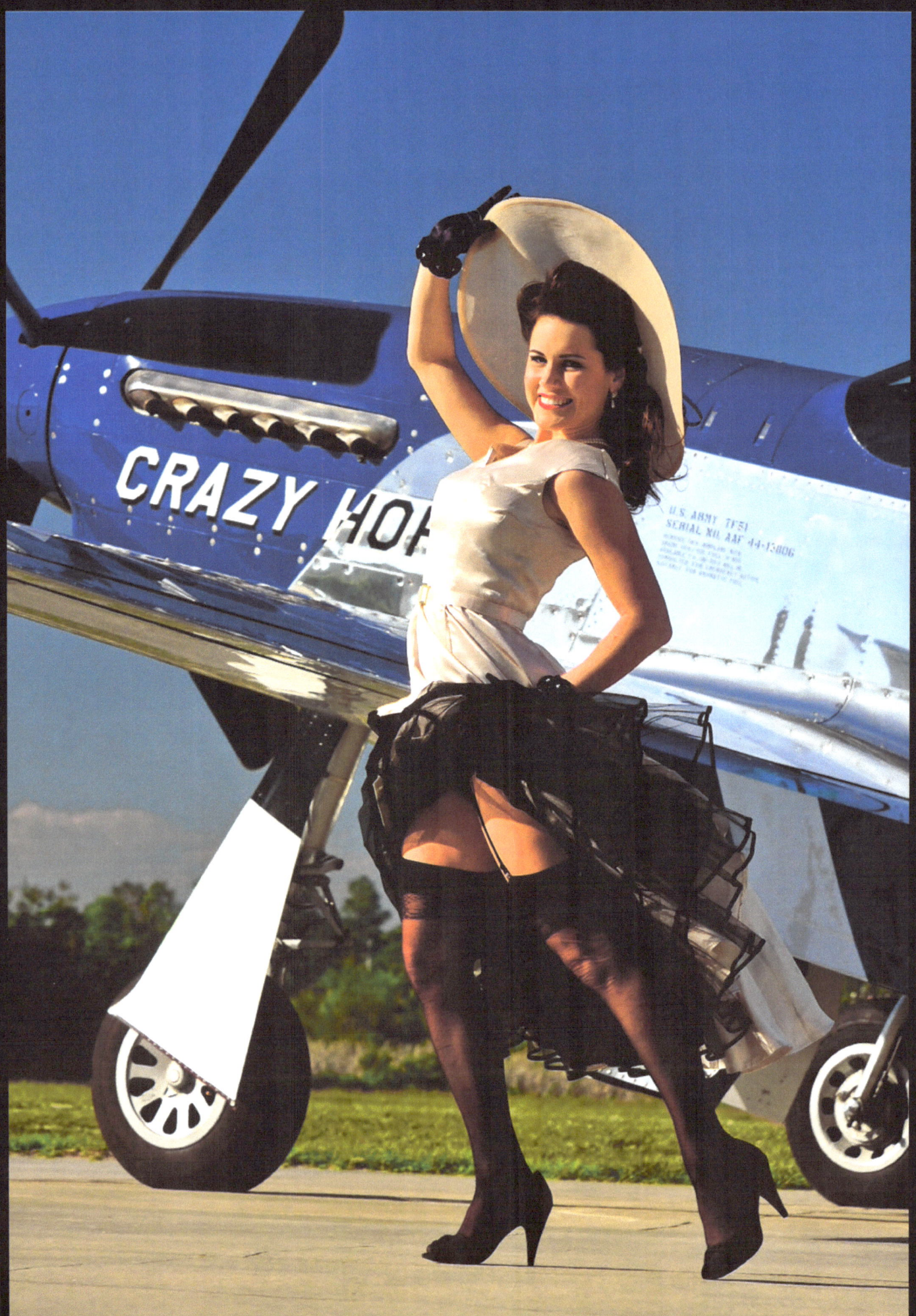

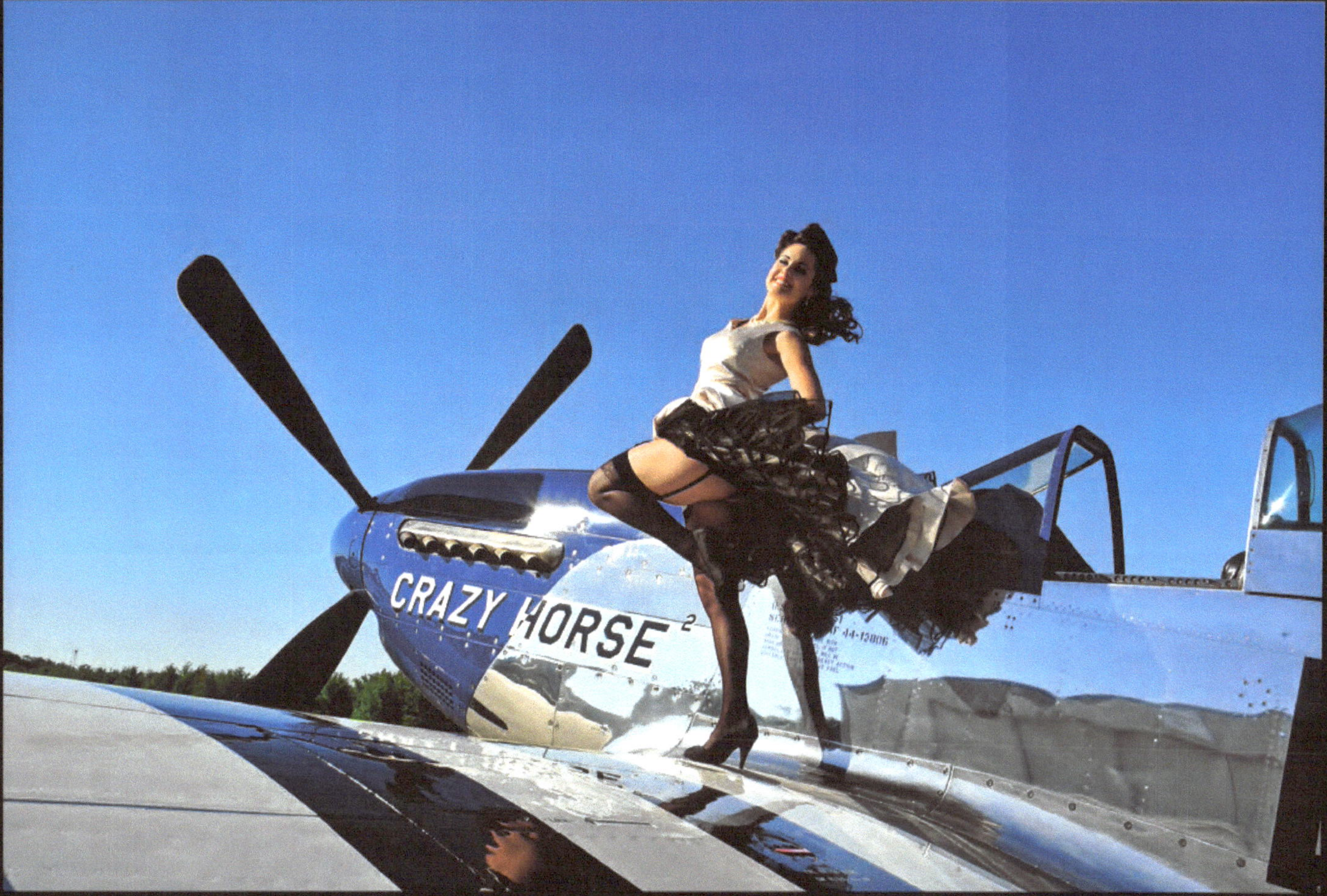

Lexi

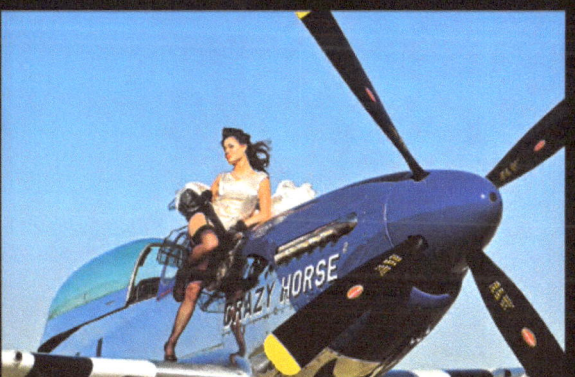

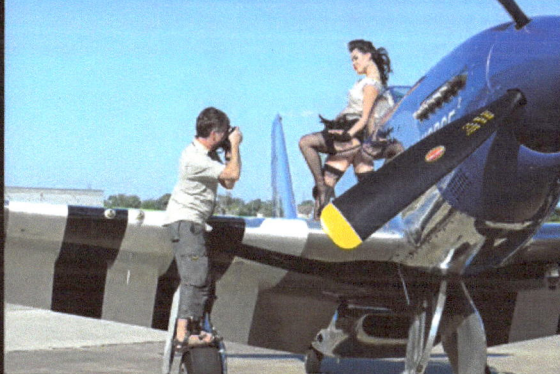

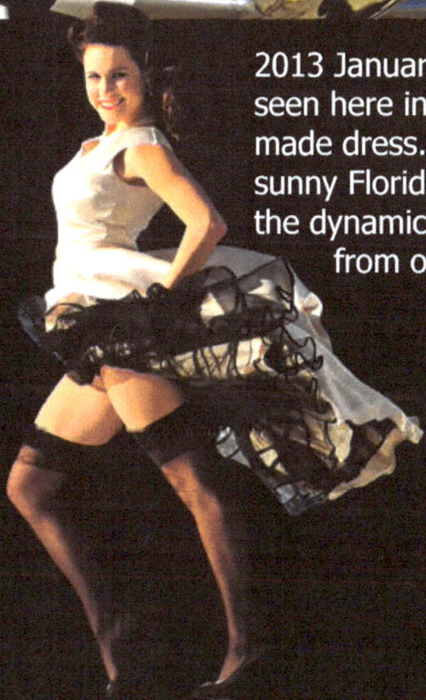

2013 January/February pinup girl Lexi seen here in a 1940's inspired custom made dress. The windy conditions on this sunny Florida afternoon helped creating the dynamic action in this popular photo from our 2013 Mustangs edition.

The "Crazy Horse 2" is one of the beloved P51-D's of Stallion 51's Mustang duo. One of only 16 dual control Mustangs left in existance she now serves to train civilians the thrill of flying a WWII Warbird. Both Mustang's reside at the Stallion 51 training facility in Kissimmee Florida.

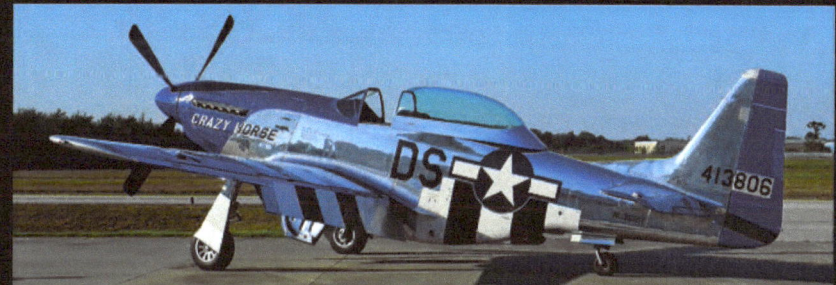

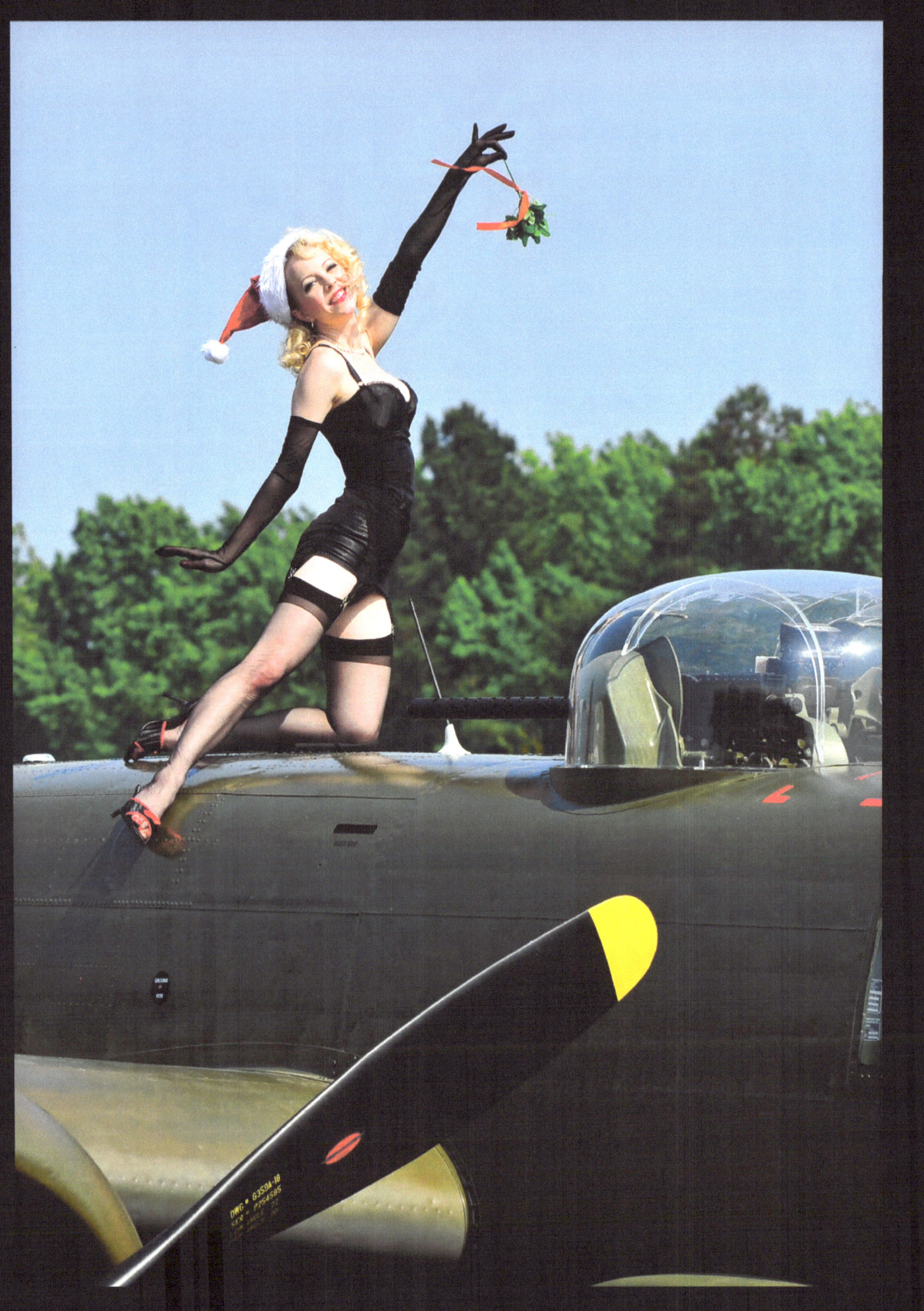

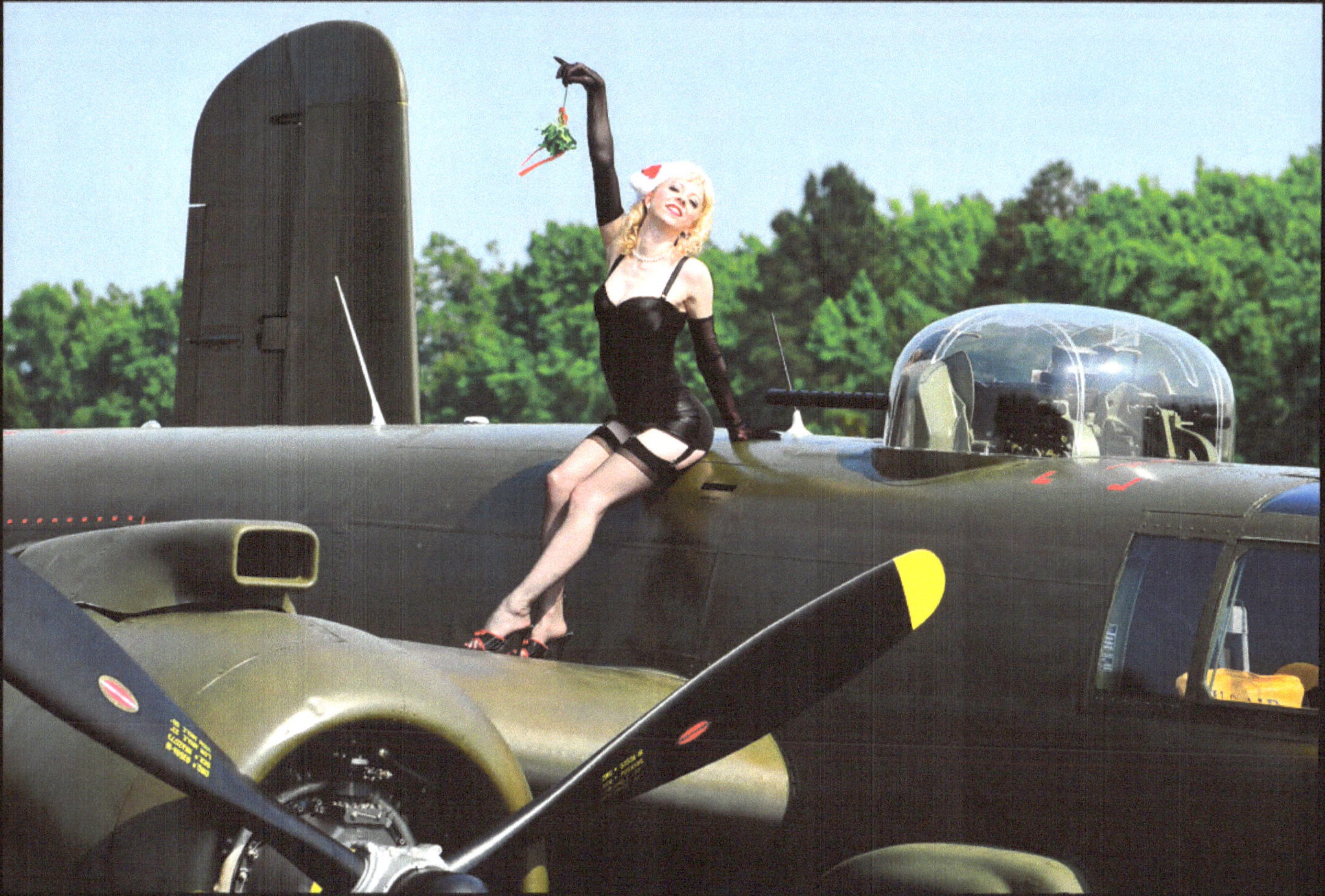

TAMMY

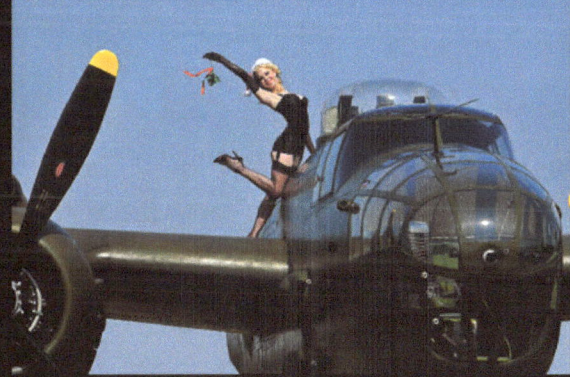

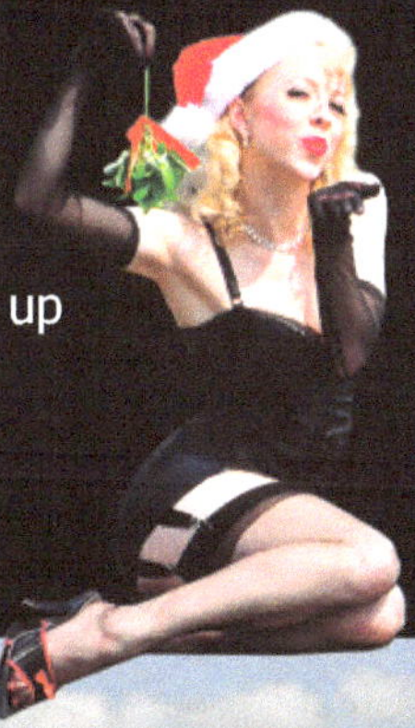

Constructed as a B-25J, "Wild Cargo" spent a long time derelict in a bone yard in Alpharetta, Georgia. Before being scrapped she was picked up by the Military Aviation Museum in Virginia and brought back to life to her full glory.
She now stands as one of the best restoration projects of any air worthy B-25 in the country.

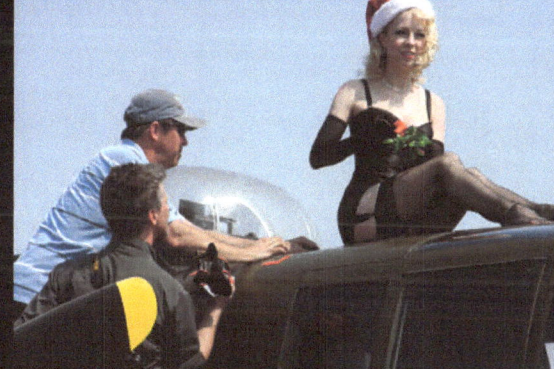

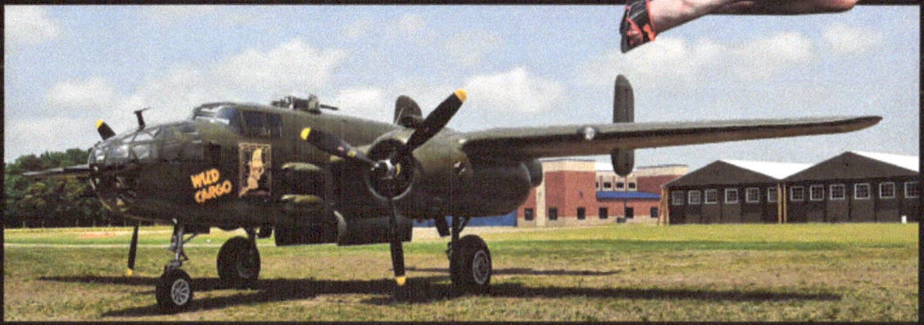

December 2012 pinup girl Tammy is a girl of many talents. Not only is she a great model, she is also a dancer and an actress. We were so impressed with Tammy's ability to pose that we brought her in as a choreographer to help our future pinup girls with the classic retro poses and as one of our returning models in our 2014 and 2015 calendars.

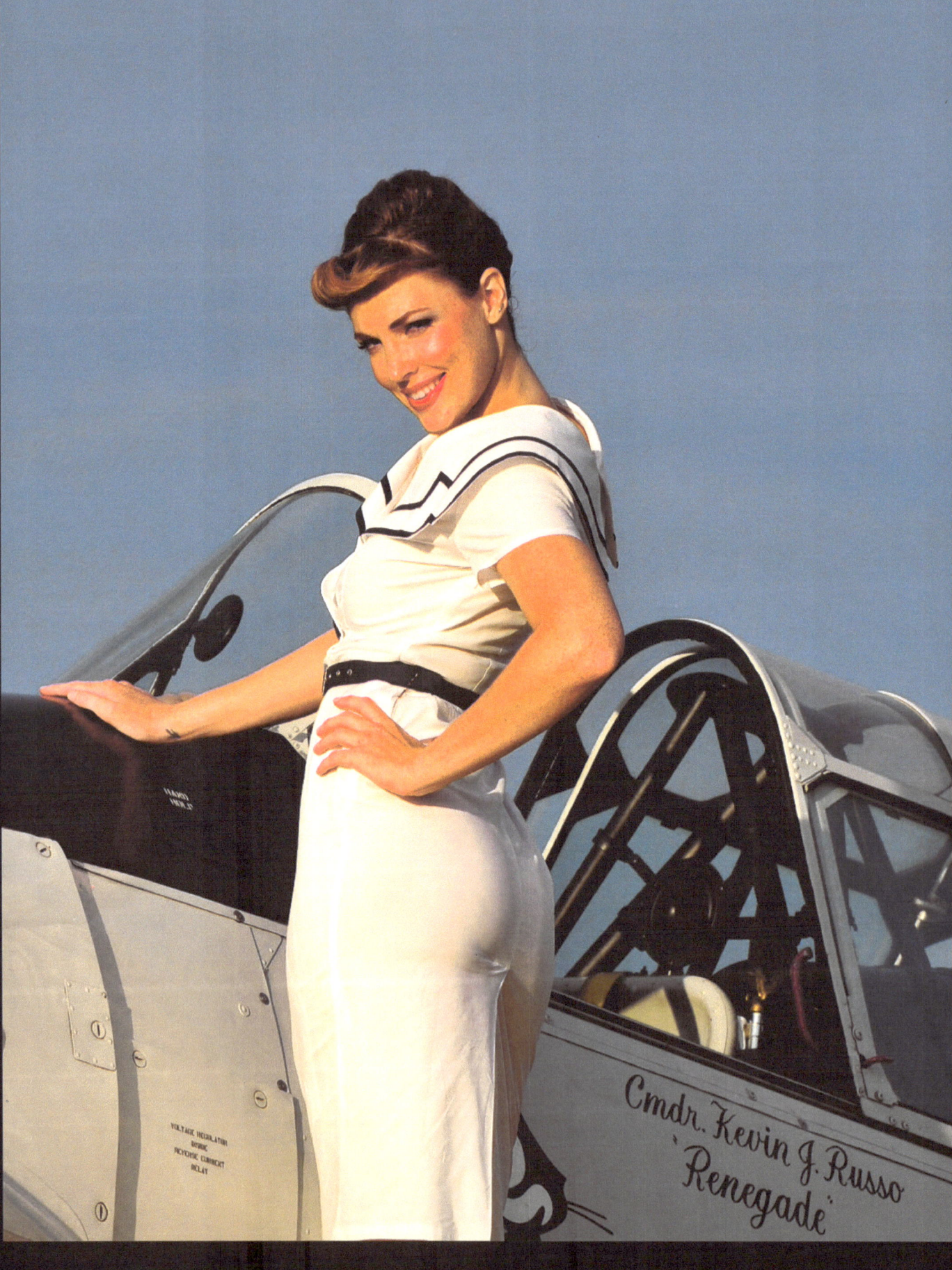

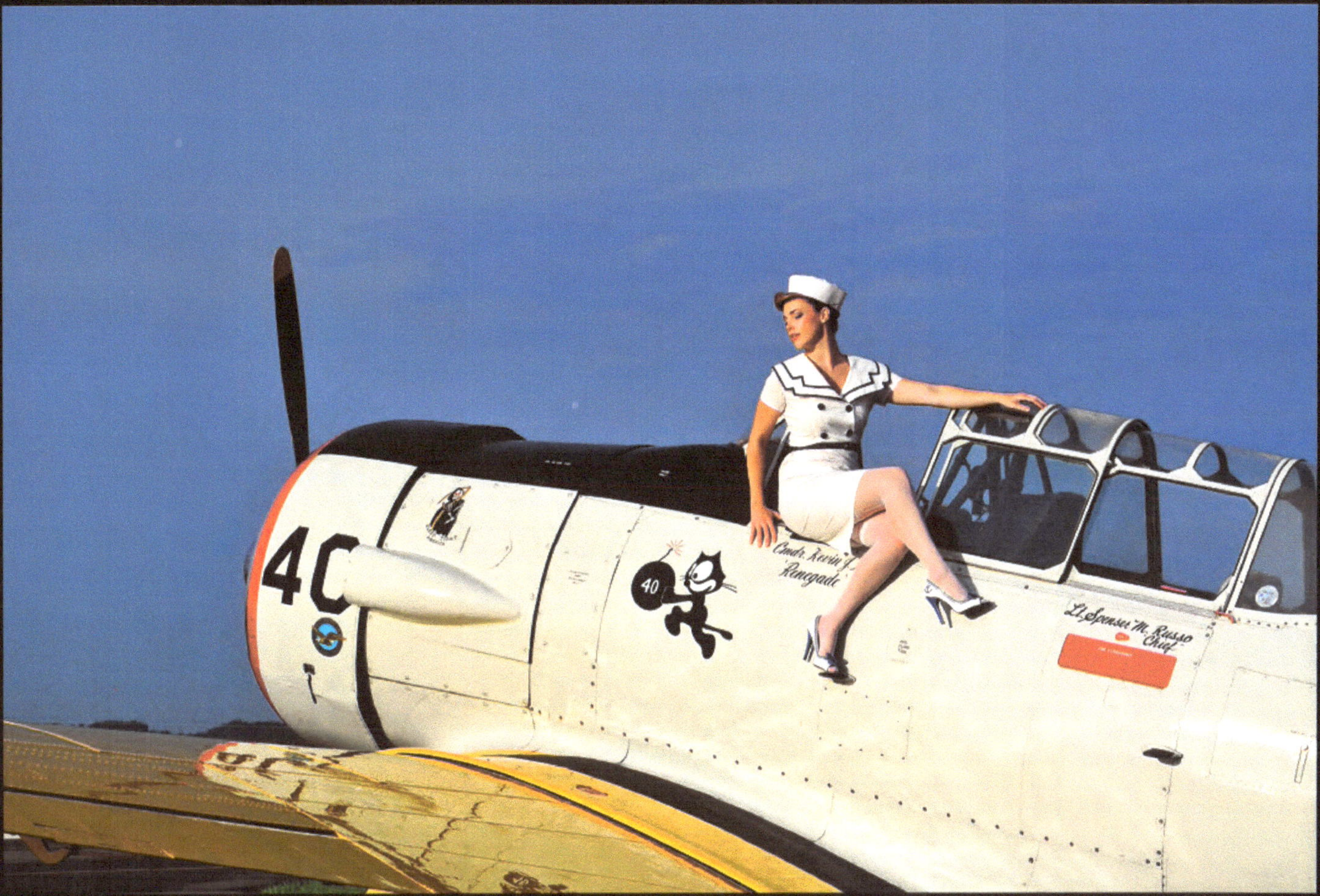

CLAIRE

North American aviations T-6 was one of the most important aircraft of WWII as it served to train new pilots and it became legendary in its reliability. This T-6 is an SNJ naval model and is one of the most pristine still flying in the air show circuit today. Owner Kevin Russo is a skilled acrobatic pilot and does more with the T-6 than any other I have witnessed. Keep your eyes out for Kevin at an air show near you for one of his beautiful performances.

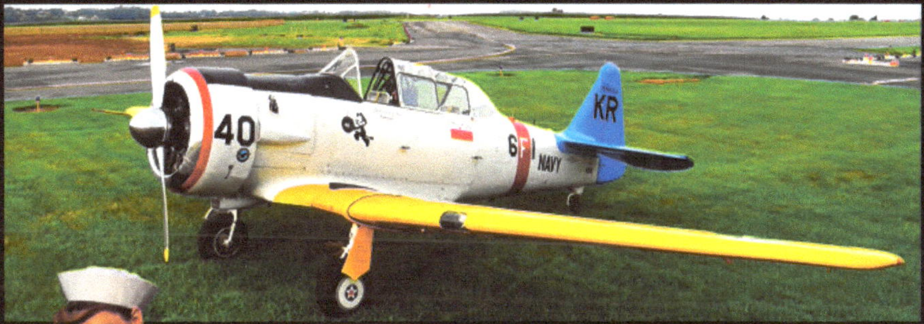

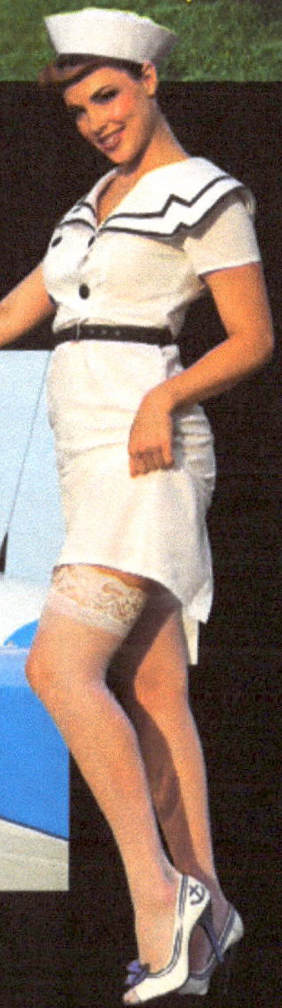

Pinup girl Claire turned out a truly classic Navy pinup girl. Cast as one of our first girls in 2011, Claire was a big hit when she traveled to some of our promotional events including the "Hot to Trot" party in California.

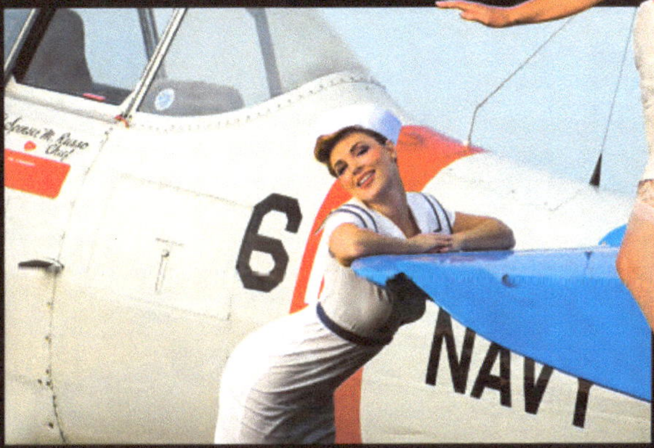

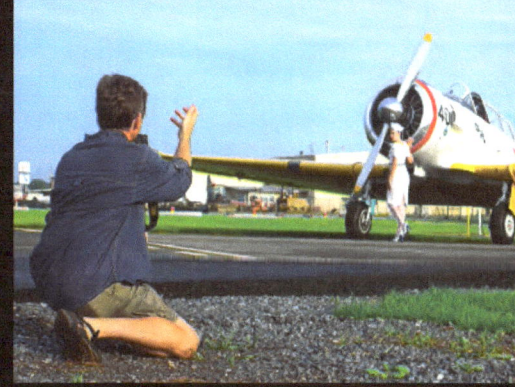

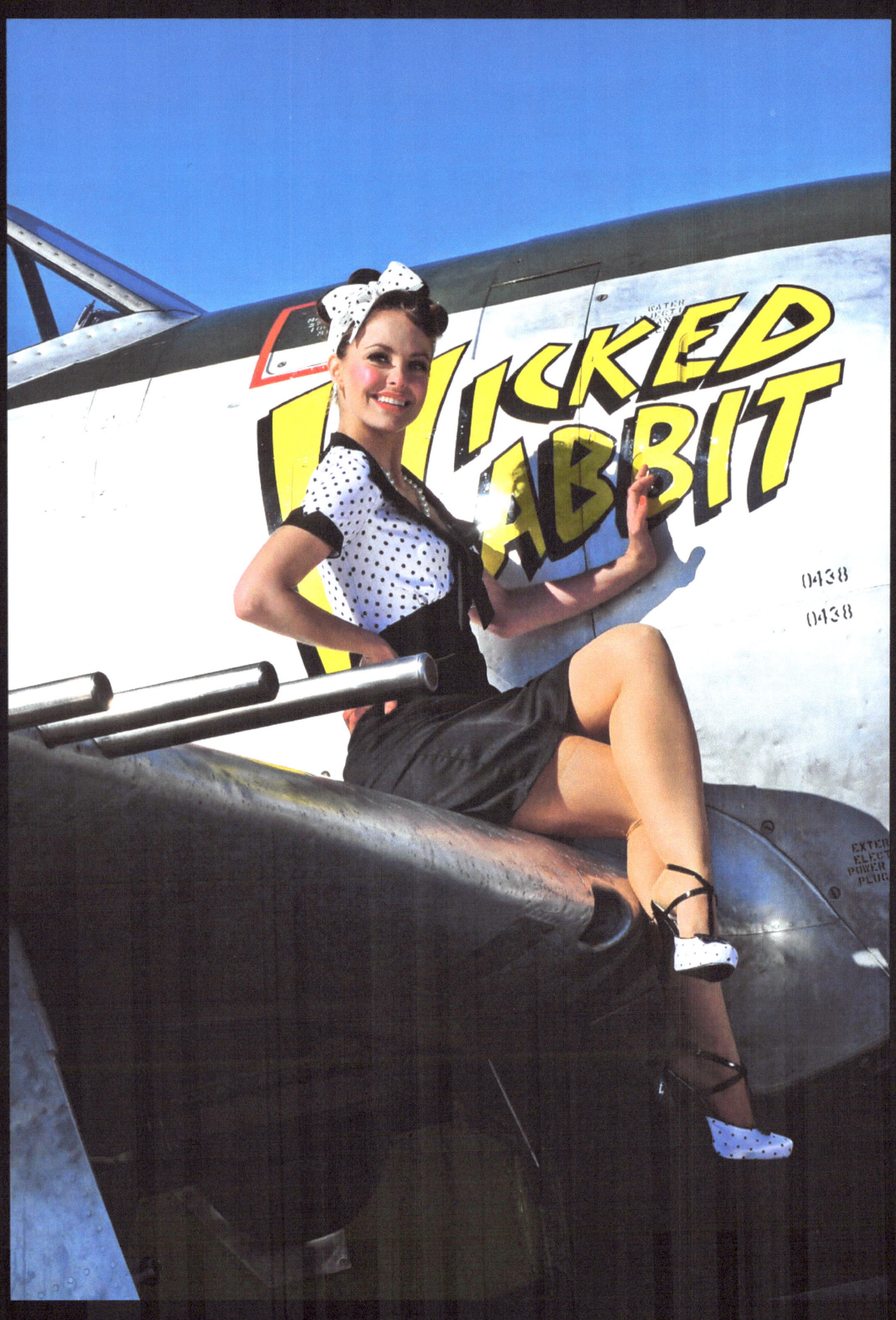

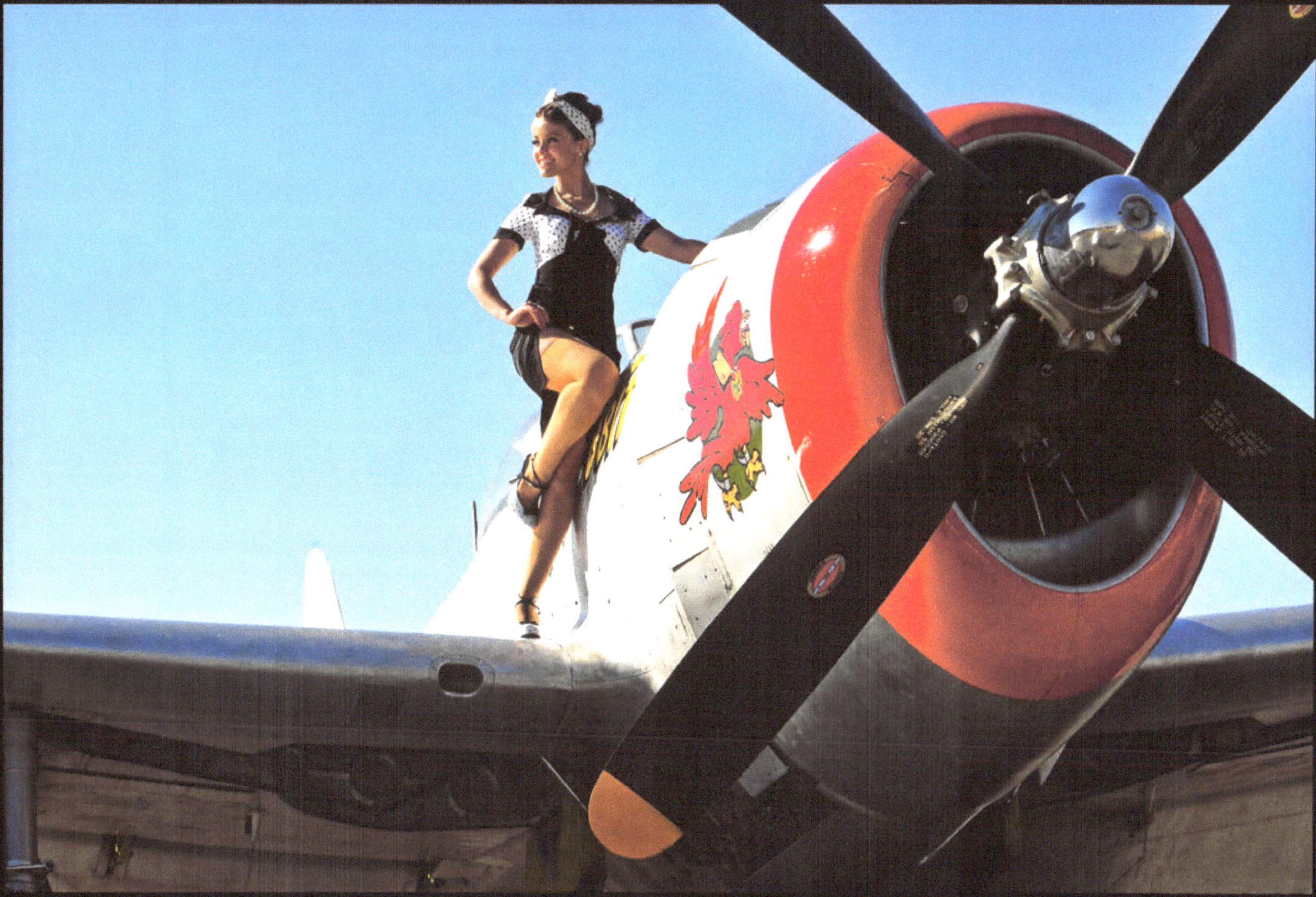

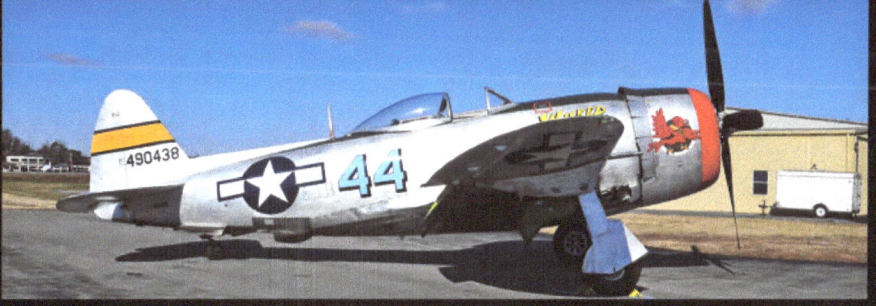

WHITNEY

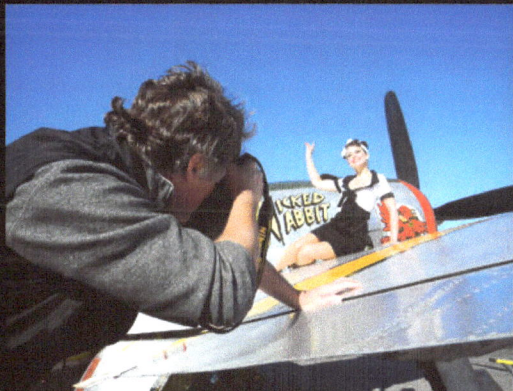

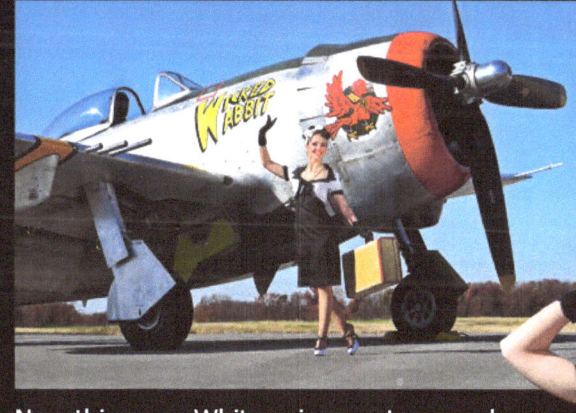

The "Wicked Wabbit" is the exquisitly maintained sister ship of "Hun Hunter", the duo of P-47's that resides at the Tennessee Museum of Aviation. These two P-47's are dressed in the 57th fighter group paint scheme. This particular aircraft was name after James C. Hare.

New this year, Whitney is an actress and model who found us and drove all the way from Chicago to our shooting location in Tennessee. She had to brave the 30 degree weather in the early morning but managed to recreate a truly authentic 1940's look.

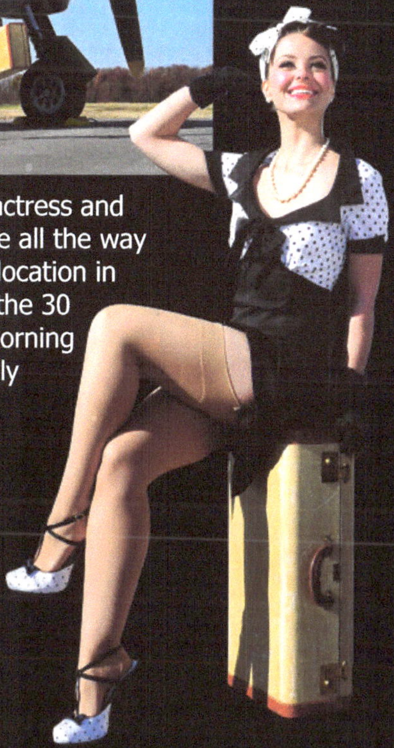

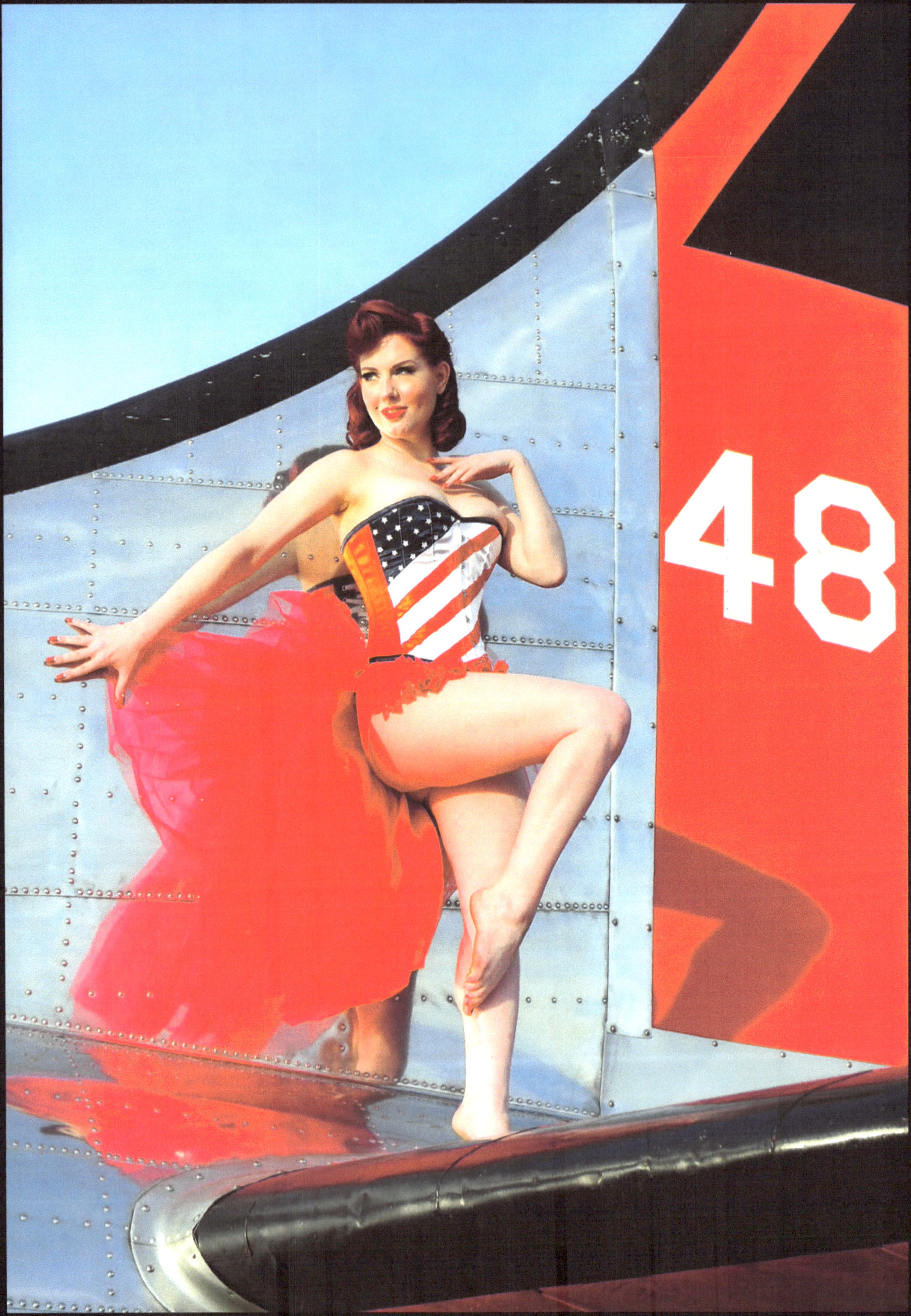
48

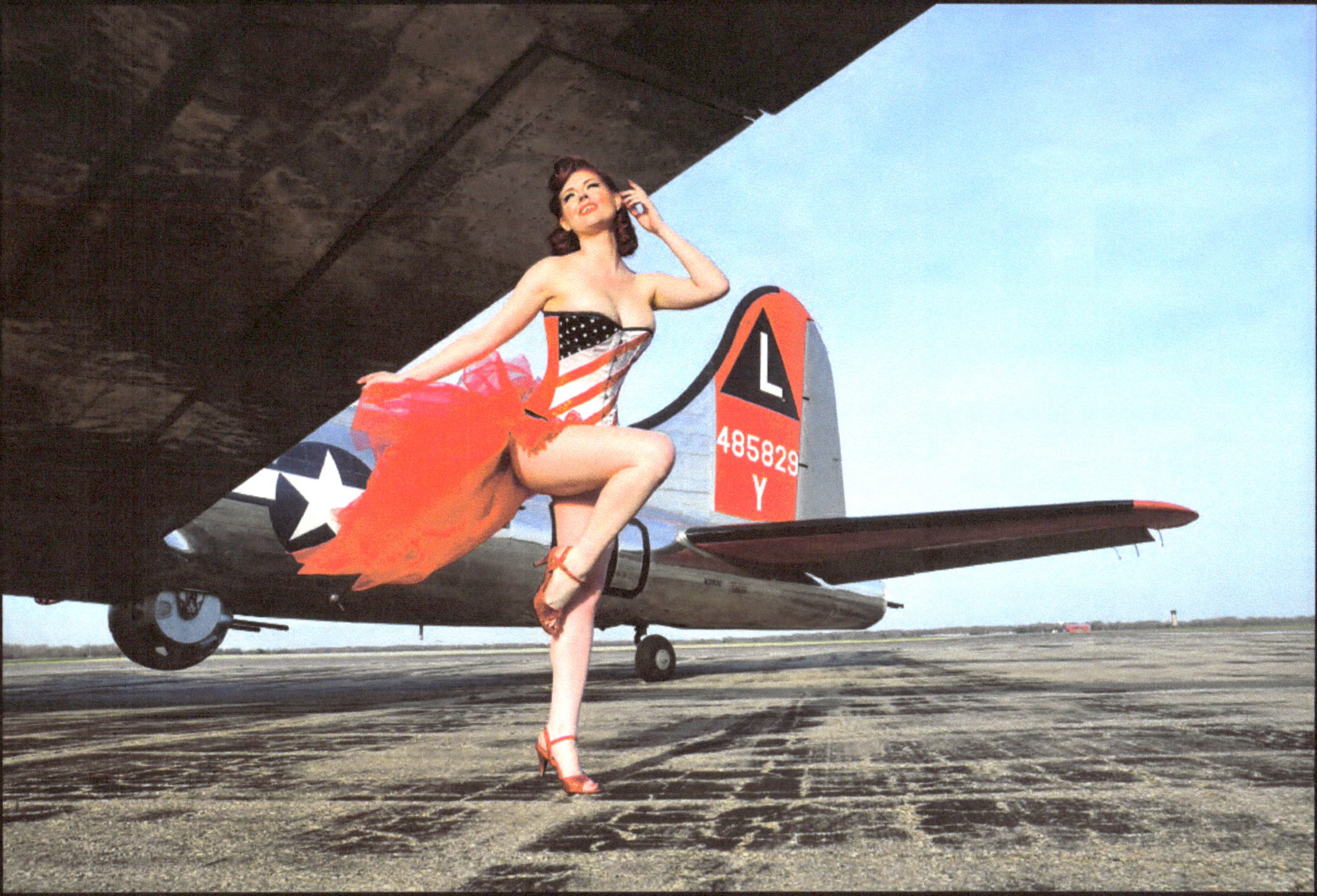

Angela

The "Yankee Lady" is the proud flagship of the Yankee Air Museum in Michigan. This B-17 was once a fire fighter in Arizona and carried out many other civic duties. With great vision she has been transformed into a patriotic legend to carry on the history of the B-17 Flying Fortress.

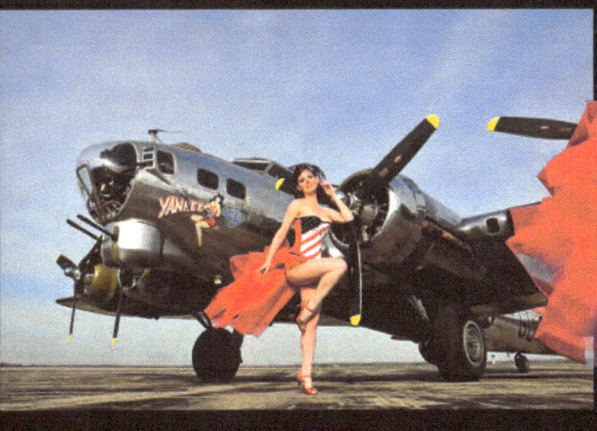

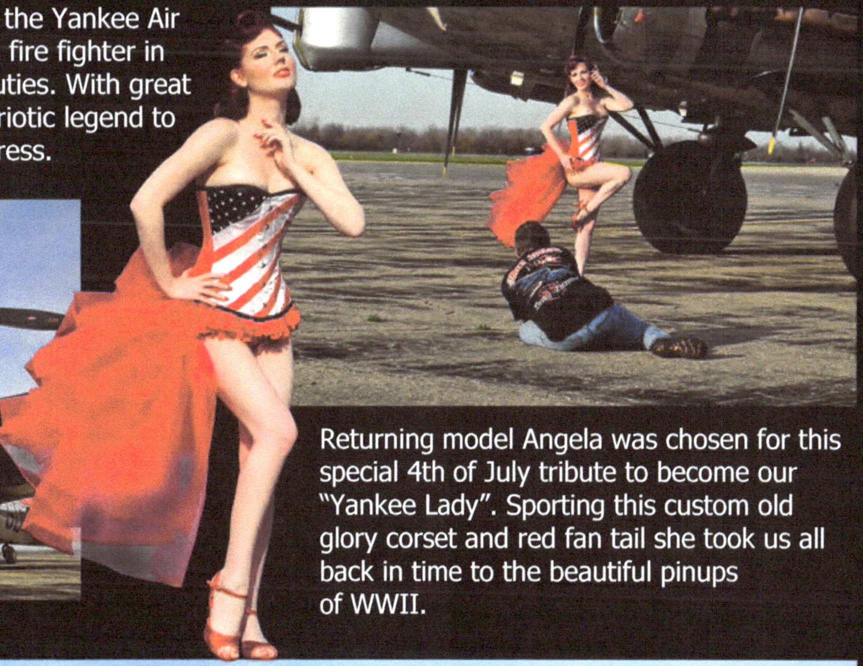

Returning model Angela was chosen for this special 4th of July tribute to become our "Yankee Lady". Sporting this custom old glory corset and red fan tail she took us all back in time to the beautiful pinups of WWII.

Today the "Yankee Lady" travels nation-wide to give the rare opportunity to take a ride on this historic legend. Watch the skies in a town near you as she makes her way across the air show circuit.

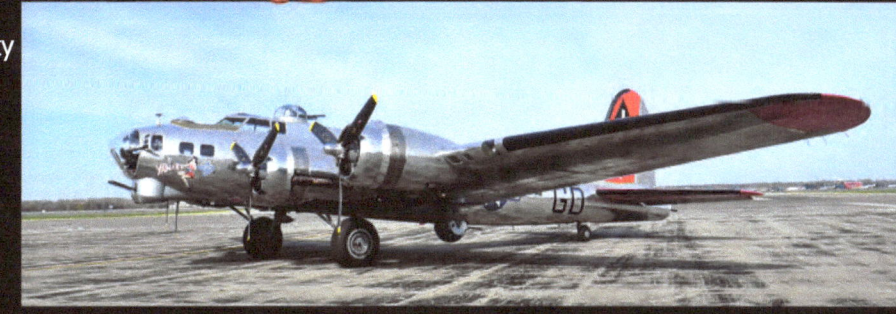

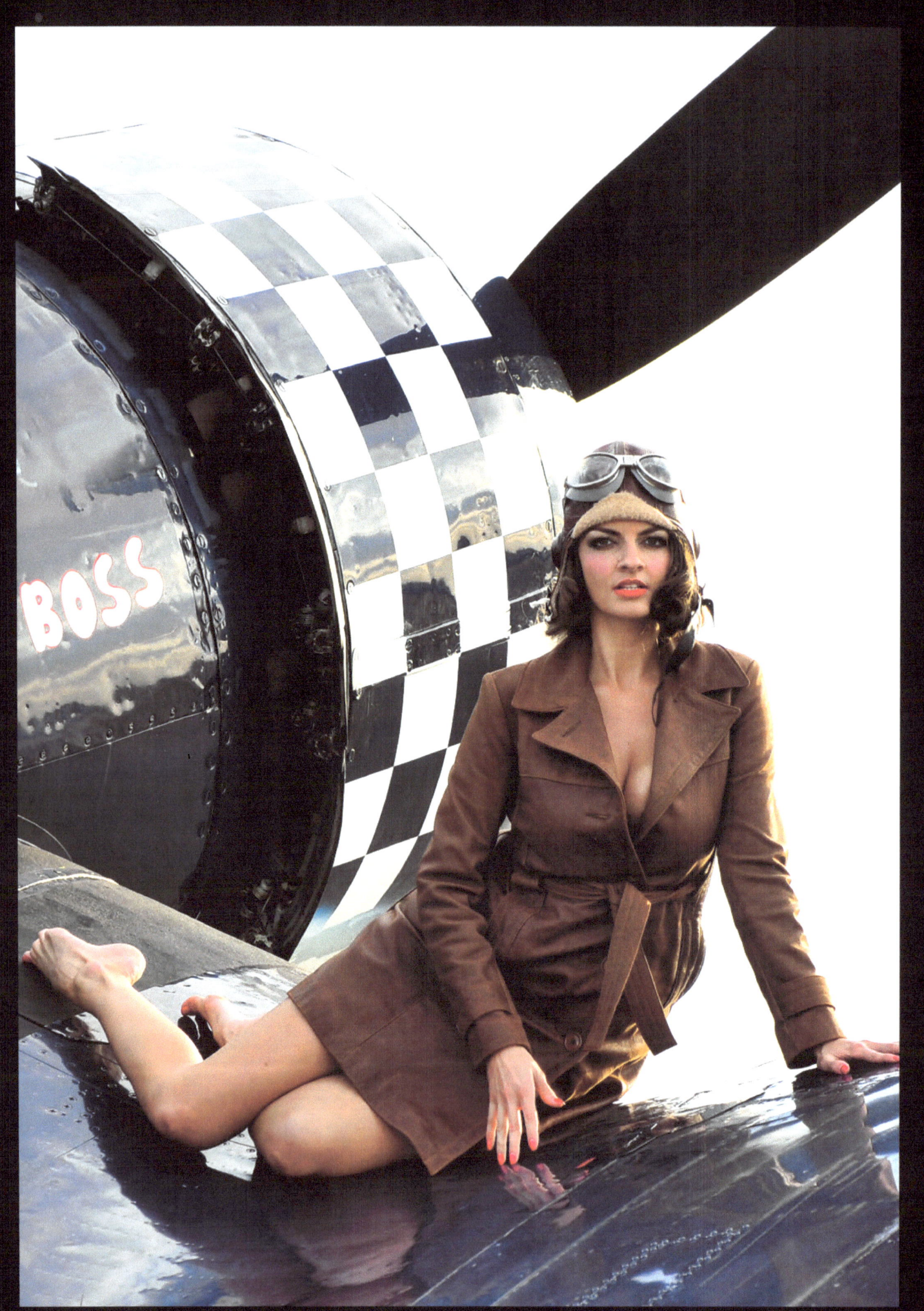

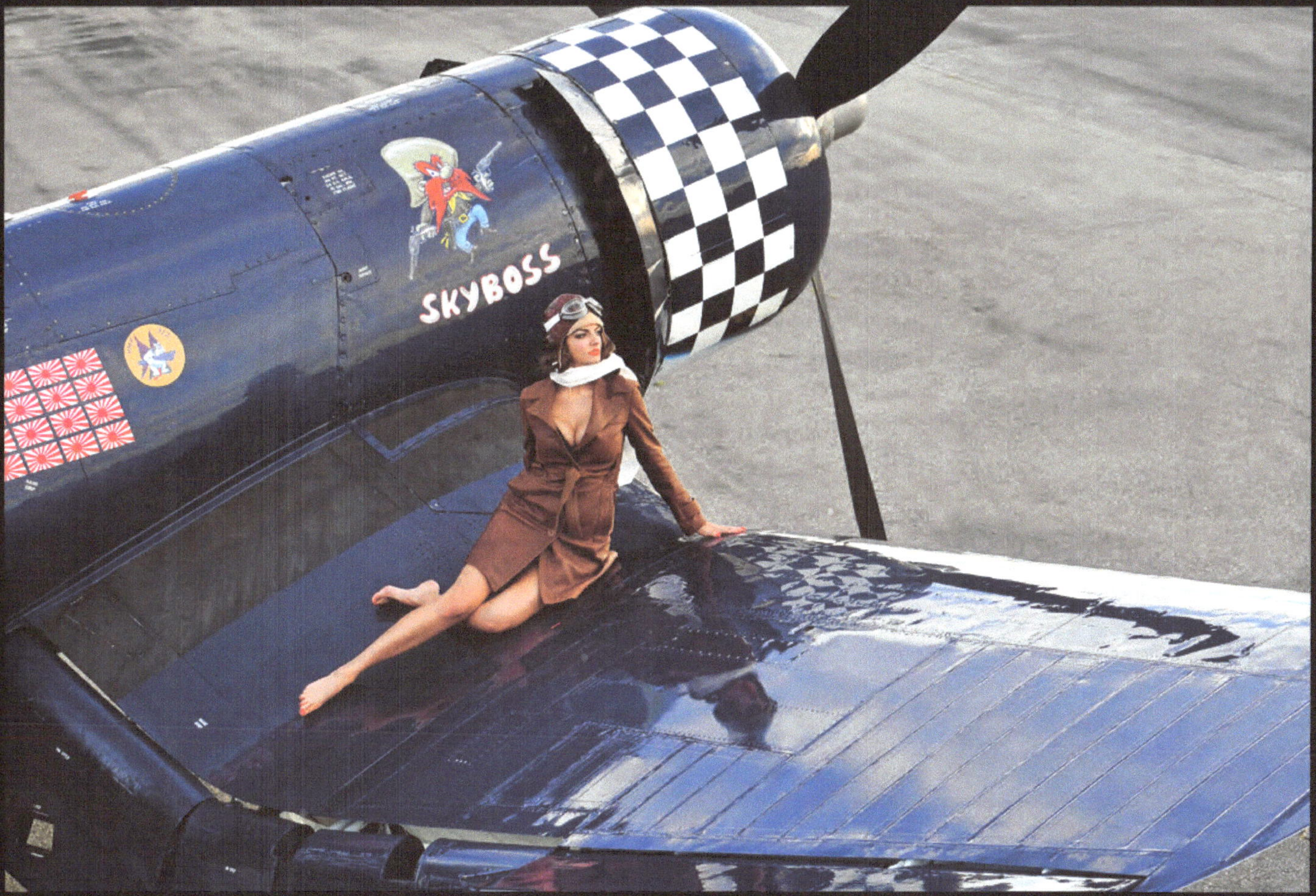

Rikki

Made famous by the 1970's hit TV show "Baa Baa Black Sheep", the Vought F-4U Corsair also known by its enemies as the "Whistling Death" was one of WWII's premier fighters. The gull wing design gave clearance for the massive propeller to land on aircraft carriers. Used primarily by the Marines and the Navy. "Skyboss" resides at the American Airpower Museum on Long Island.

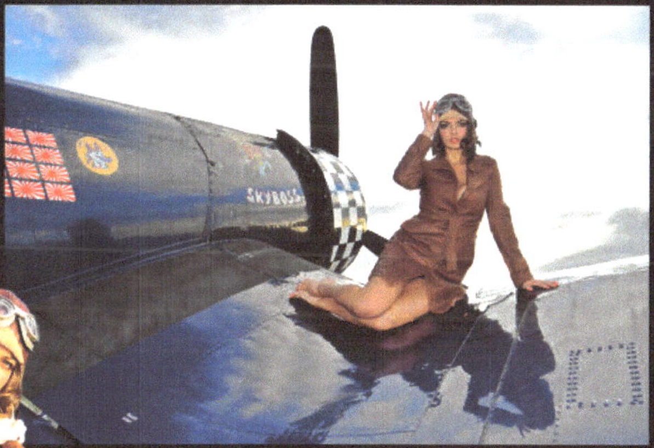

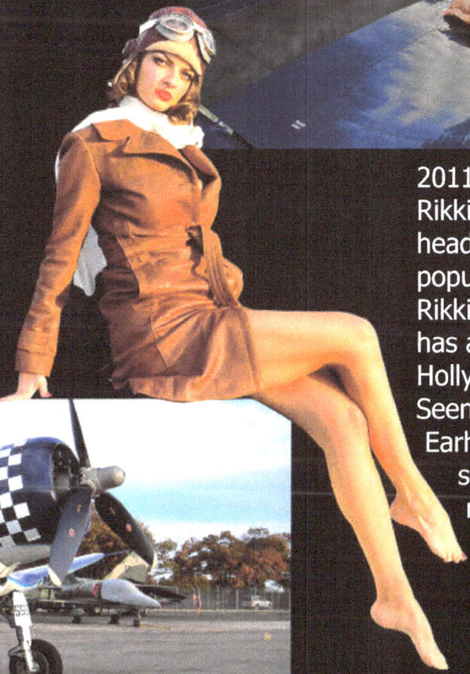

2011 February pinup girl Rikki did more than turn heads as one of our most popular pinup girls to date. Rikki is a small town girl but has all the qualities of a Hollywood starlet.
Seen here in an Amelia Earhart replica jacket she pulls off the perfect retro aviatrix.

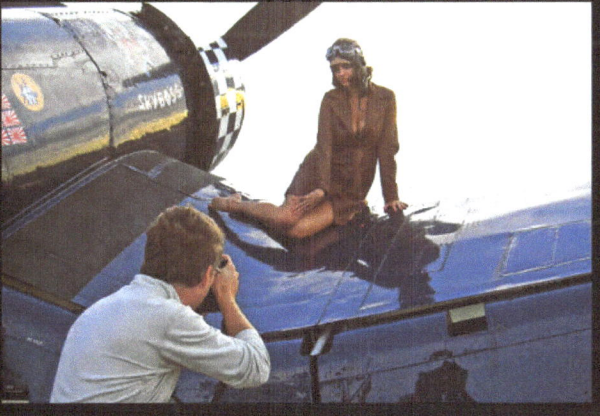

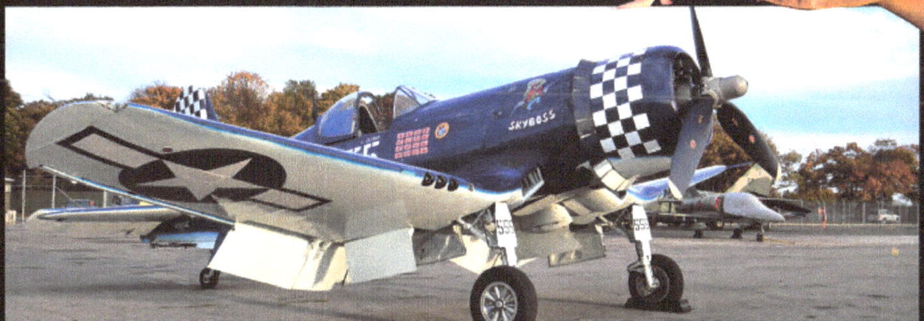

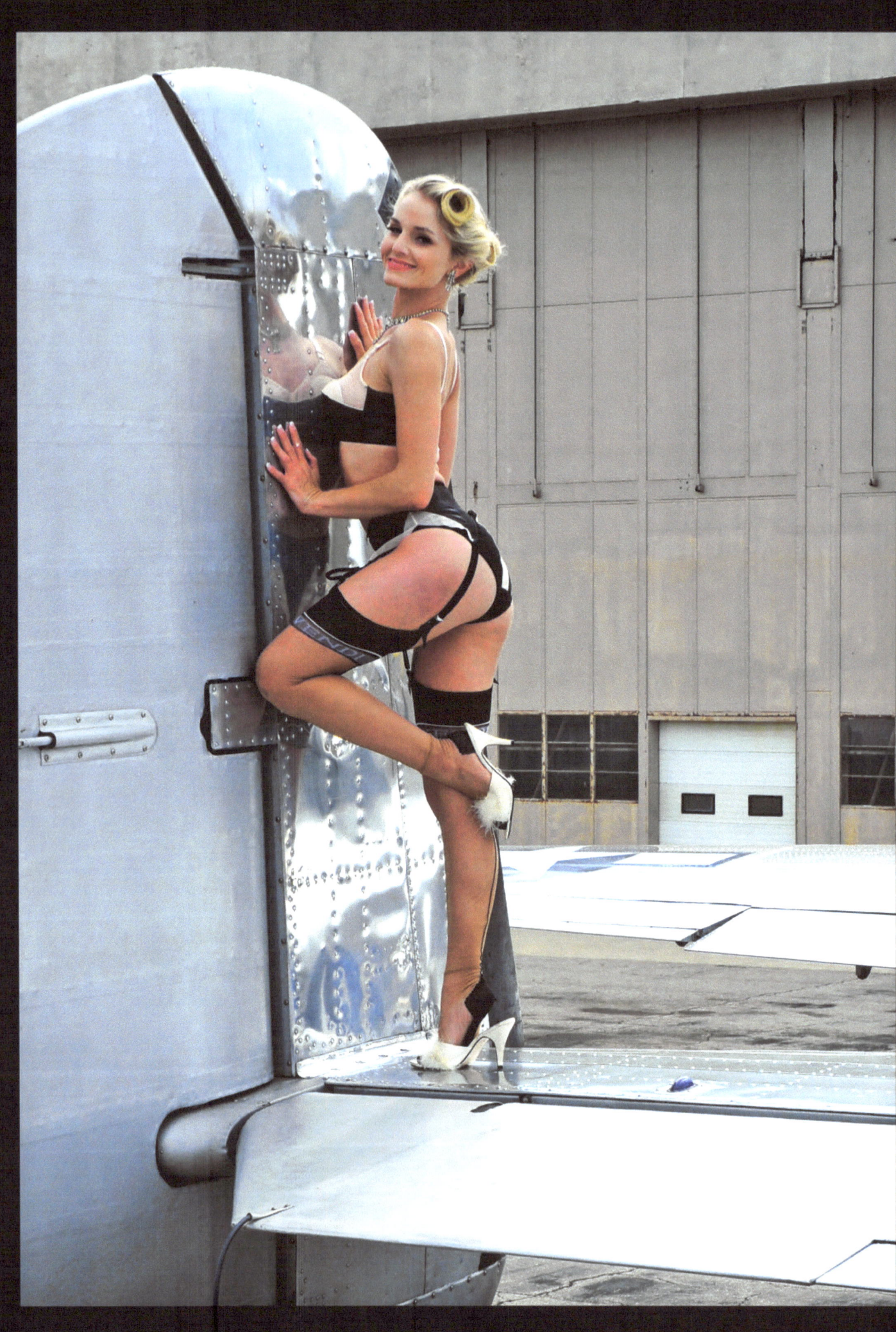

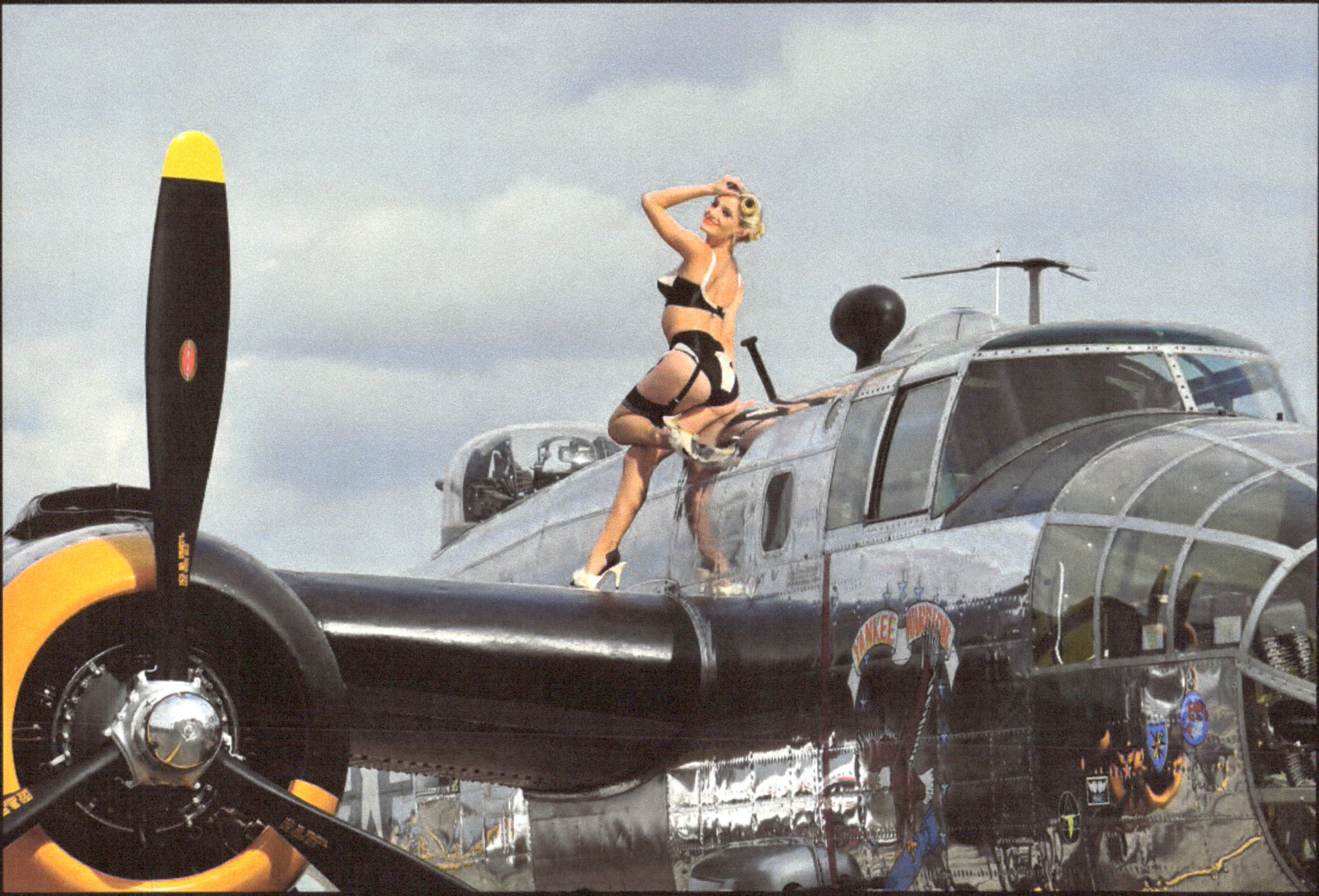

LIZ

2013 cover model Liz returns as one of our sexiest pinup girls to date. Liz, an experienced full time model from Houston Texas has become one of our most popular models with her ravishing cover shot on the 2013 all Mustangs edition. Liz appears as our February 2014 pinup girl.

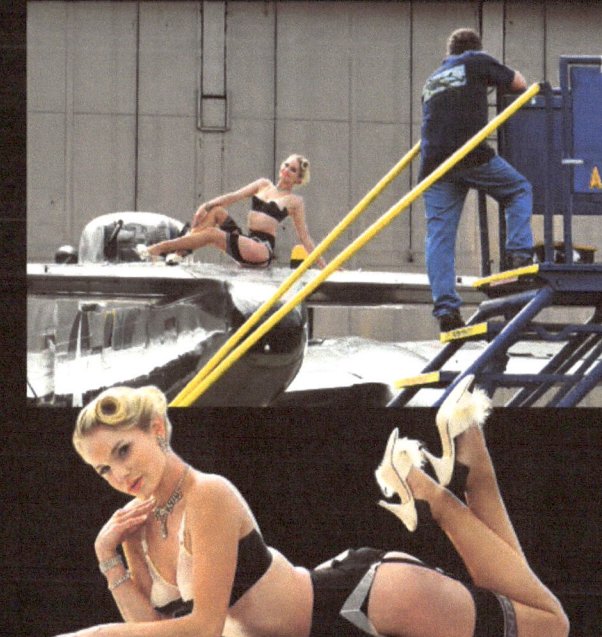

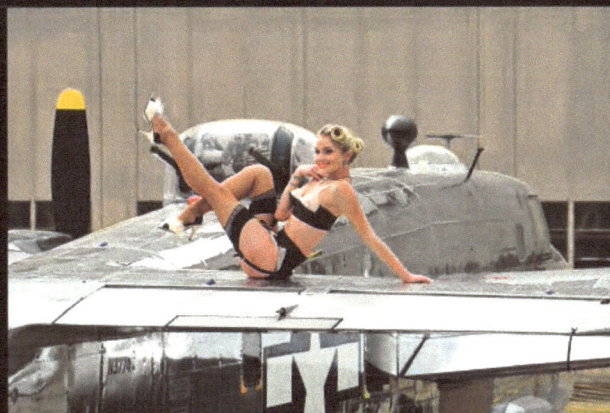

Nicknamed the "Yankee Warrior" this B-25 Mitchell has its home with the Yankee Air Museum in Ypsilanti Michigan. This proud veteran saw combat in all the theaters of WWII and she remains in service today as a testament to her legendary design.

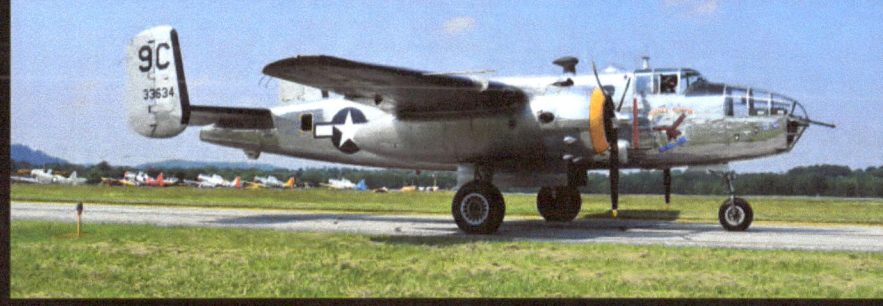

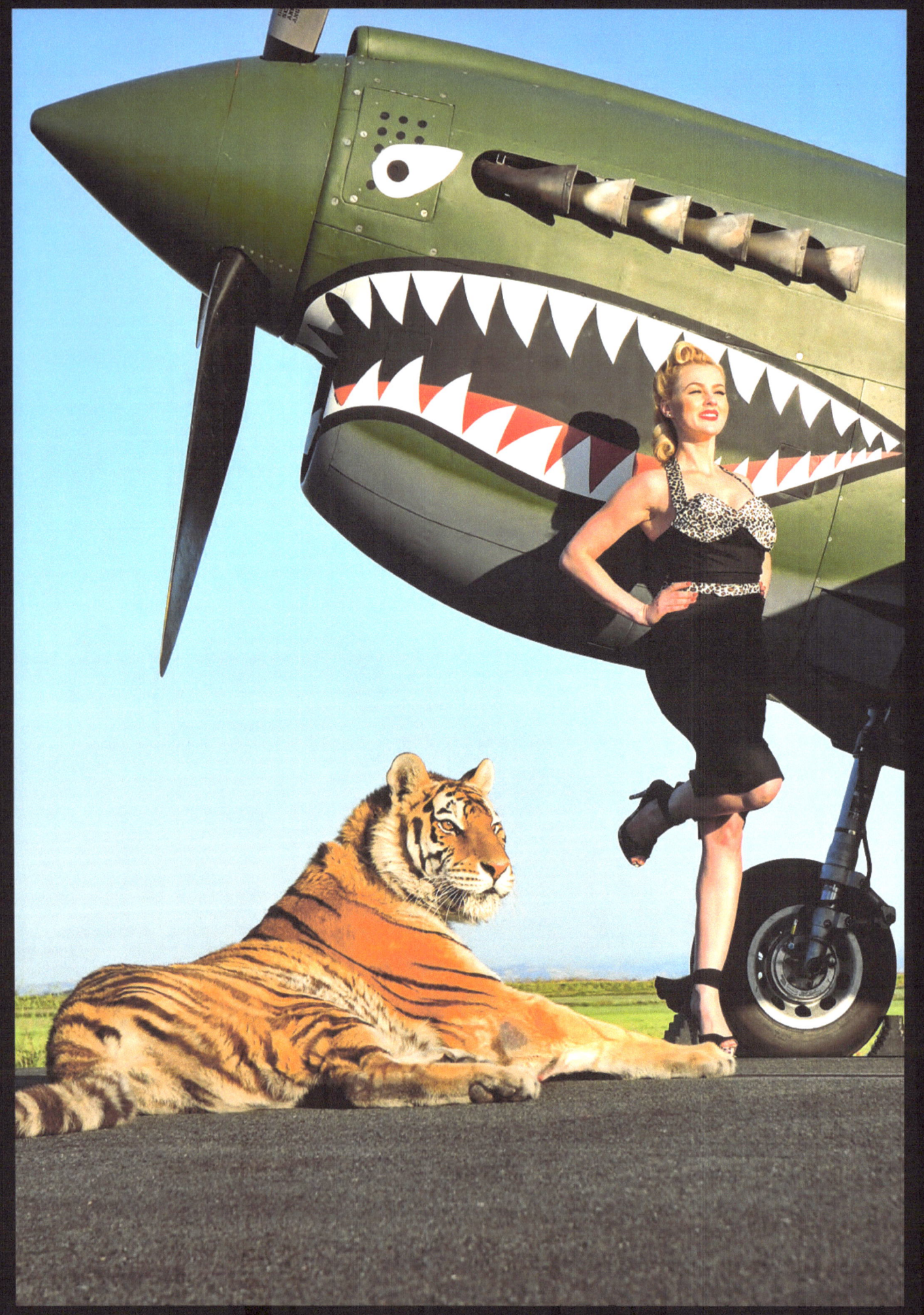

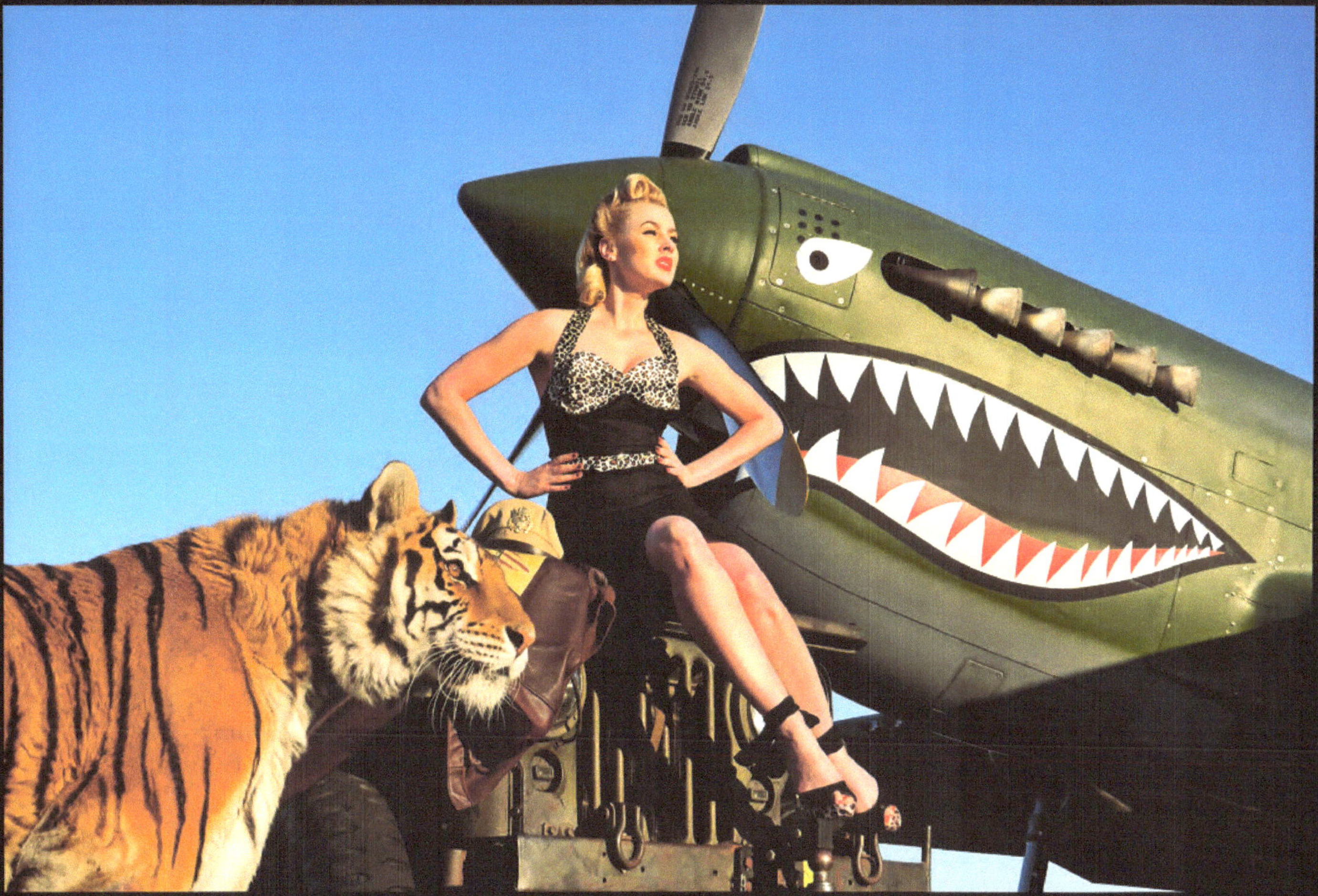

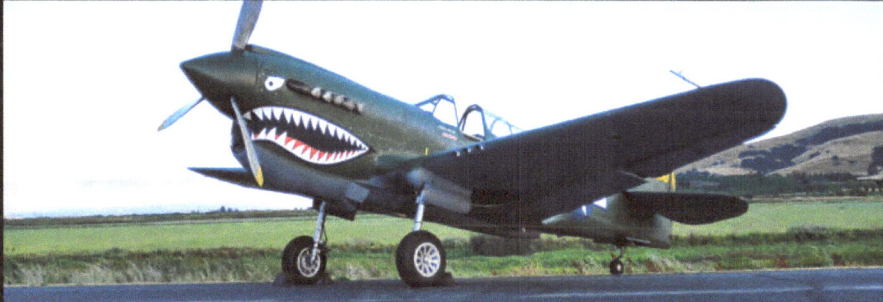

Karolina & Asia

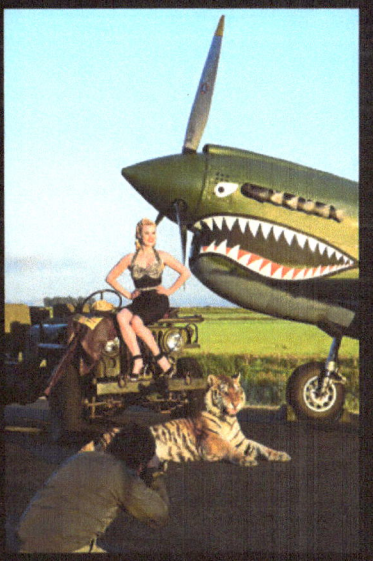

The Vintage Aircraft Company in Sonoma California was excited to feature their beautiful P-40 Kittyhawk stationed at Schellville Airport. This is one of the last remaining dual-control Kittyhawks in the world.

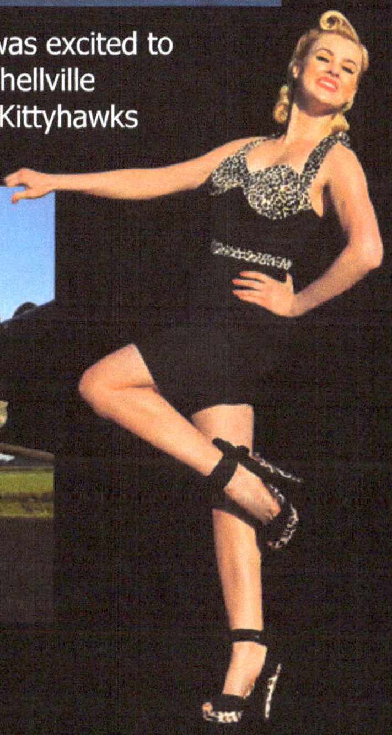

In this tribute to the AVG "Flying Tigers", we contracted a Hollywood show cat to come on location in Sonoma for our photo shoot. Returning 2012 pinup girl Karolina was nervous and a bit apprehensive about working with Asia, our Siberian tiger, but after getting acquainted they both performed brilliantly in this homage to the famed "Flying Tigers" of WWII.

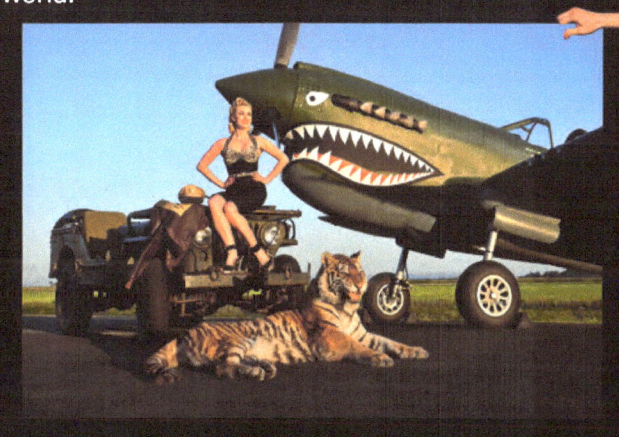

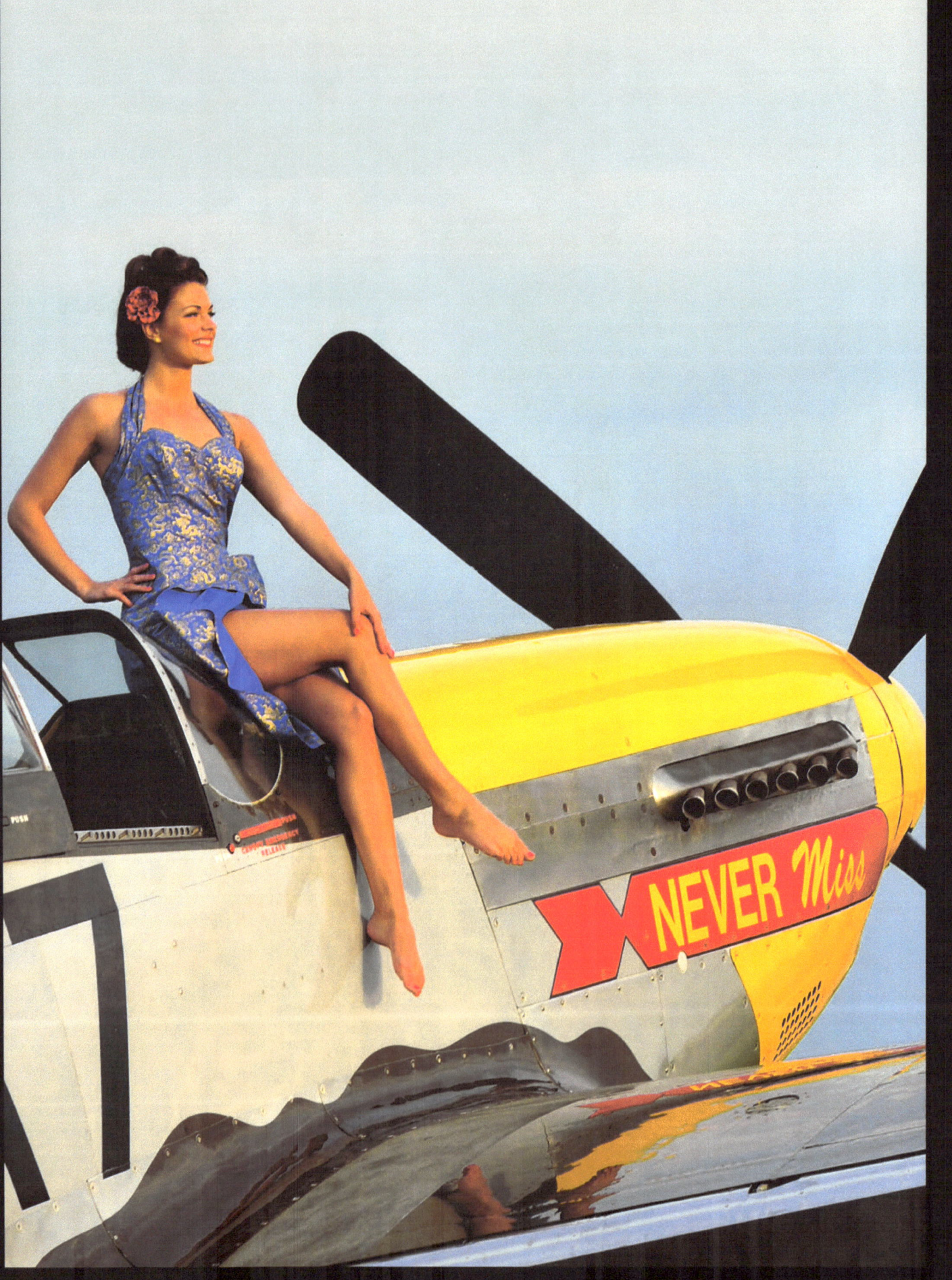

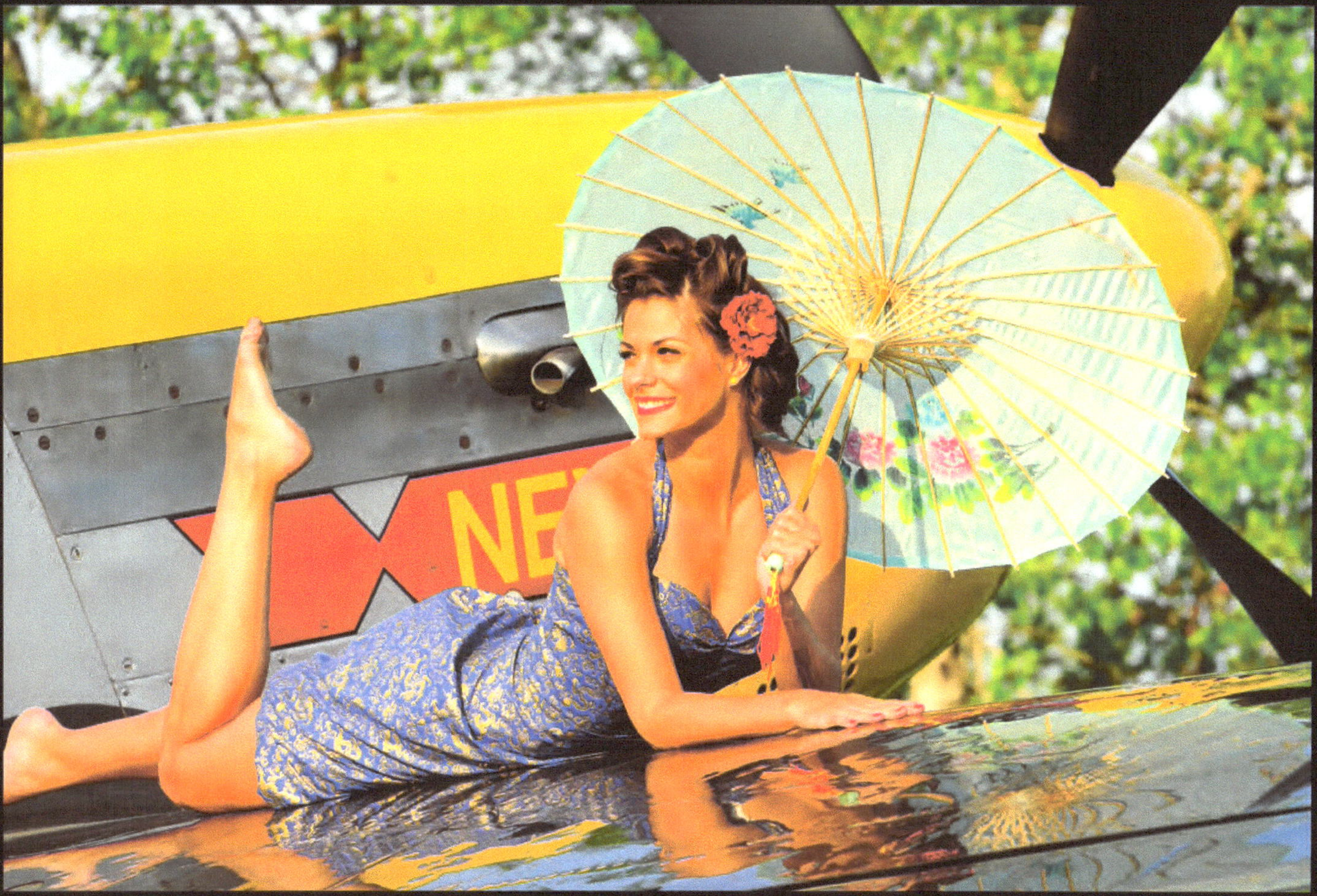

LAURA

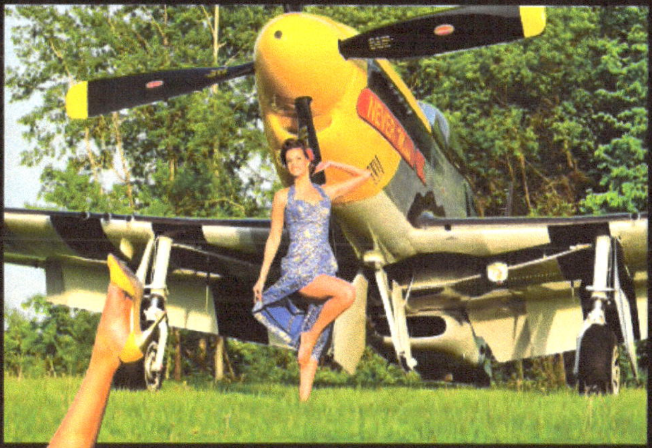

November/December 2013 pinup girl Laura is a true classic beauty. This Pennsylvania native had no pinup experience prior to working with us, however she turned out one of the most authentic and classic shots of the season.

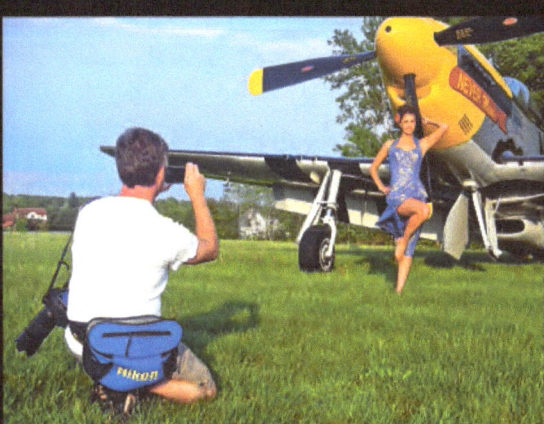

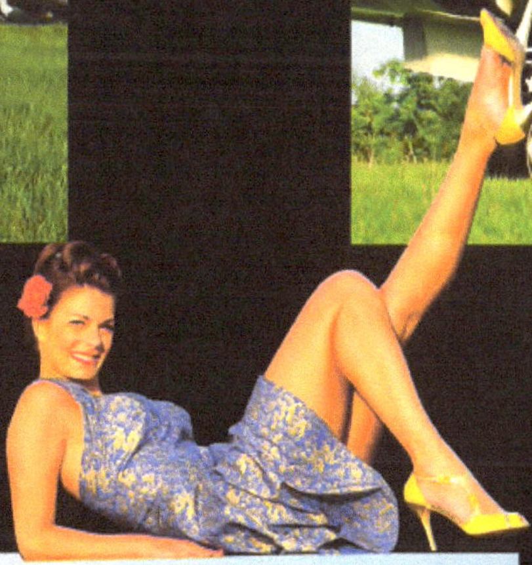

The P-51D "Never Miss" first saw the light of day on March 9th of 1945. Delivered to the 8th Air Force in the European theater of operations, she went on to play a part in the D-Day operations. As is evident in these photos you can still see her stripes. Operating out of upstate New York, "Never Miss" can be seen in action in many East Coast regional air shows.

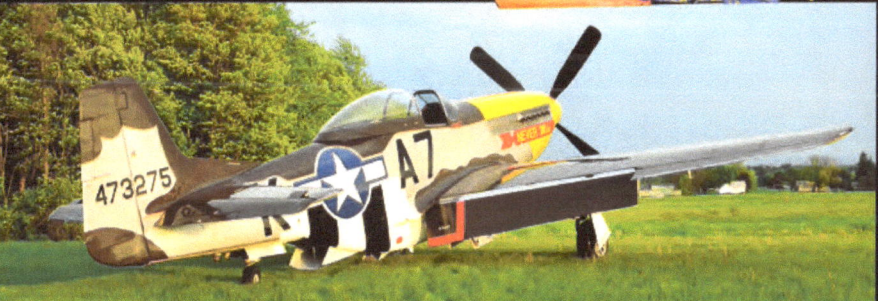

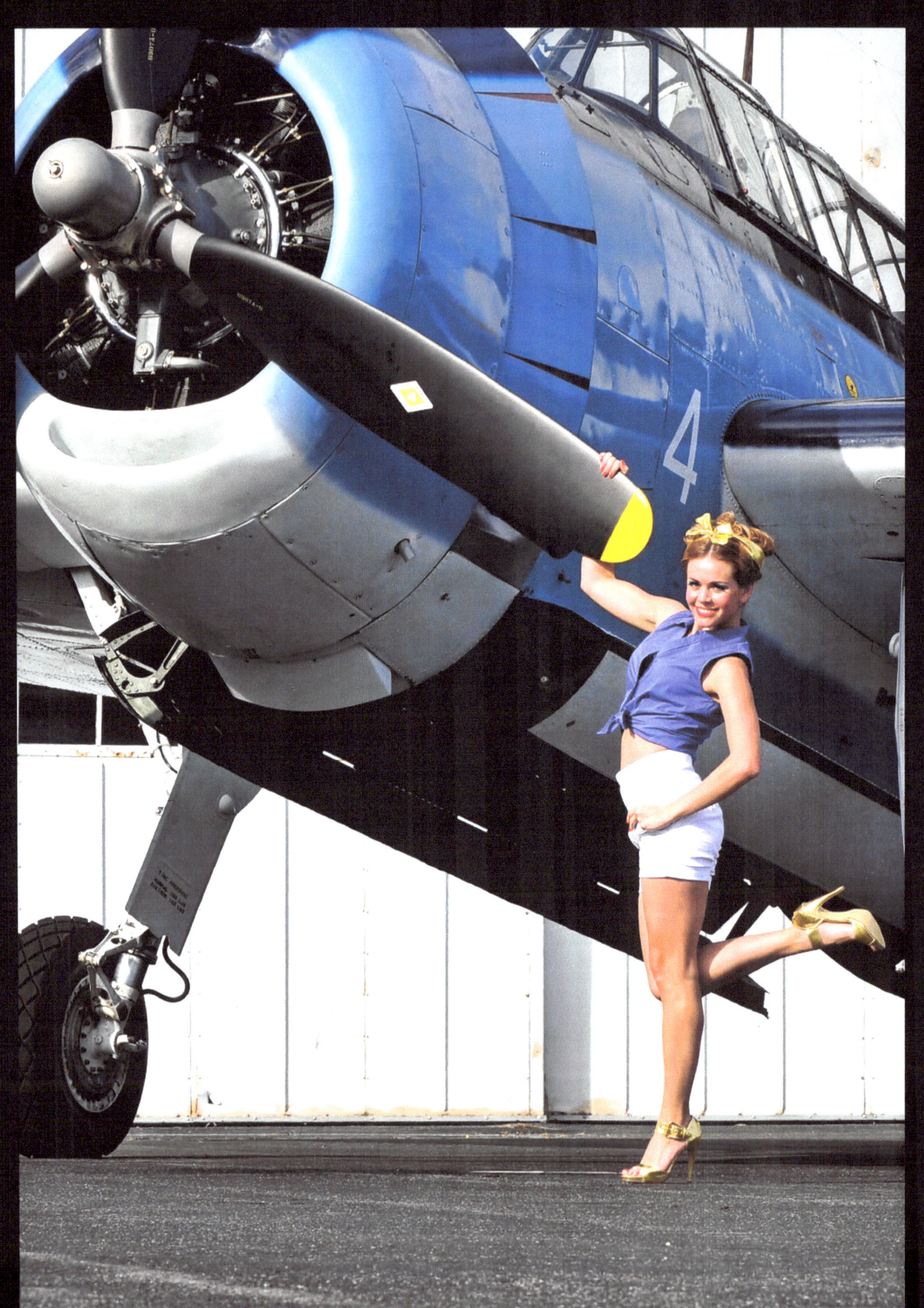

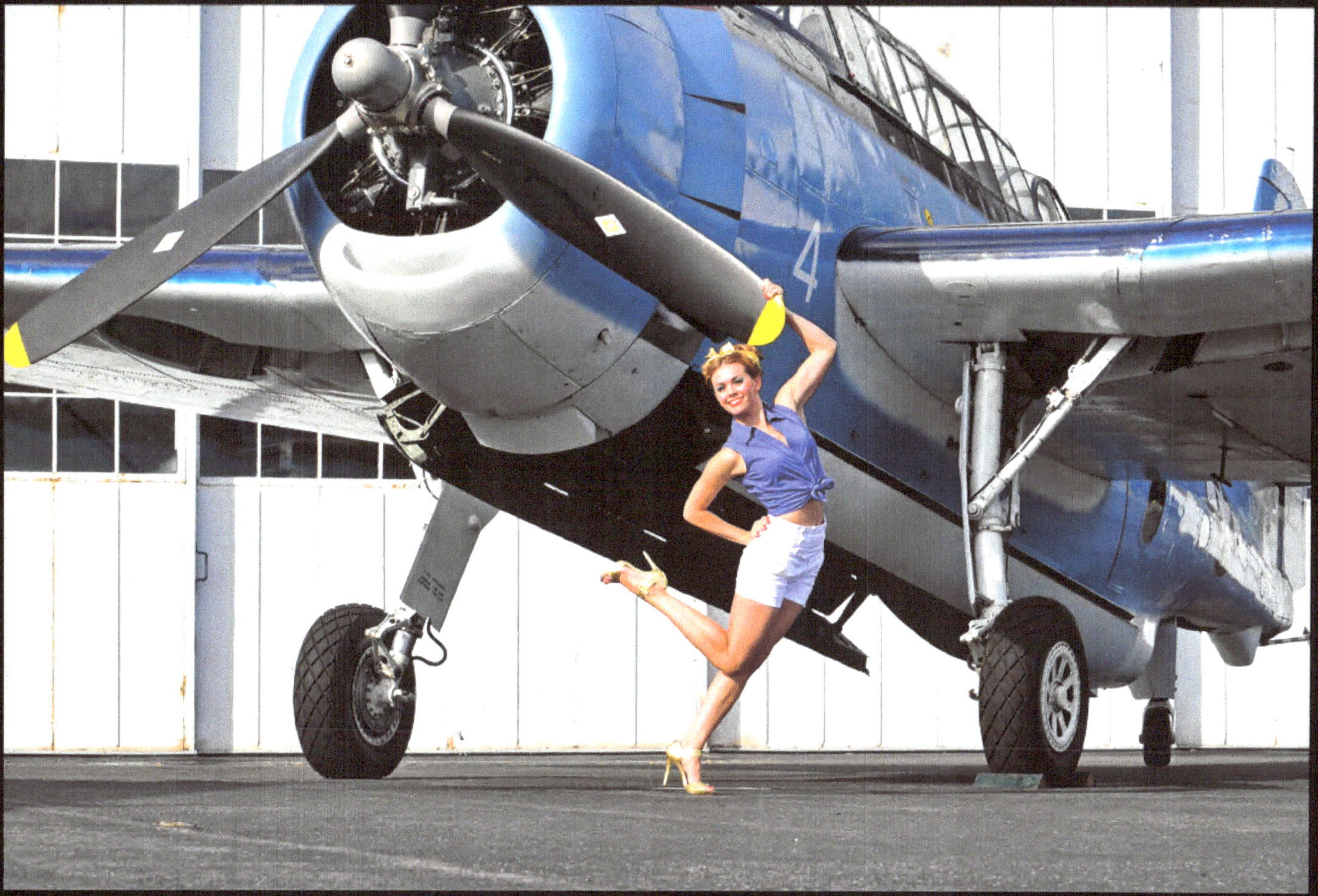

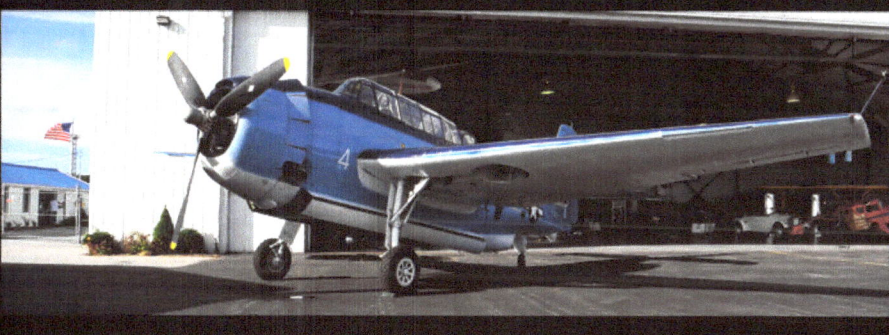

Kat

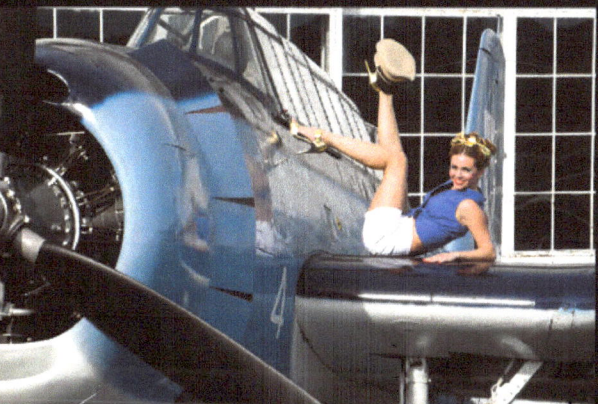

2011 April pinup girl "Kat" Ekaterina makes a superb model with her experience as a professional dancer, she has no problem with those pinup poses. Kat's pose with a traditional crush cap is inspired by an original Alberto Vargas pinup painting.

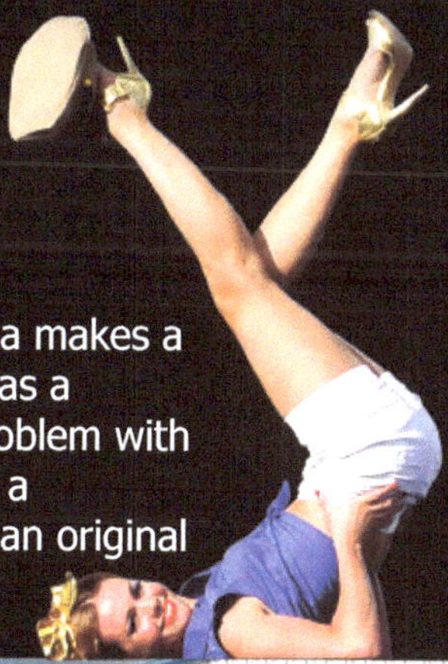

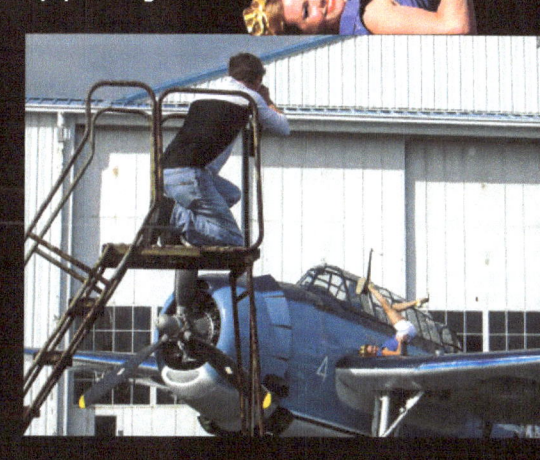

One of the few remaining TBM-3 Avengers still flying today, this beautiful example lives at the Mid Atlantic Air Museum in Reading Pennsylvania, where it is flown regularly at regional air shows. She has been painstakingly restored to the original VT-23 squadron from the USS Langley. The TBM is a surprisingly large aircraft whose

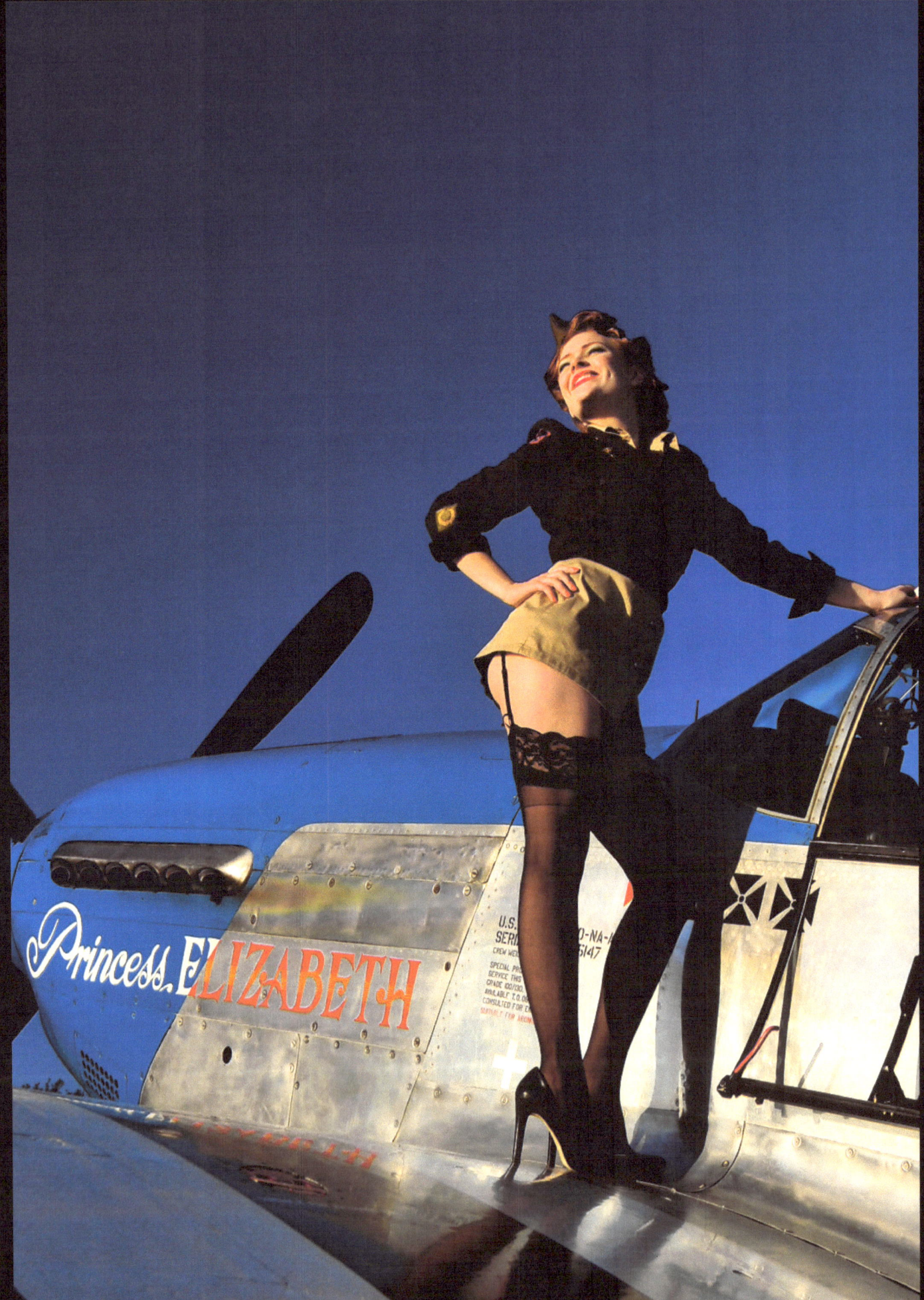

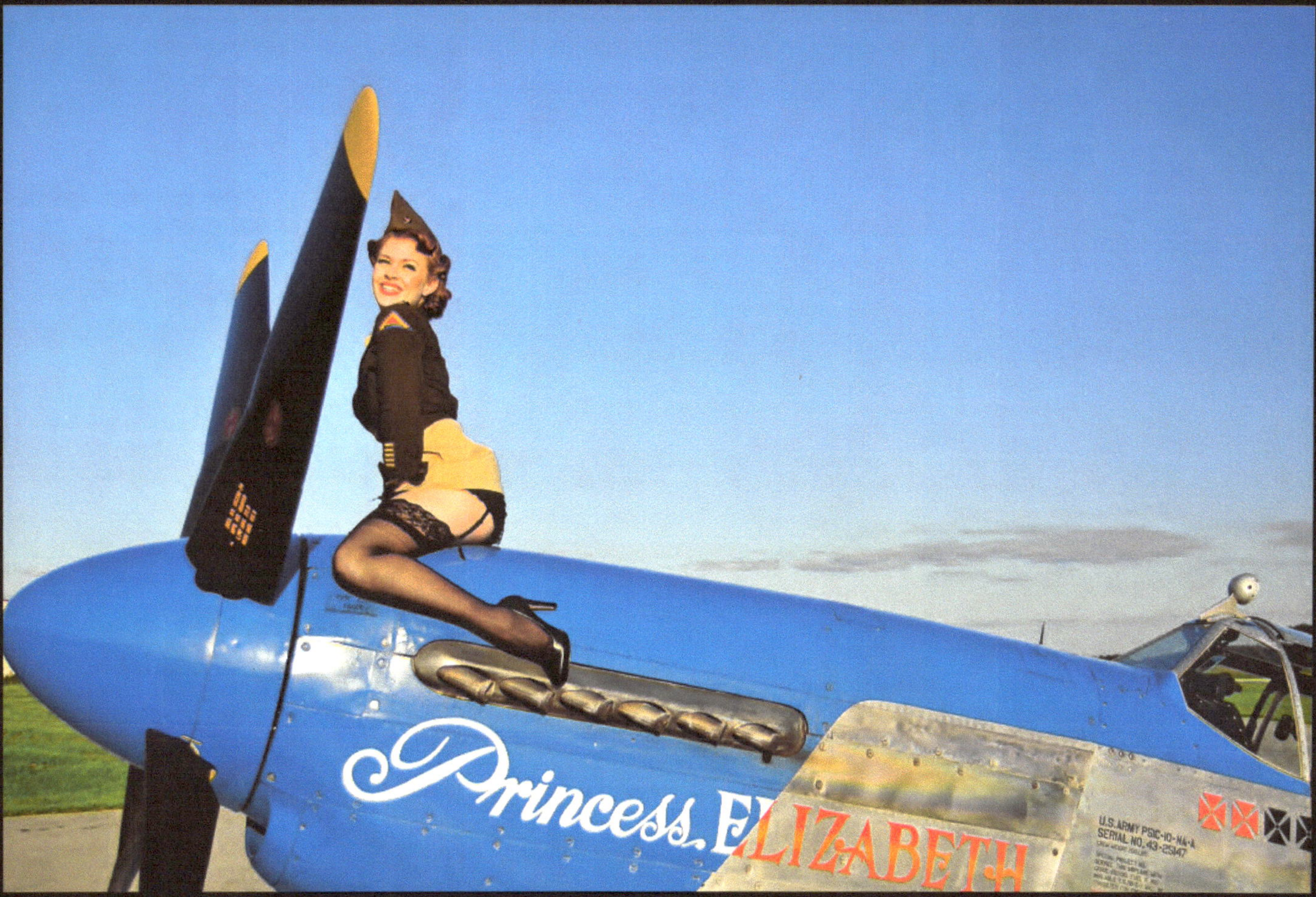

KATE

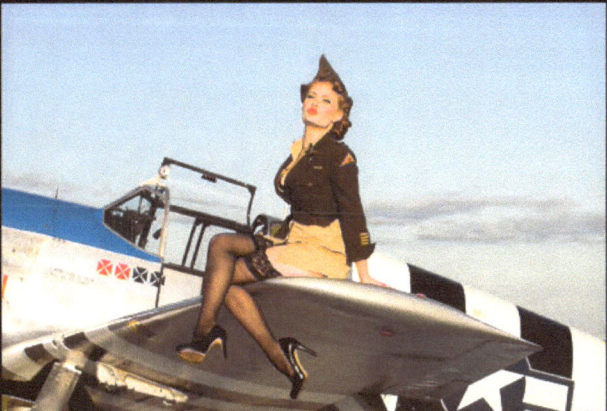

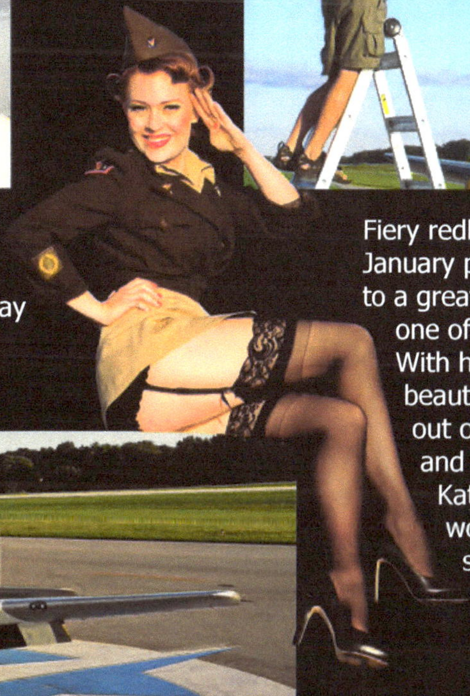

The P-51C "Princess Elizabeth" was part of the Horsemen team at the time of our shooting. Owned and operated by the Friedkin family in Dallas TX. She is a true beauty. Painted with D-Day invasion stripes, it's so nice to see this European veteran alive and well. Take notice this early model's canopy unlike the late model Mustangs.

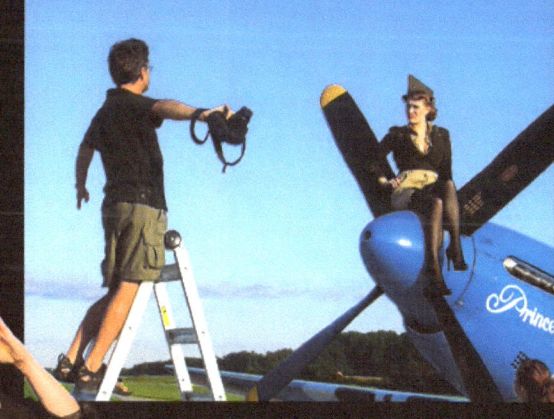

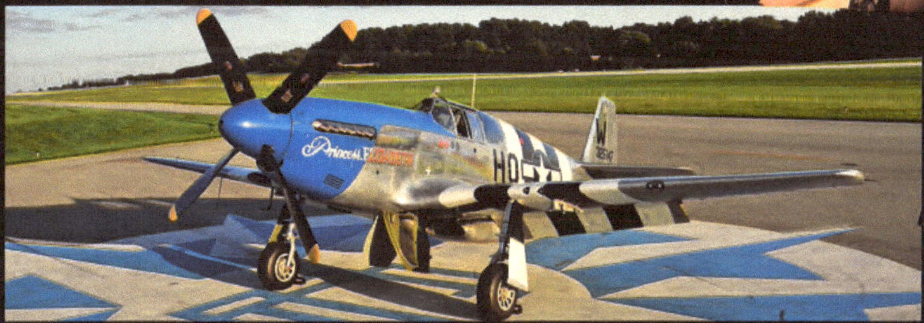

Fiery redhead Kate, 2011's January pinup girl, was already off to a great start when she became one of our models.
With her classic features and beautiful red hair she turned out one of our most authentic and classic 1940's pinup girls. Kate is so ambitious, last we heard she was skydiving and doing stunts in Hollywood movies.

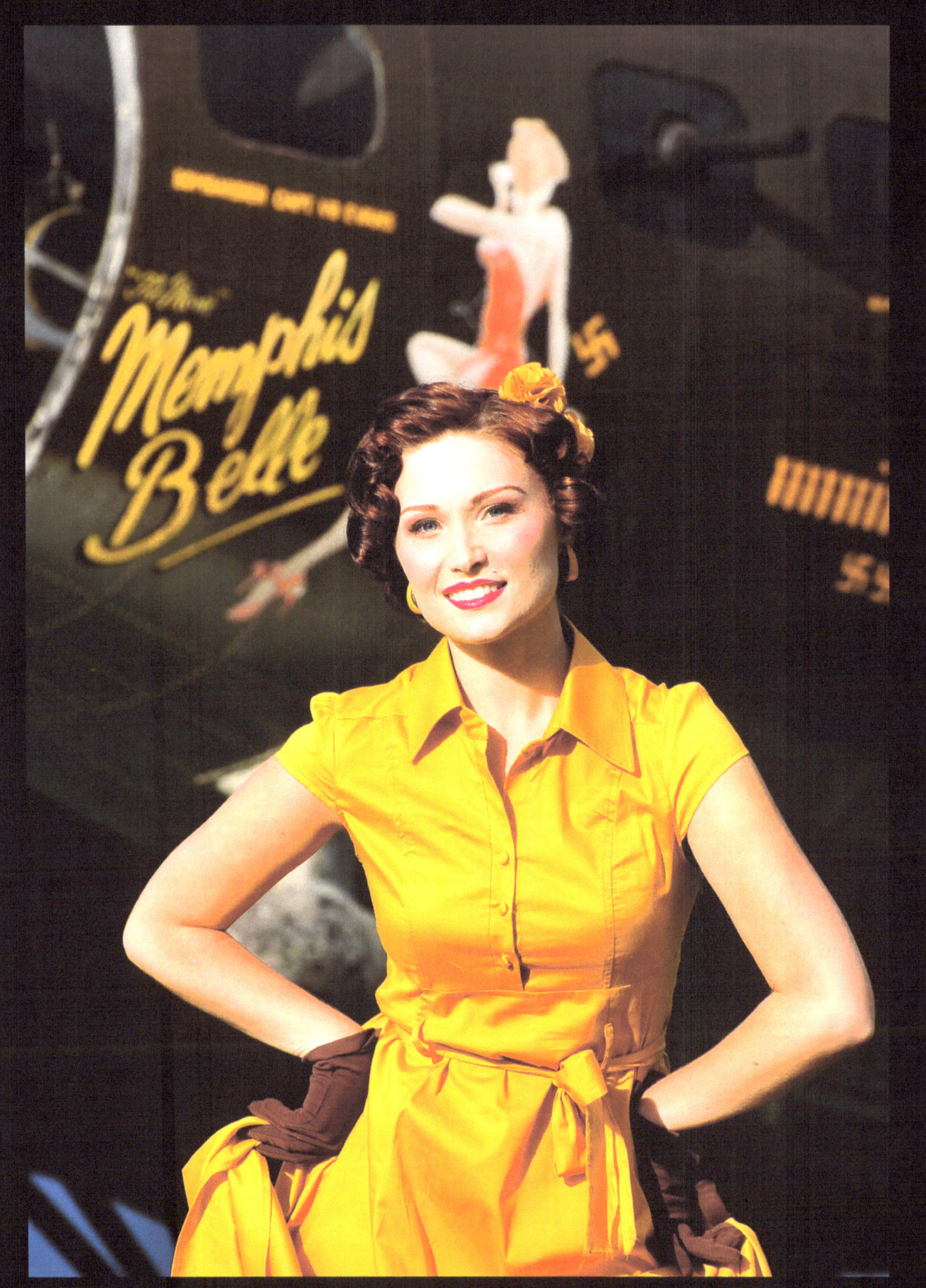

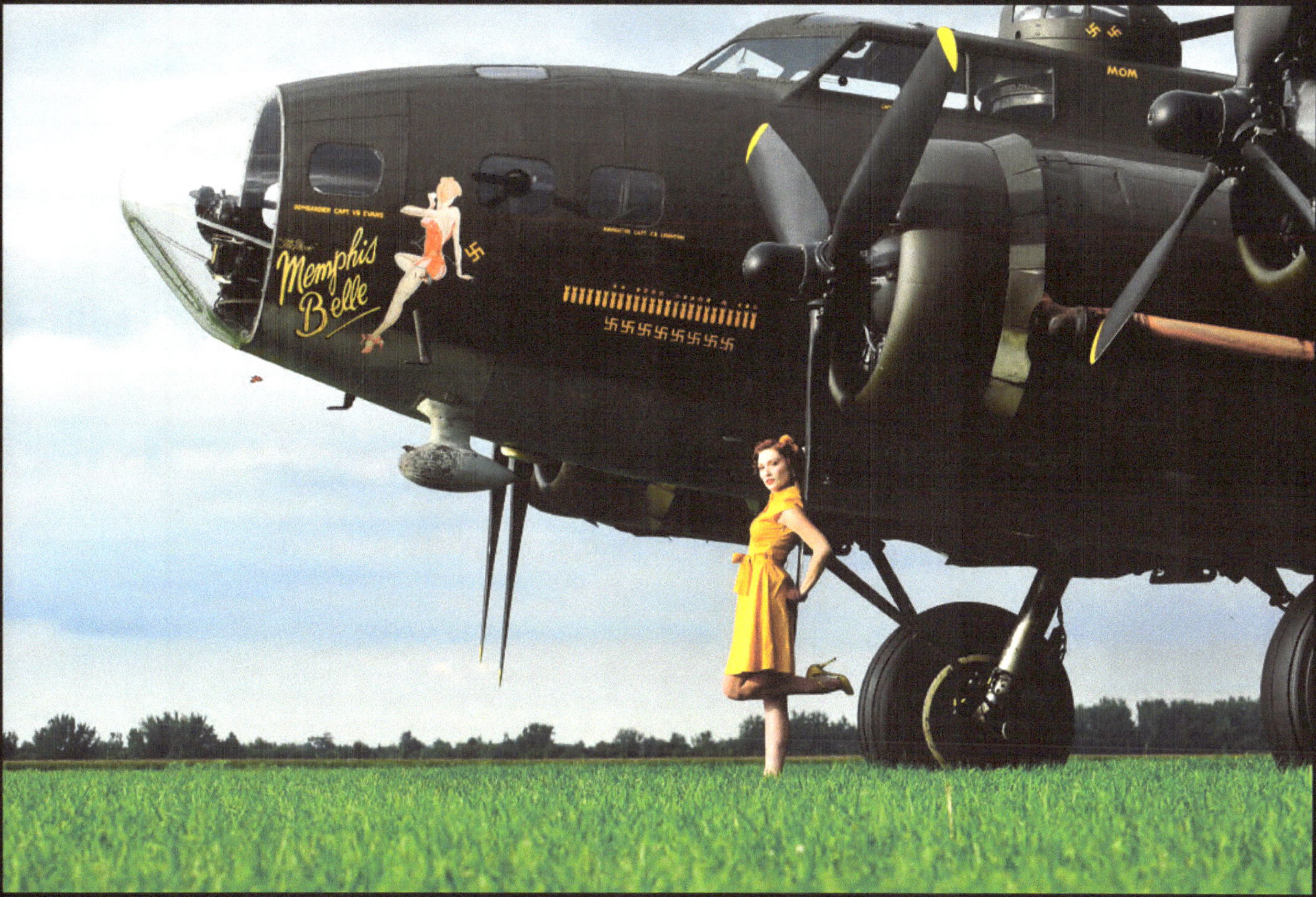

PAIGE

2012 cover model Paige is a diamond in the rough. She actually found us and we gave her a chance and it was the best decision we ever made! A truly classic girl from the past.

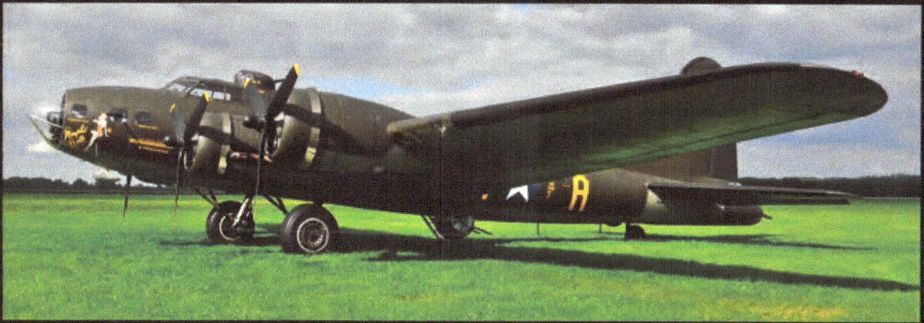

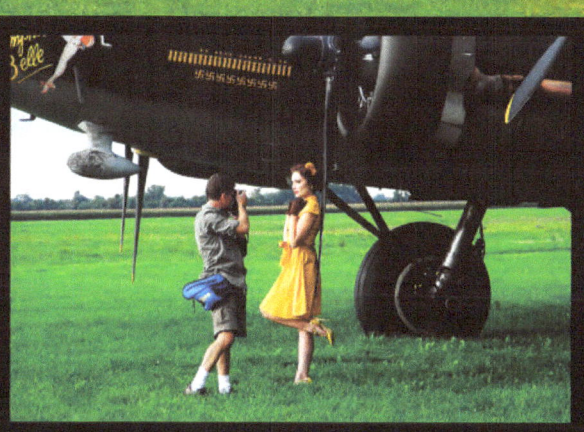

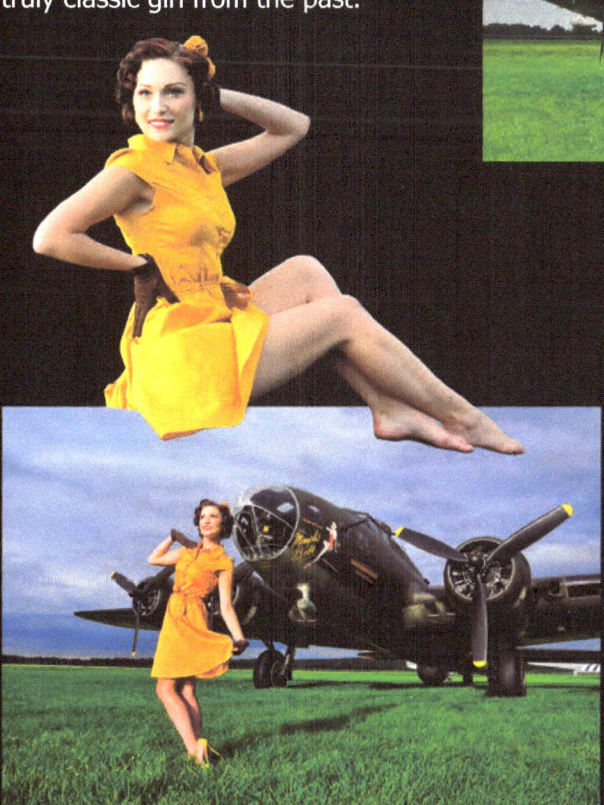

The B-17 "Memphis Belle" is in fact not the real McCoy. However, she's a real B-17. This particular model was repainted and used in the hit 1990 film of the same name. She now travels the country educating people about this world famous plane and gives people the opportunity to take a ride and truly experience the past. Watch for her at an air show near you.

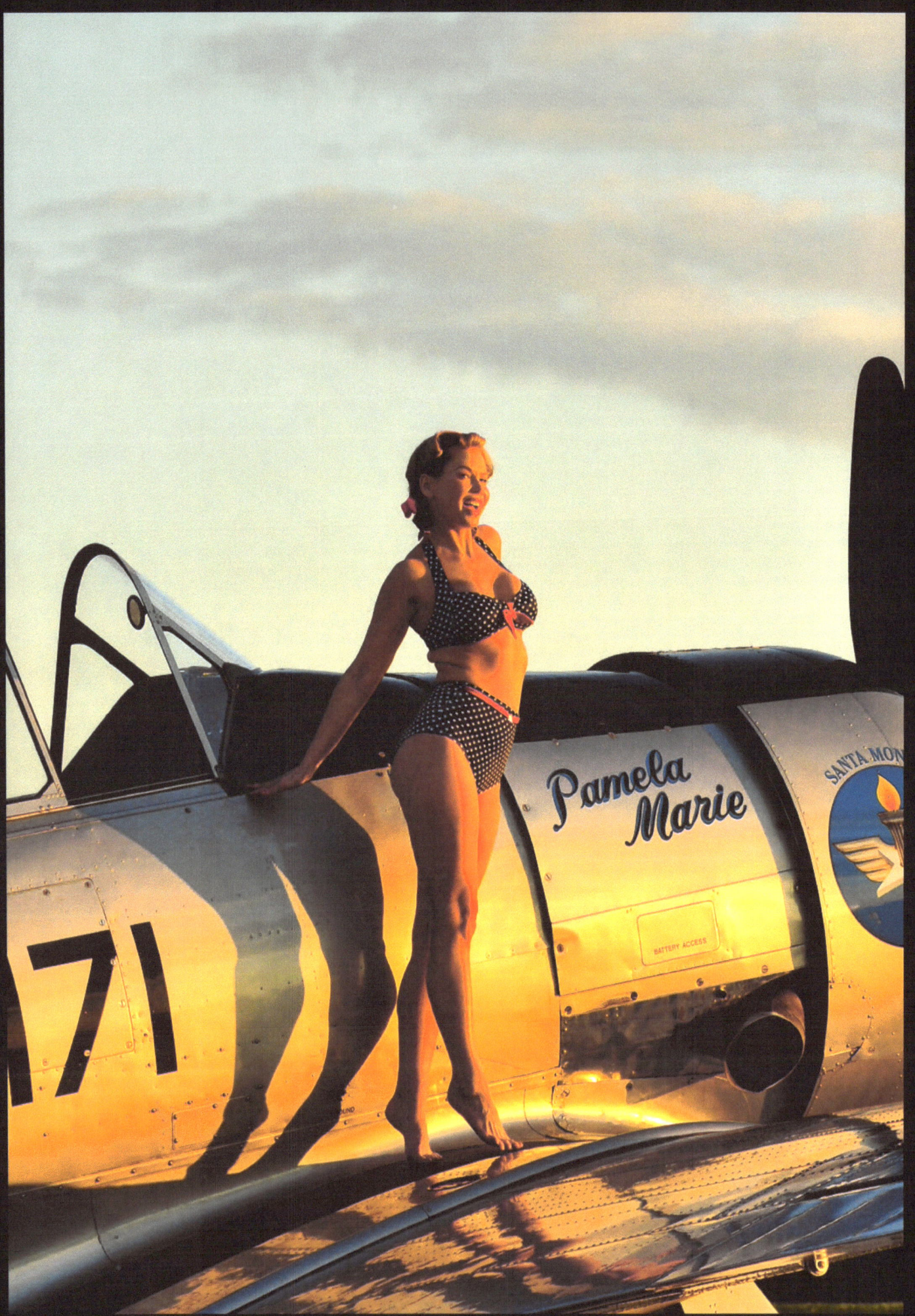

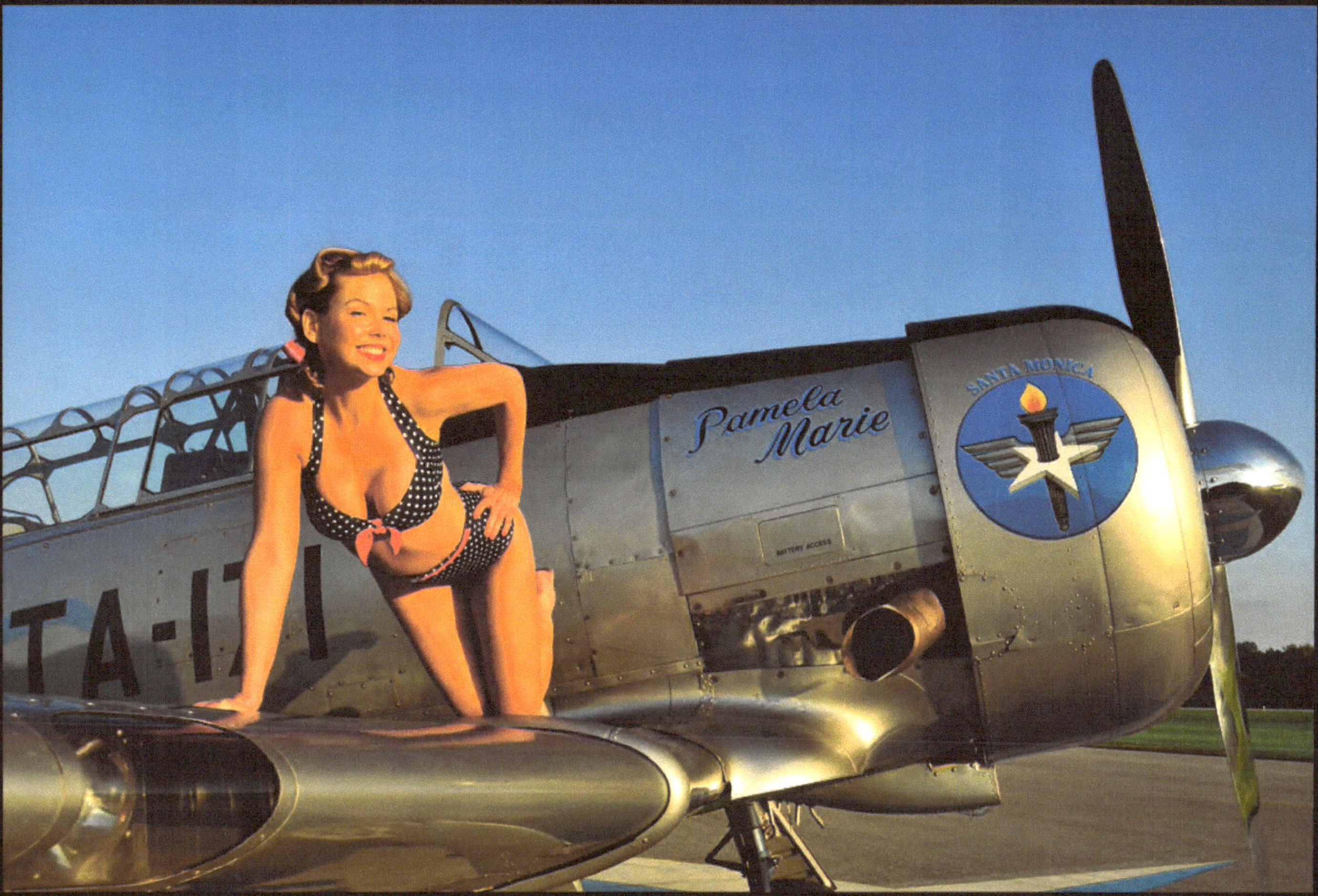

GWEN

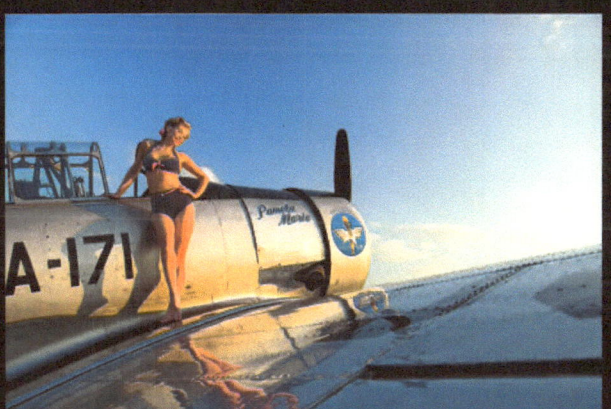

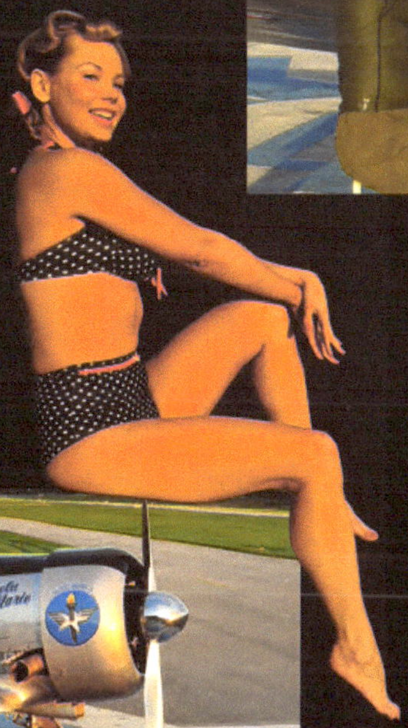

The "Pamela Marie" is a beautiful late model T-6 Texan that operates out of the north east. The markings are of the US Air Force, which used the T-6 Texan after WWII. Seen here on the aerial compass in Coatesville Pennsylvania where she lived at the time. We had great conditions that evening for our photo shoot.

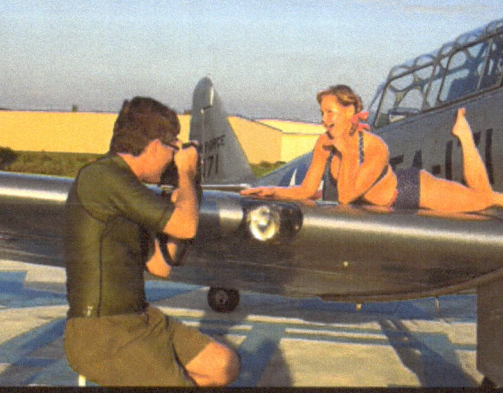

2011 June pinup girl Gwen is as sweet as pie. With her adorable all-American girl looks and charm, her photo is one of our favorite and most classic. We shot Gwen on a beautiful but chilly October evening but despite the cold gwen smiled the whole time and was a real professional.

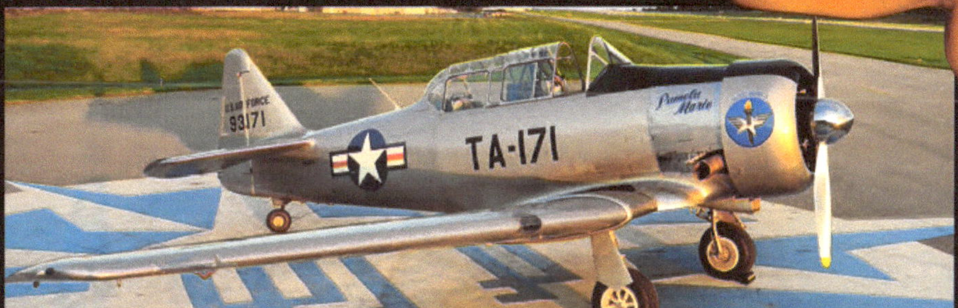

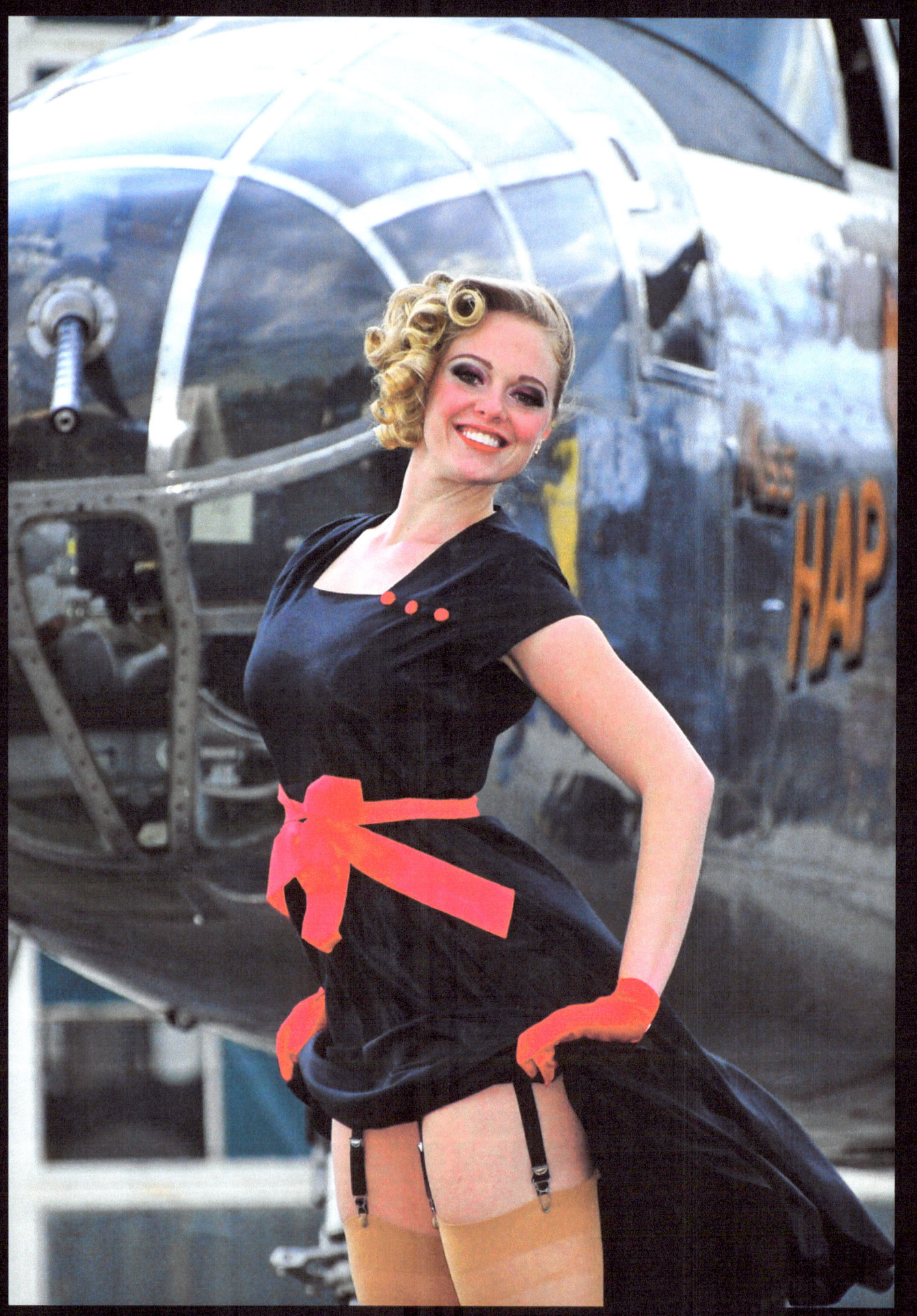

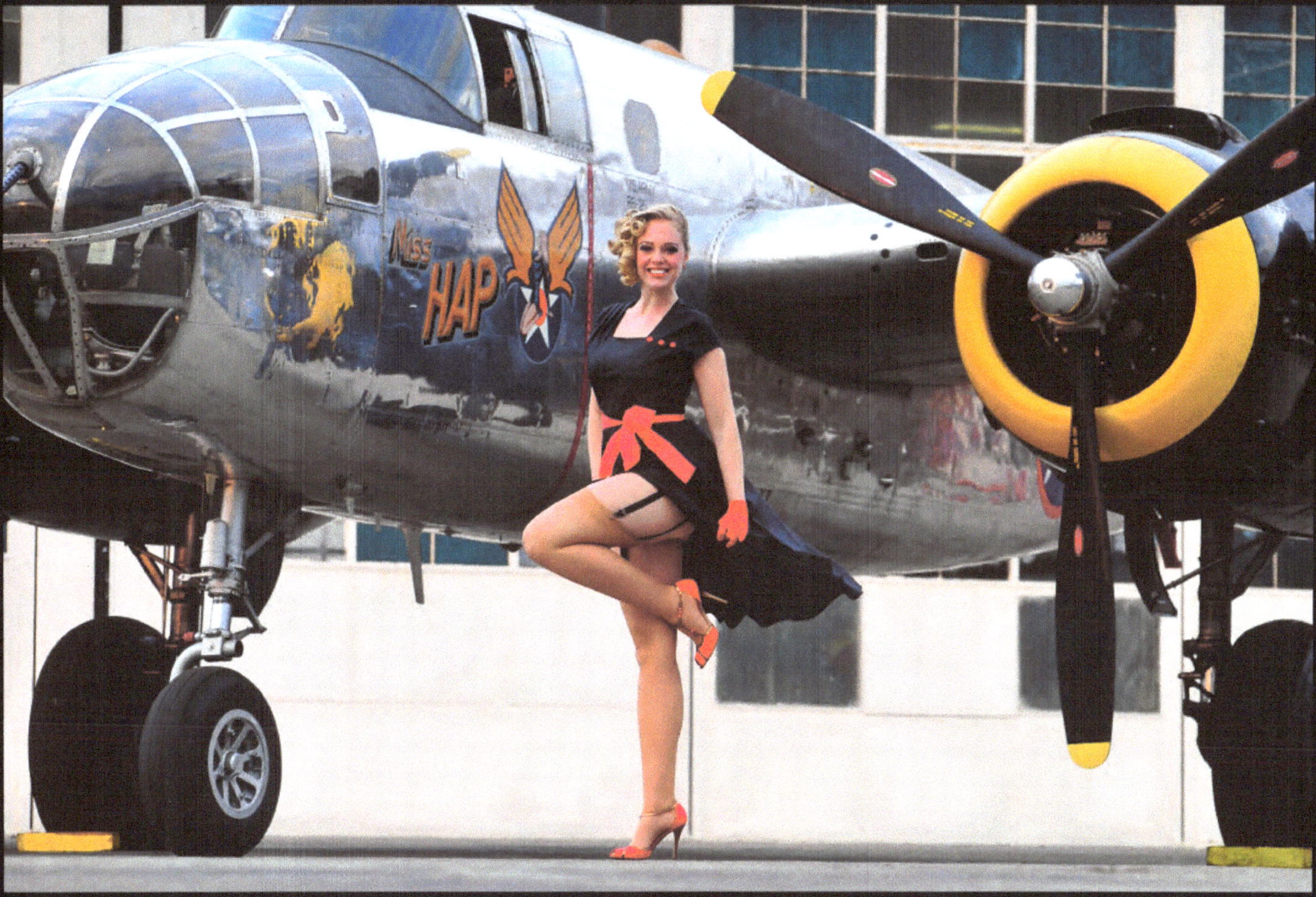

KAYCE

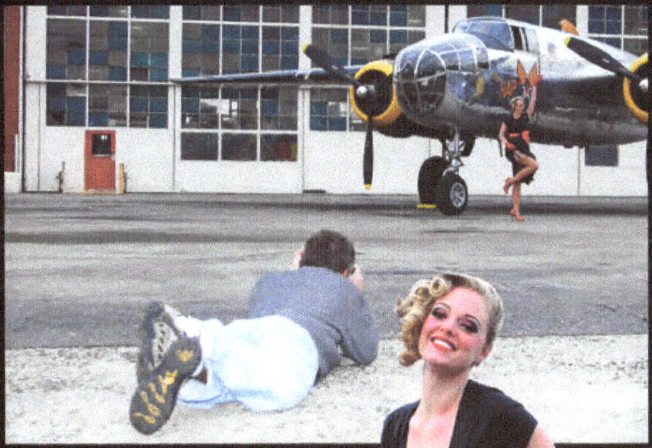

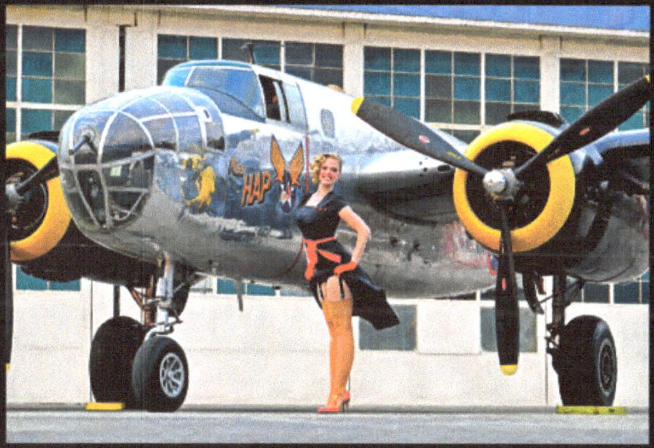

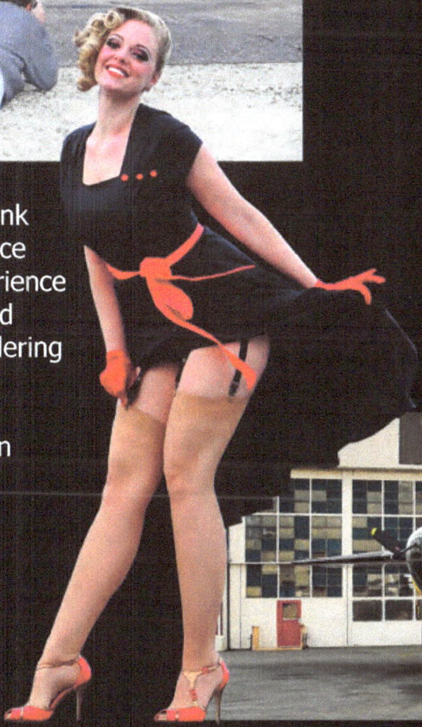

Kayce, 2012's April pinup girl, is one tall drink of water from NYC. Kayce had a lot of pinup experience before we found her and worked very well considering the challenging cold weather of New York in November of 2011 when her shot was taken.

The B-25 "Miss Hap" belongs to American Airpower Museum on Long Island. This particular B-25 was General Hap Arnold's personal airplane during the war. Other past owners of this particular aircraft include Howard Hughes. This B-25 makes regular flights for demonstrations and air shows out of Republic airport in Long Island.

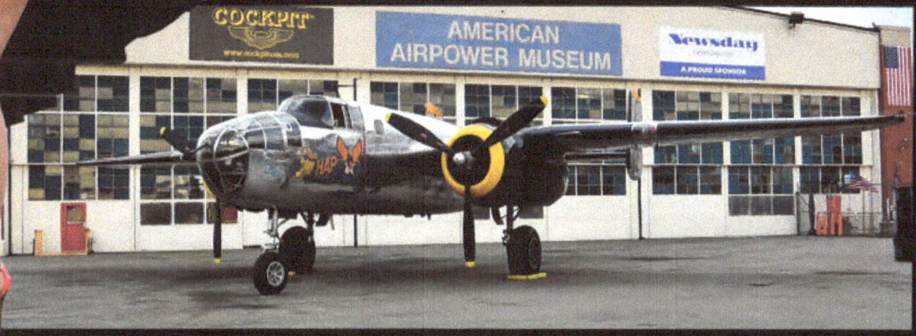

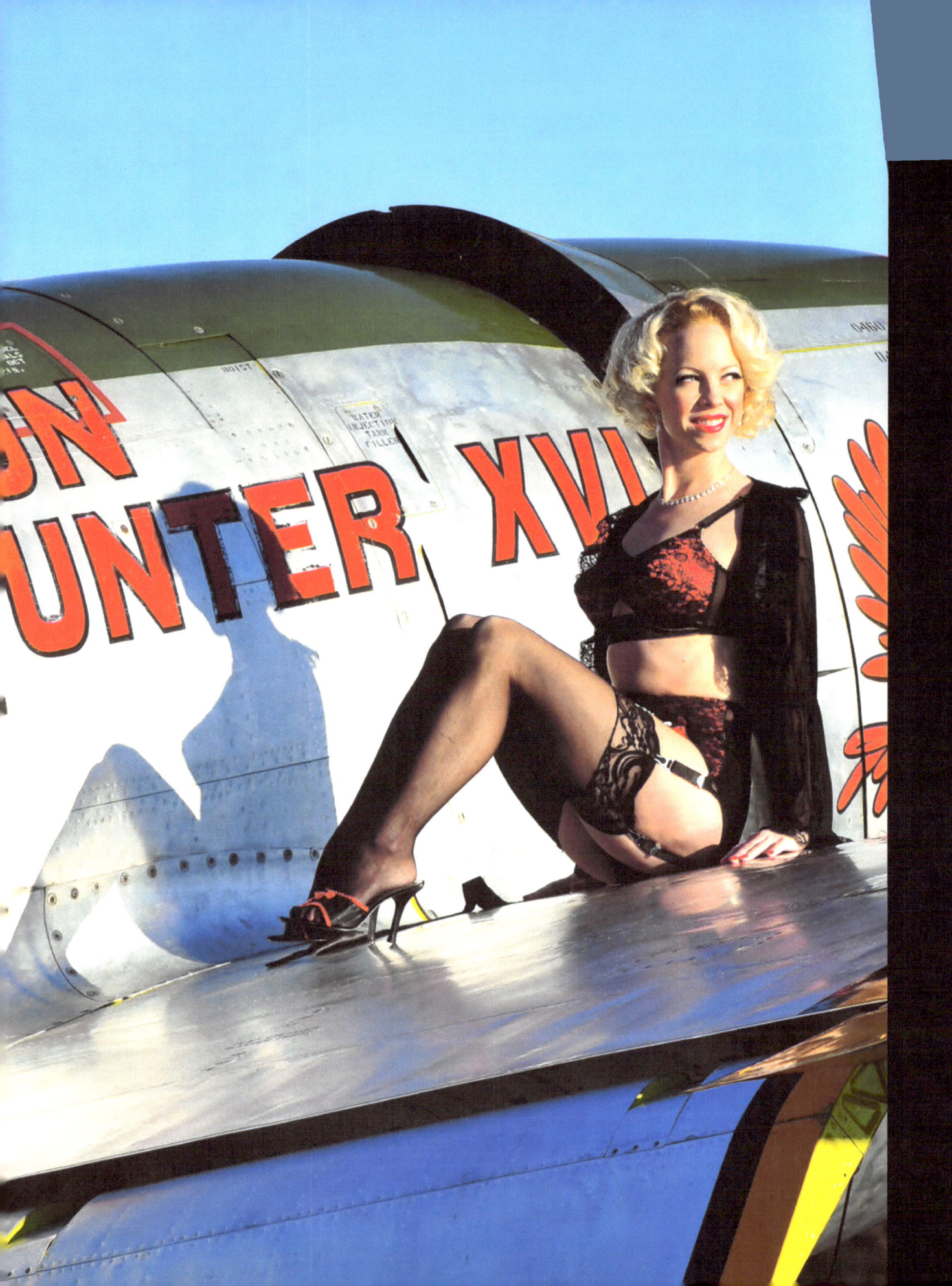

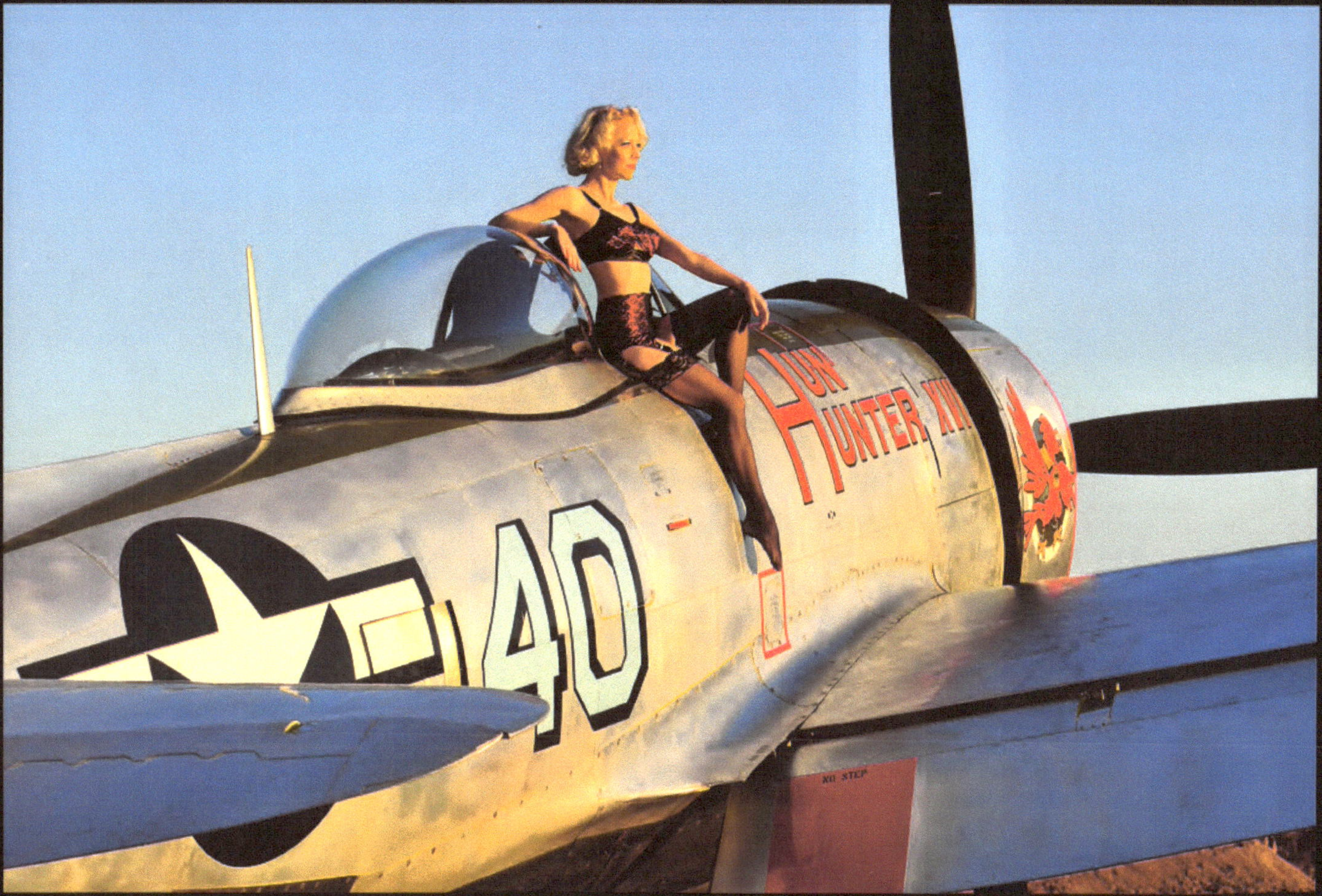

TAMMY

3 time Warbird Pinup Girl Tammy Jean is back for 2015. Tammy is a full time model, dancer and actress, appearing in many film and television projects. Tammy is our lead choreographer bringing her years of pinup experience to help create an authentic pinup recreation.

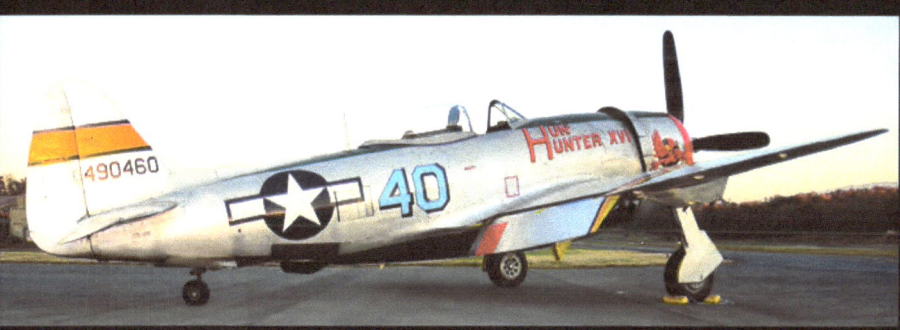

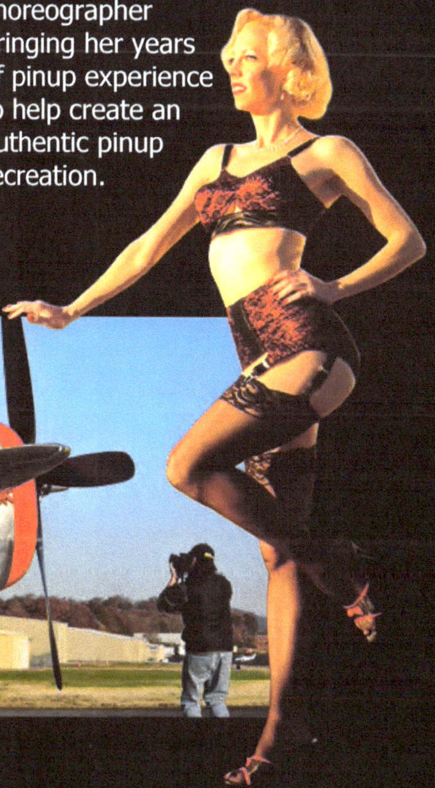

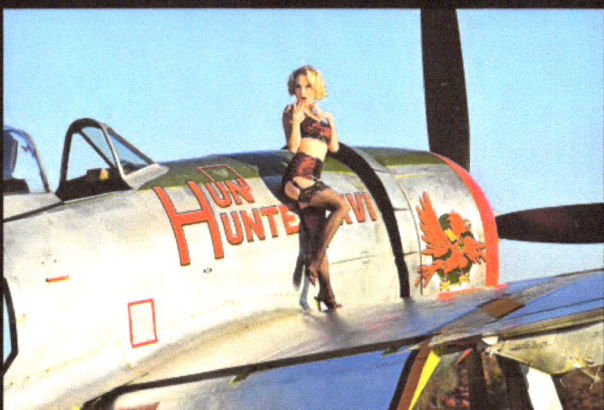

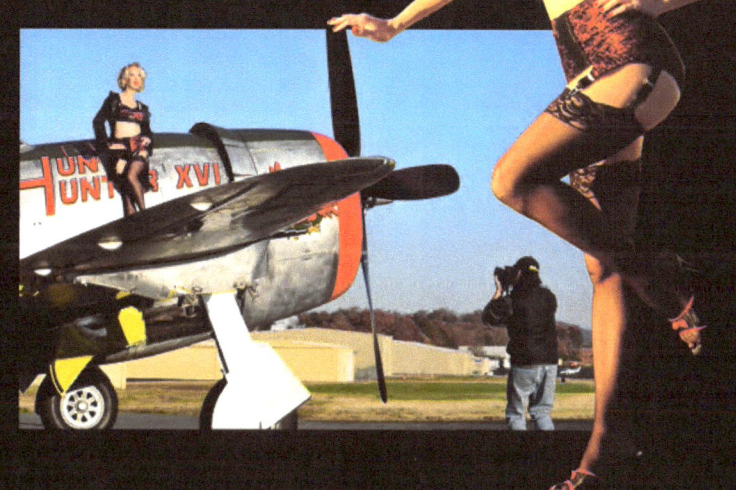

"Hun Hunter XVI" is the alter ego of her sister ship the "Wicked Wabbit" from the Tennessee Museum of Aviation. These two veteran P-47's can be seen throughout the season at many regional air shows. To witness these two classics performing is a true warbirds delight.

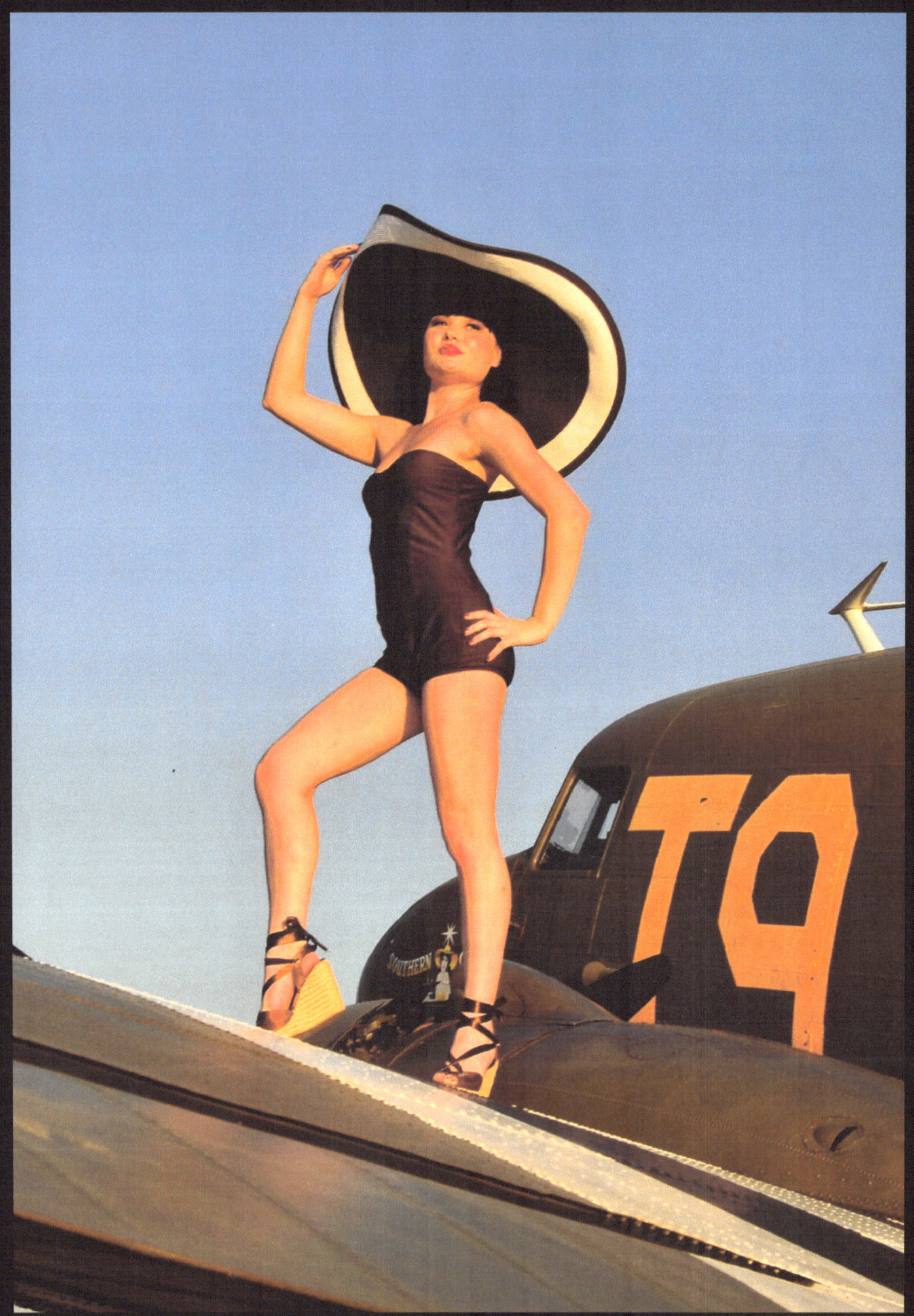

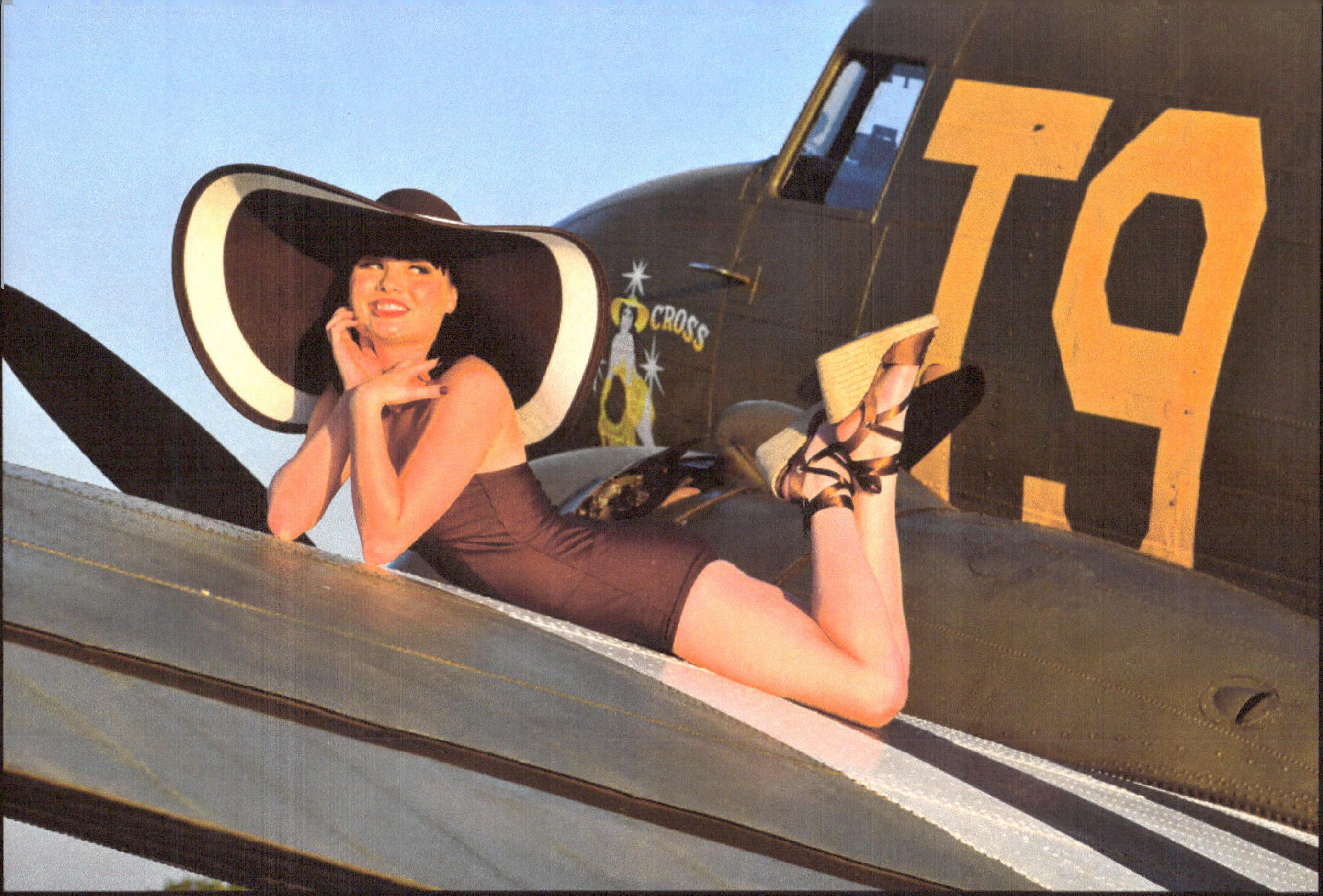

AMBER

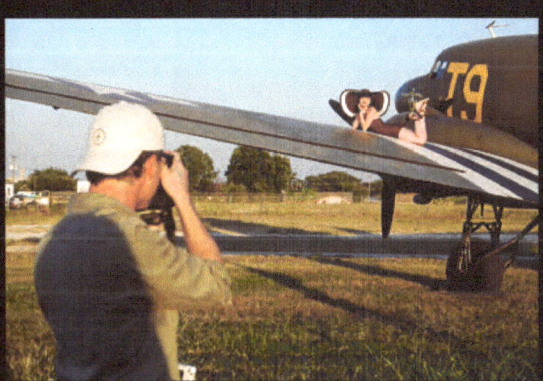

The "Southern Cross" C-47 from Vintage Flying Museum in Dallas Texas is a real beauty. Along with her name, she adorns a classic pin up girl on her nose. We were blessed with a perfect Texas sunset as we created our own Southern belle.

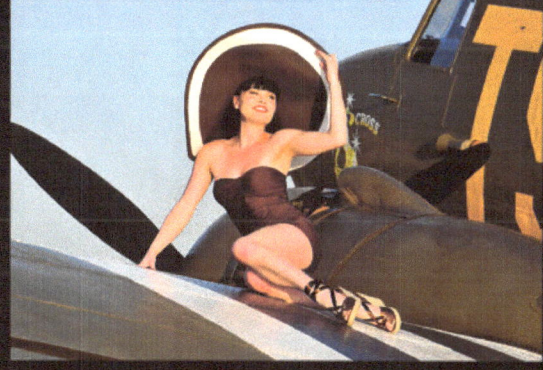

Amber is a long time pinup and burlesque artist from Texas so it was easy to transform her into our southern belle. Amber's experience came in handy as she turned out some of the best traditional pinup poses in our collection.

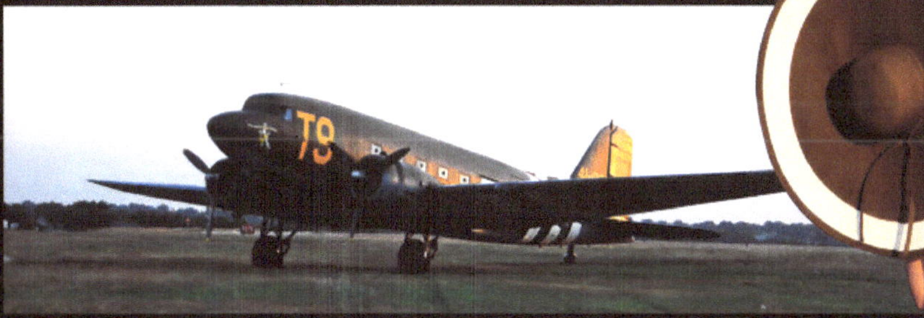

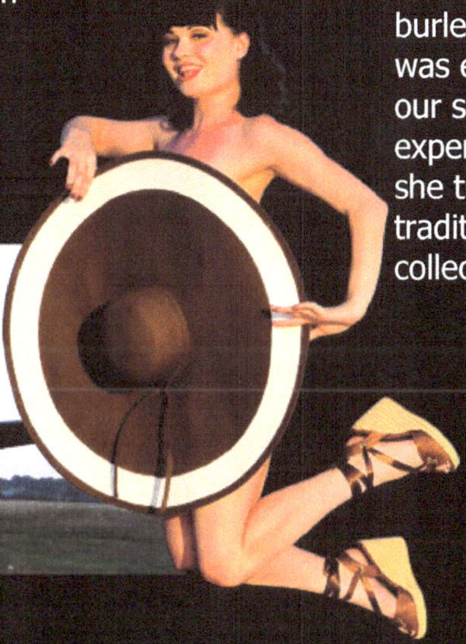

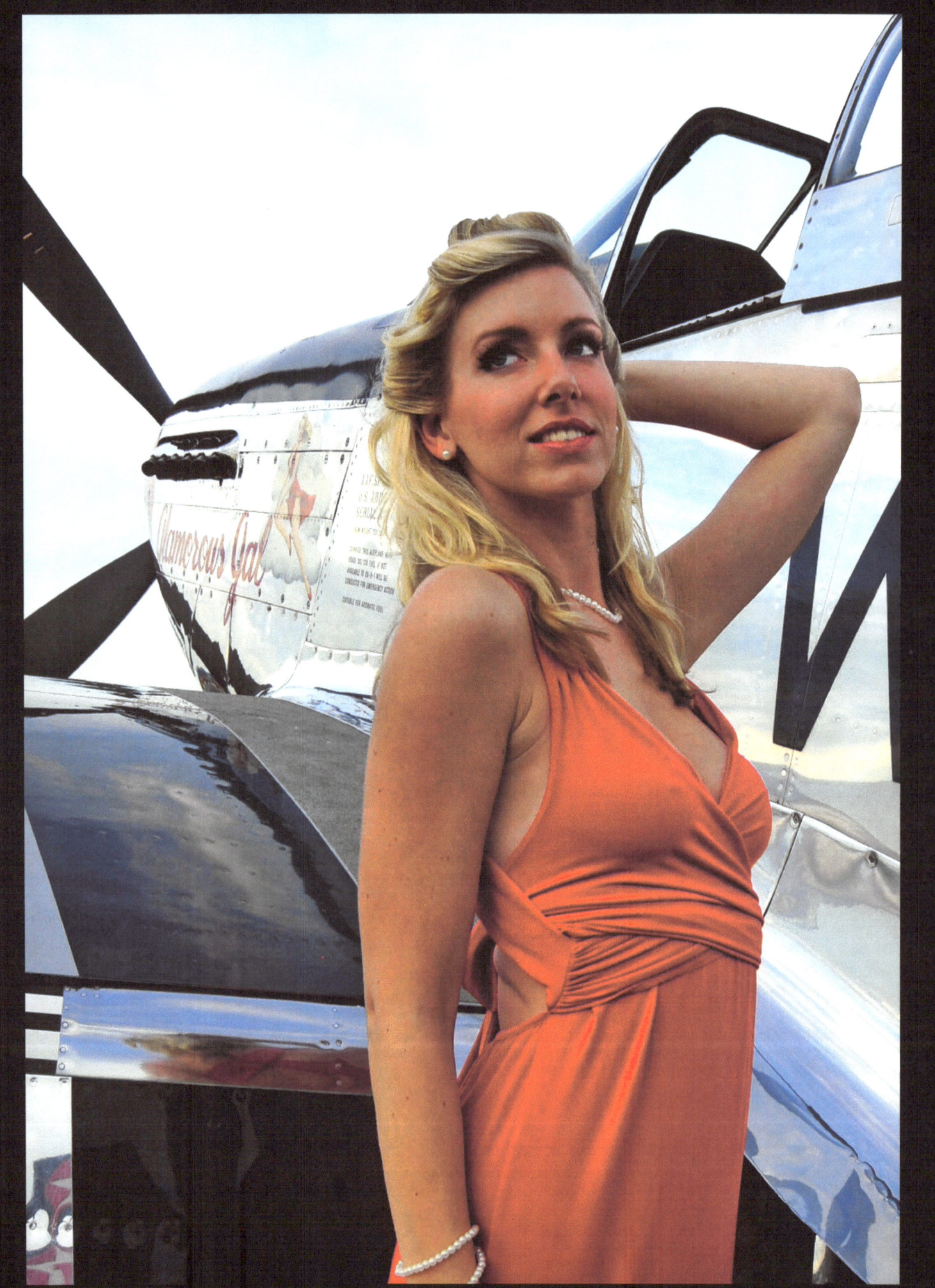

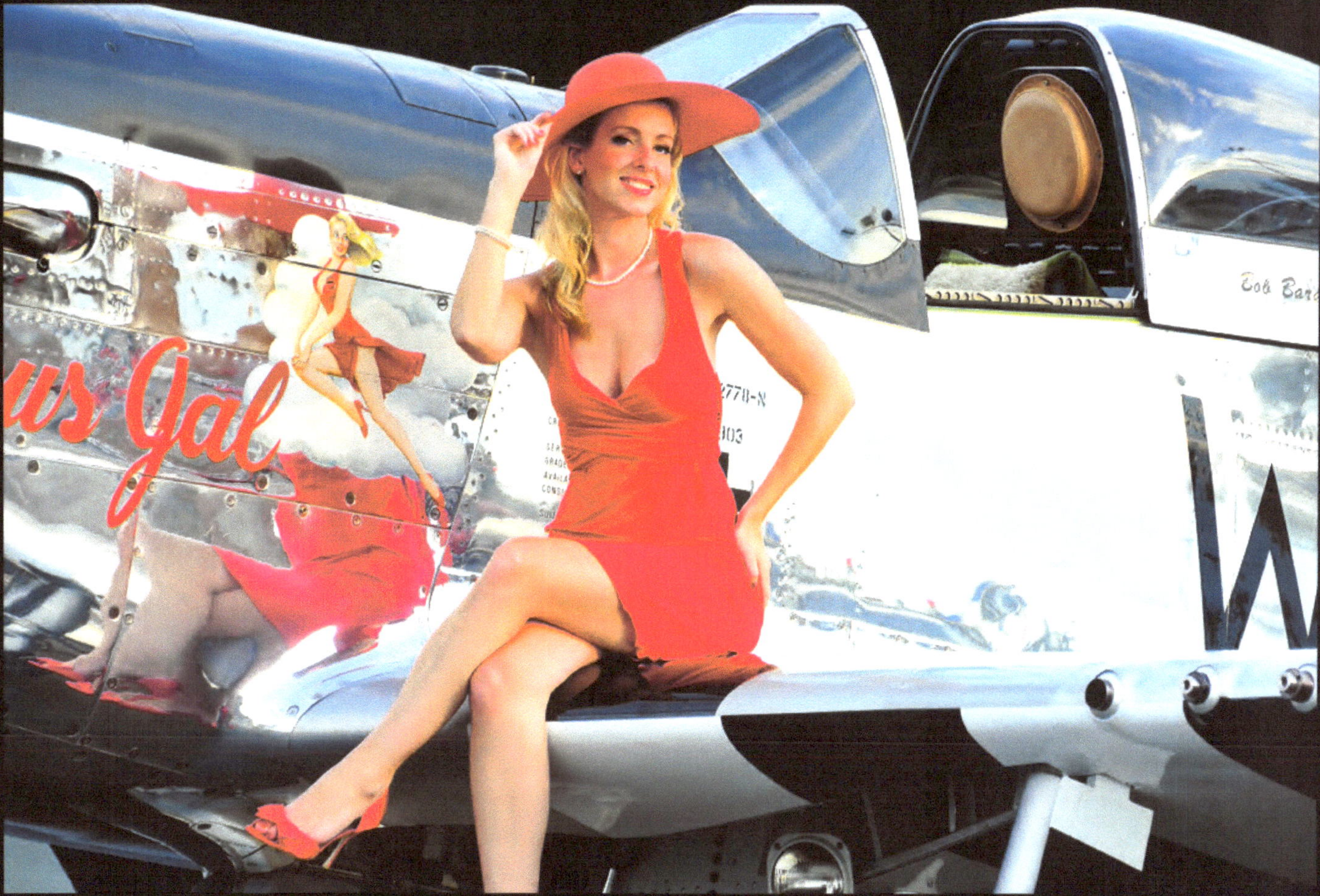

KELLY

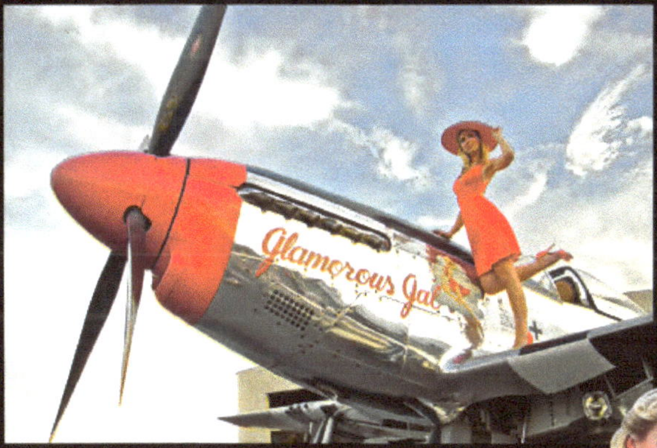

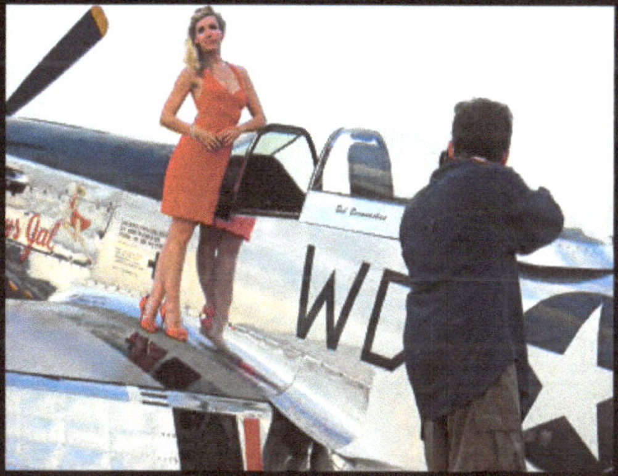

The P-51D "Glamorous Gal" which recently changed hands from Warbirds Over Long Island is a superb example of this legendary fighter plane. A regular on the air show circuit on the East Coast, the "Glamorous Gal" was known for her honor flights with the Wounded Warrior Foundation. What better way to honor our vets than a flight in this WWII hero.

December 2011 pinup girl Kelly will forever be remembered as the "Glamorous Gal". This Pennsylvania native recreated the nose-art from the "Glamorous Gal" P-51 perfectly in a gorgeous red dress that's a mirror image.

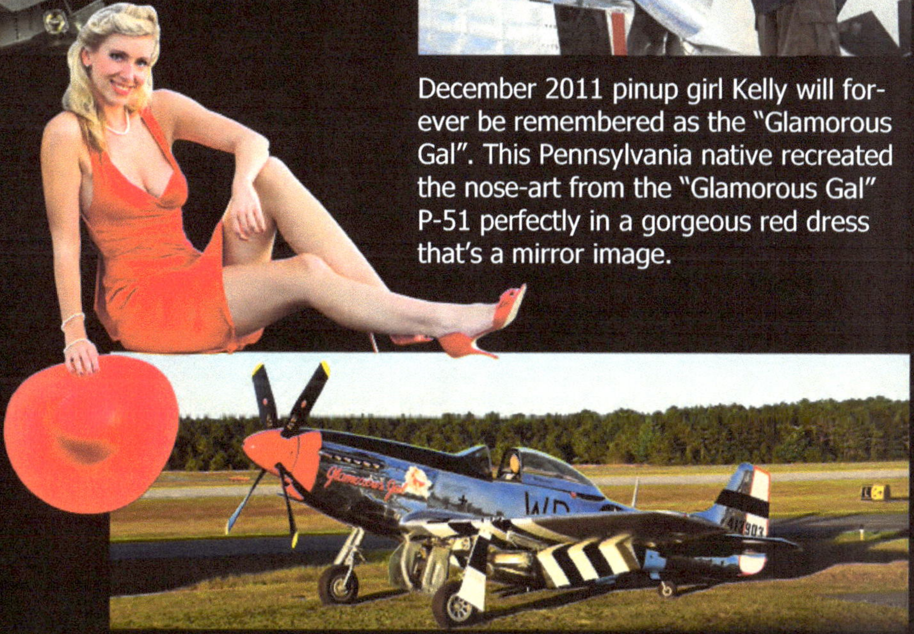

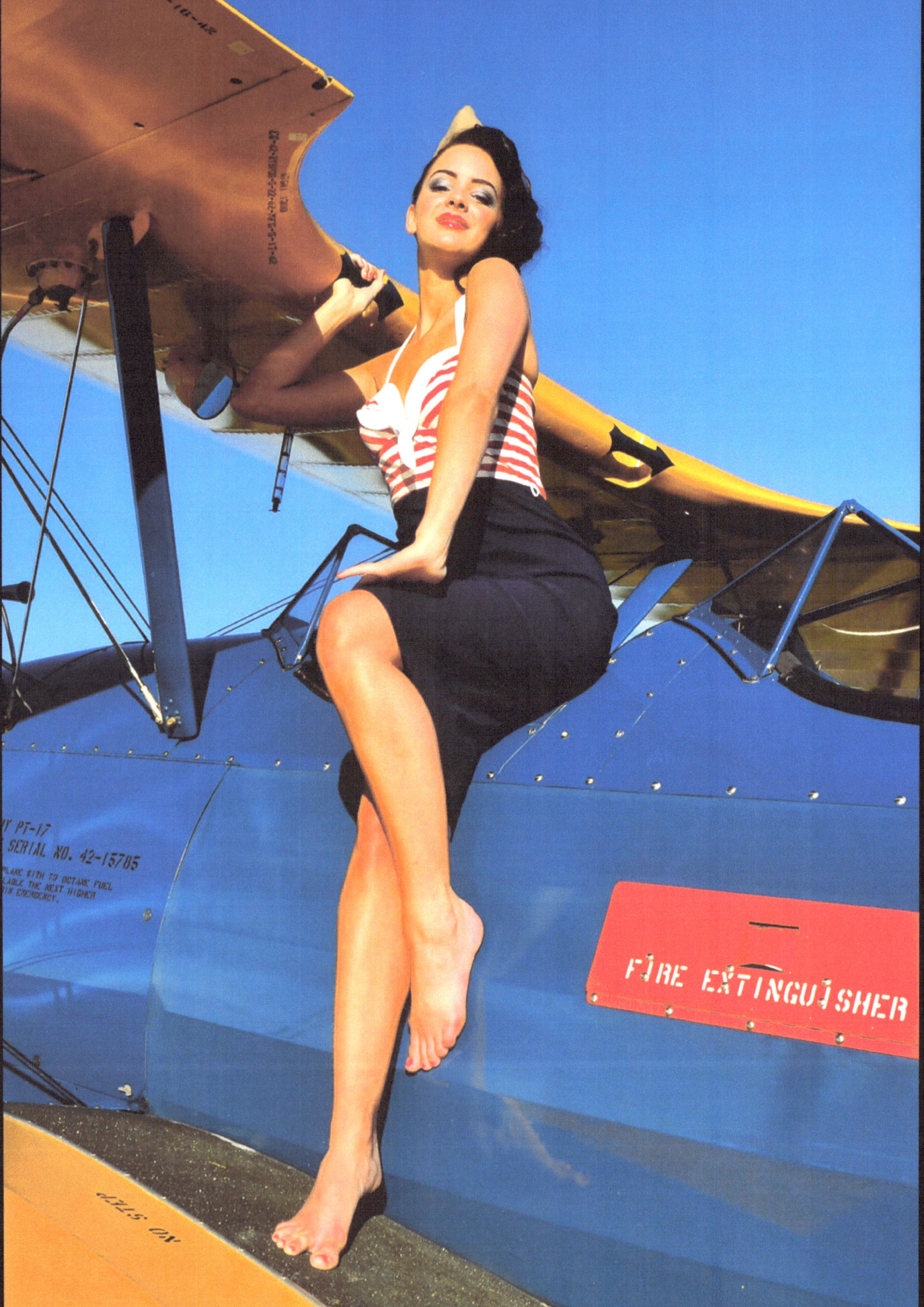

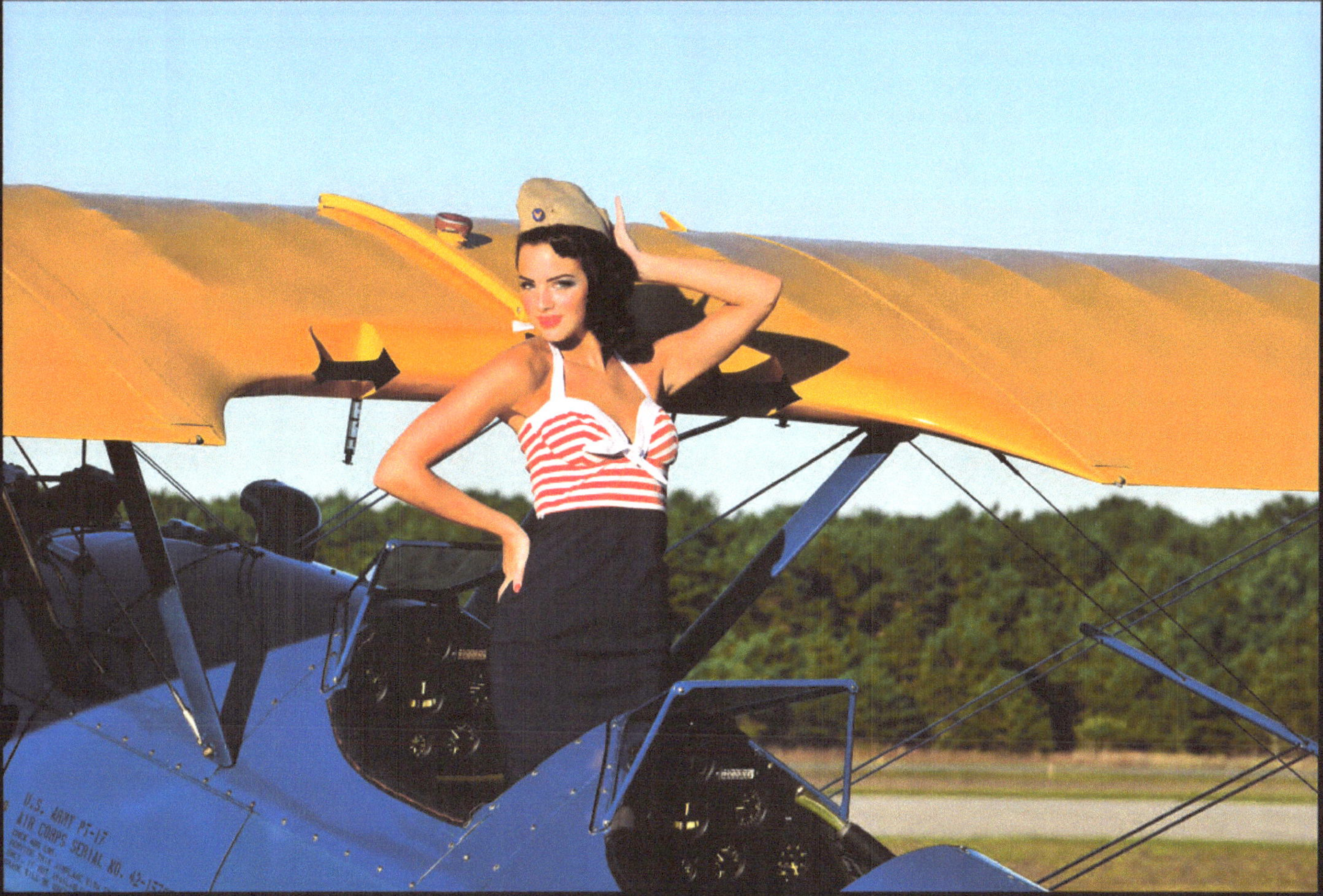

STEFANIE

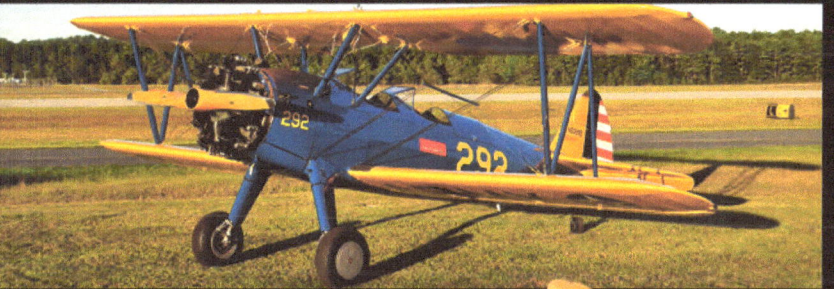

This PT-17 Stearman lives on Long Island New York. She's just another beautiful example of a perfectly maintained biplane. The Stearman was used to train cadets in the early part of the war before they went on to advanced trainers. With the reputation of one of the most stable and well-built designs, the Stearman lives on as one of the best aircraft ever built.

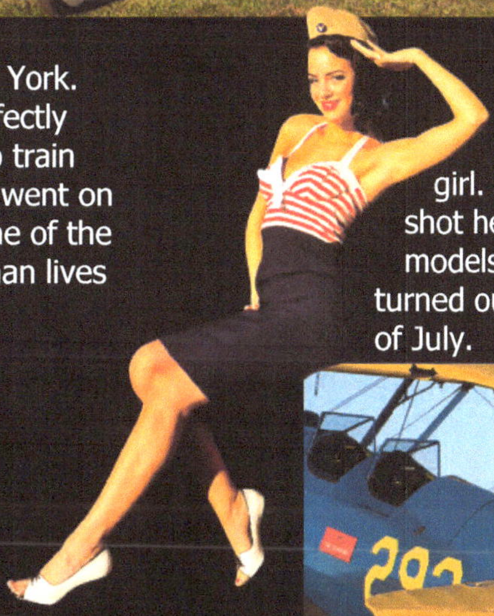

Miss July 2011 Stefanie has a truly classic look and was easy to transform into a retro pinup girl. Stefanie was only 19 when we shot her and was one of our youngest models but she took direction well and turned out a great photo for our month of July.

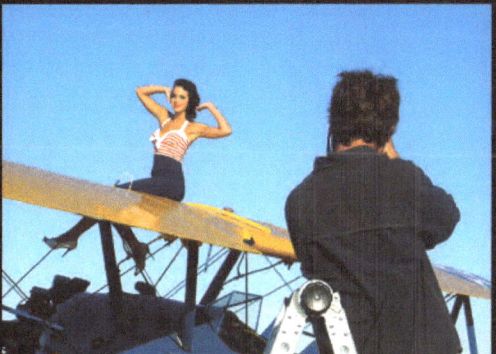

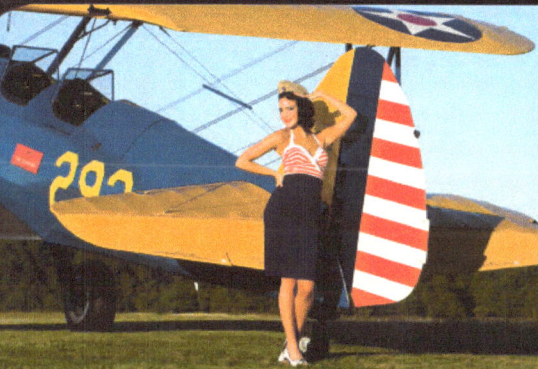

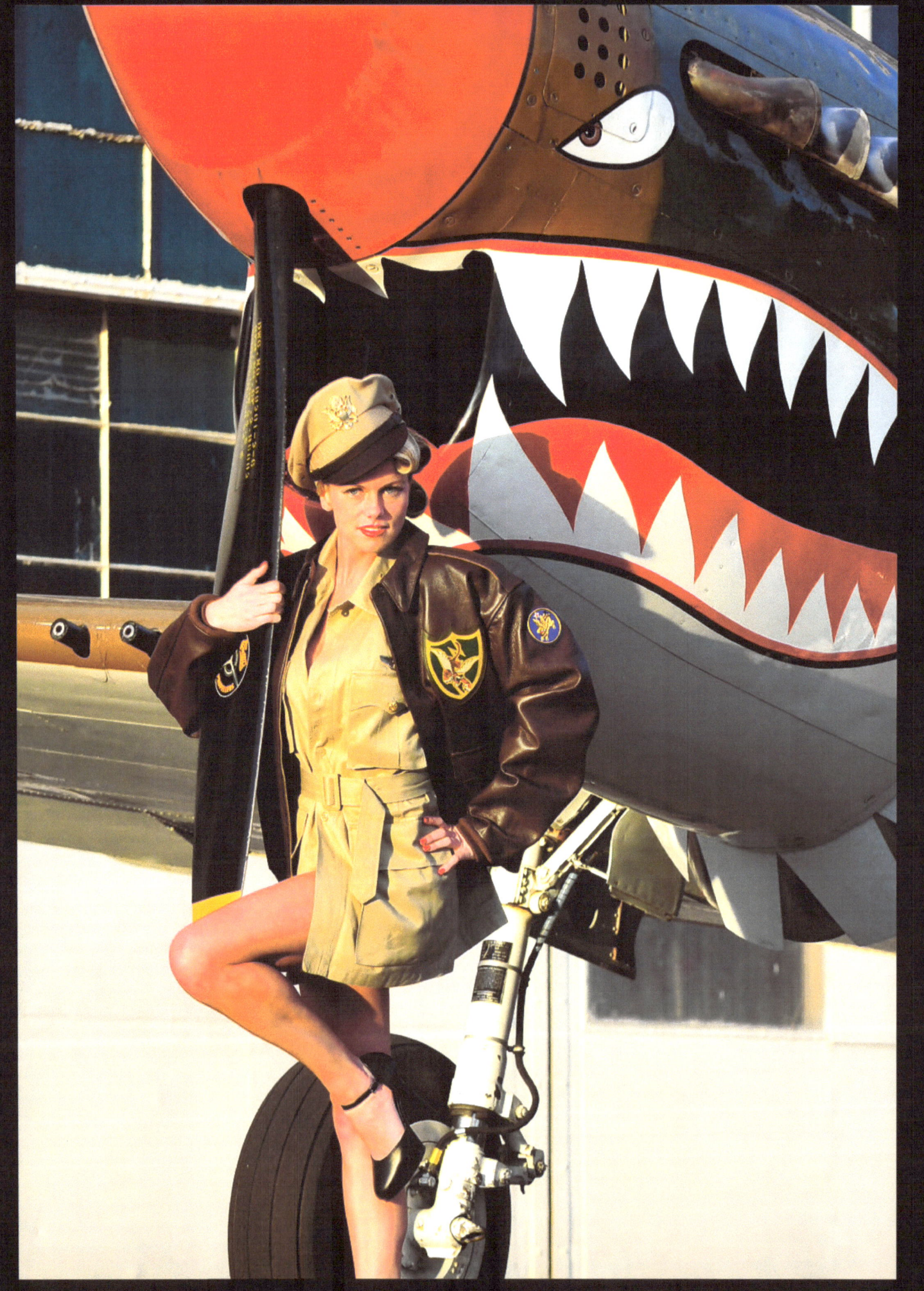

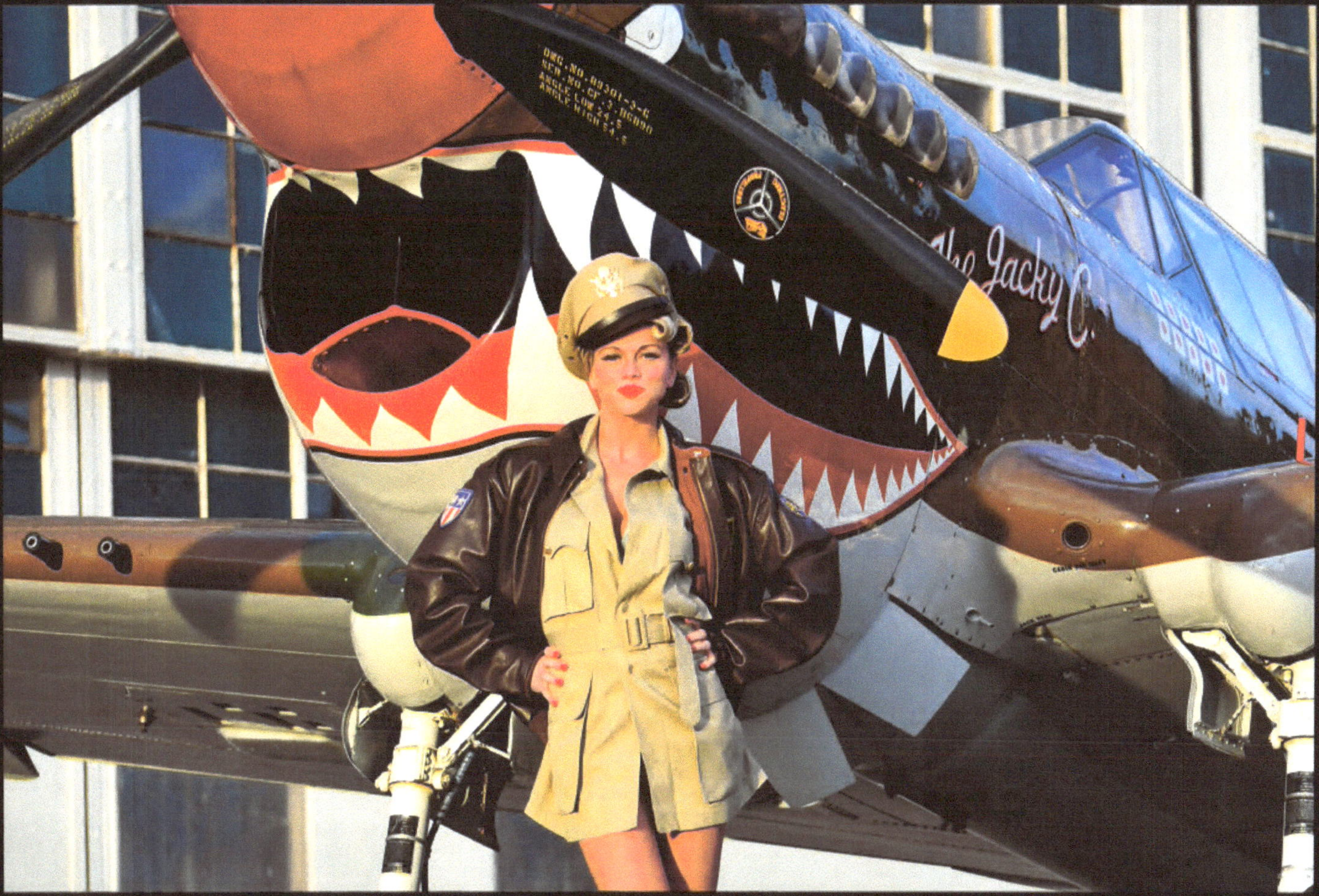

KATIE

The "Jacky C" as she's known, is one of the finest examples of flight worthy P-40's left. Dressed in the classic "Flying Tigers" 23rd paint scheme, this P-40 is in good hands at the American Airpower Museum on Long Island. Keep an eye out as she makes appearances at many regional air shows.

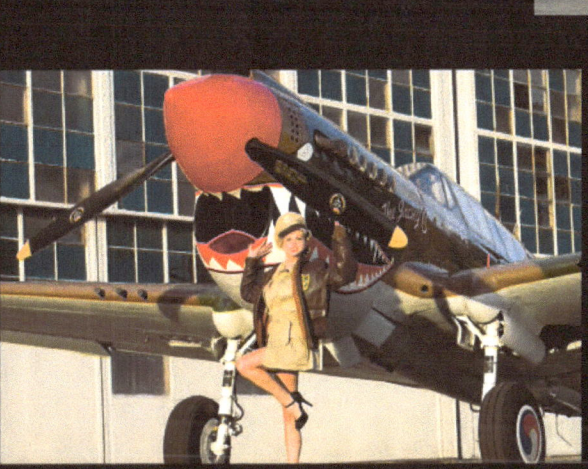

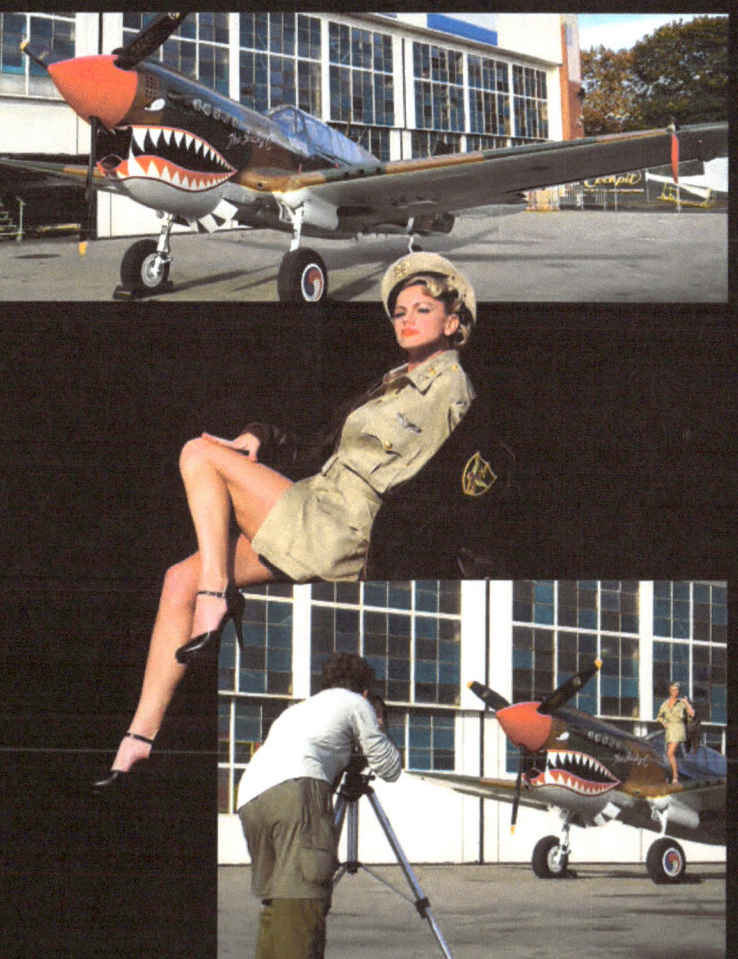

Katie, our 2011 September pinup girl, appears in an authentic 23rd fighter group leather jacket along with a classic crush cap of that era. This photo shoot is special to me as it celebrates my favorite aviators, the "Flying Tigers".

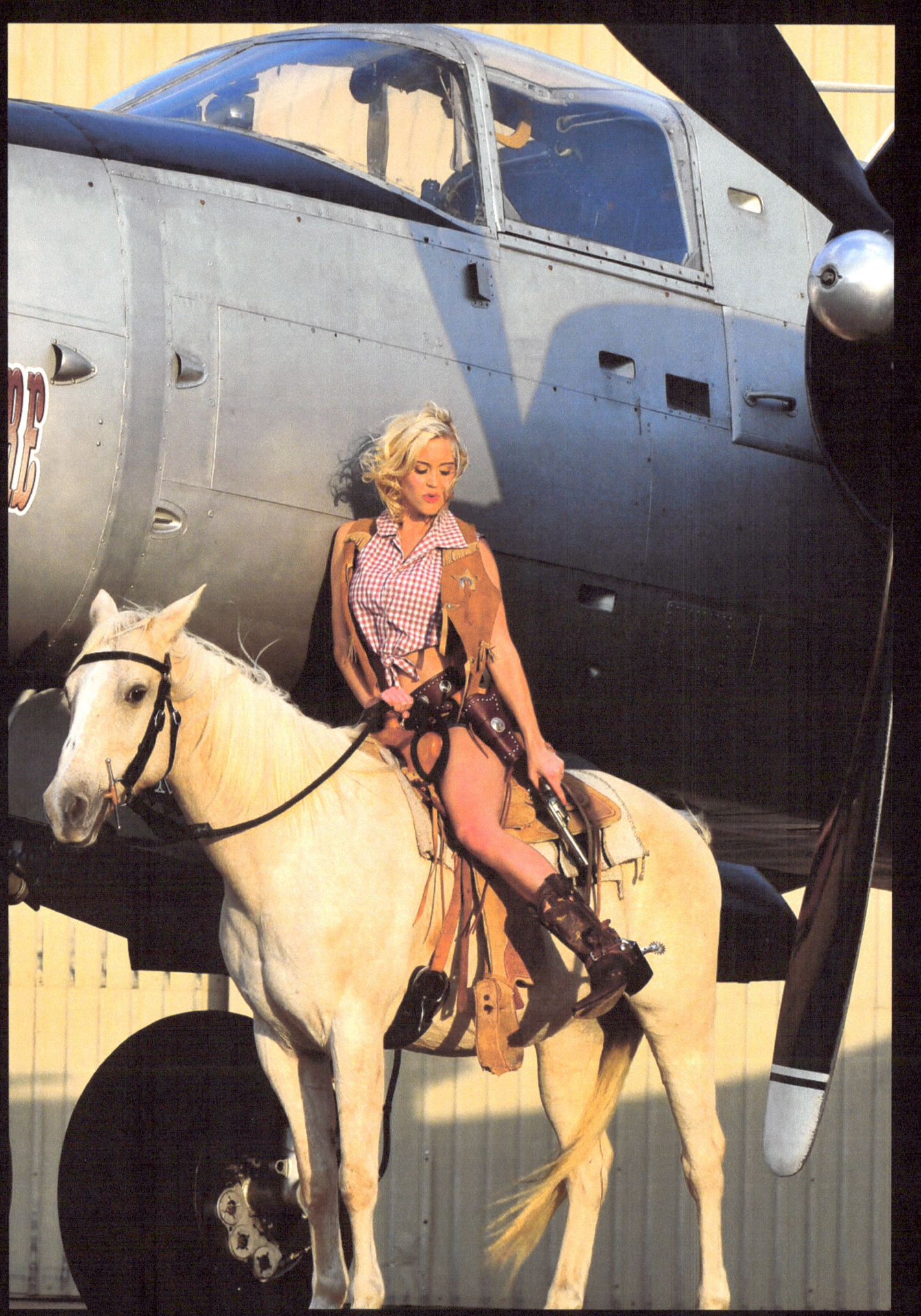

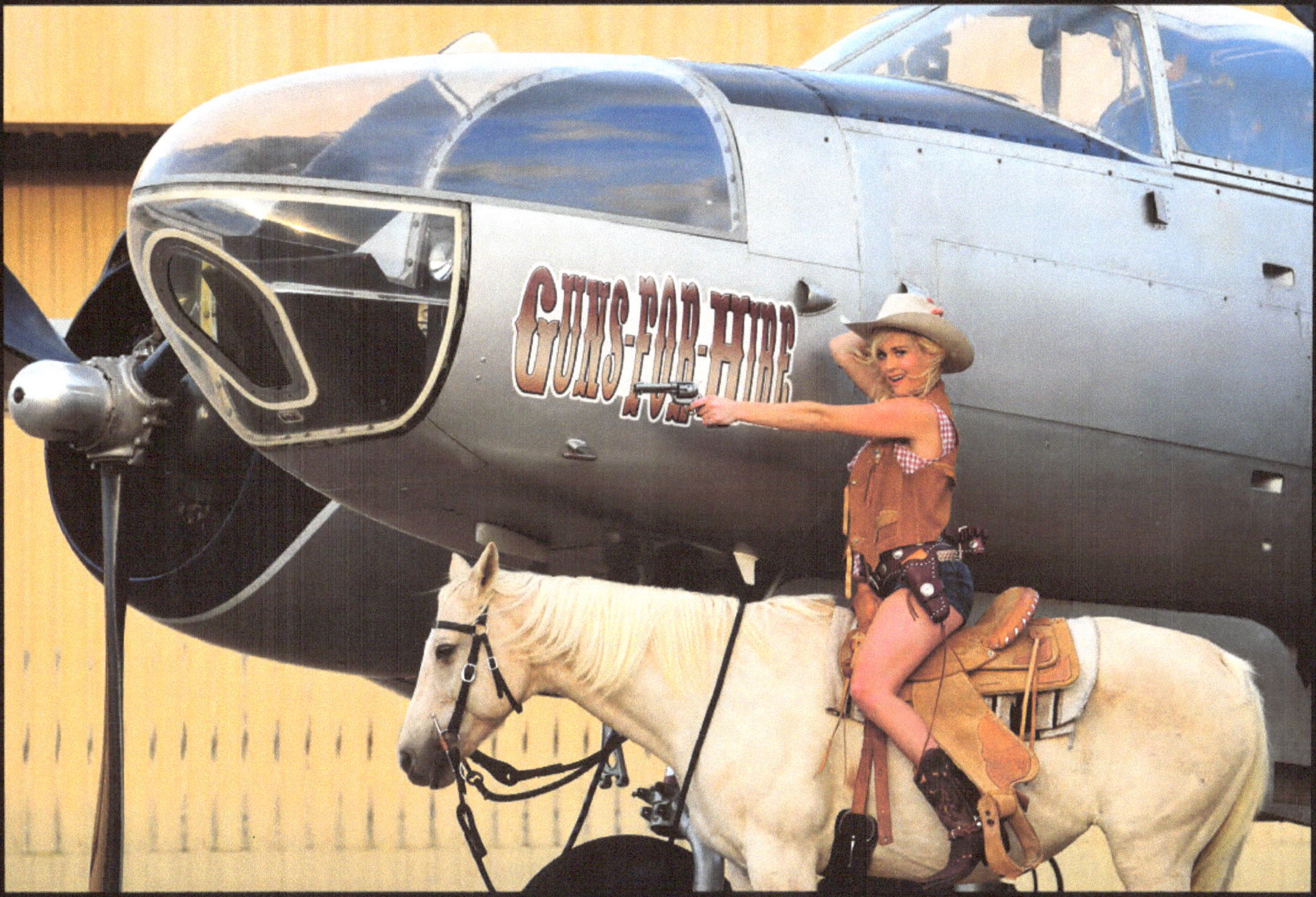

LAUREN

September 2012 pinup girl Lauren appears with our only A-26 to date. "Guns for Hire", how appropriate. Originally there was no horse in our concept but I met a local wrangler who offered to bring the steed on location for us, which made for a very exciting shoot. Although Lauren had little experience with horses, she managed to hold her own as the horse got spooked by other aircraft starting up nearby.
Definitely a shoot I will not forget.

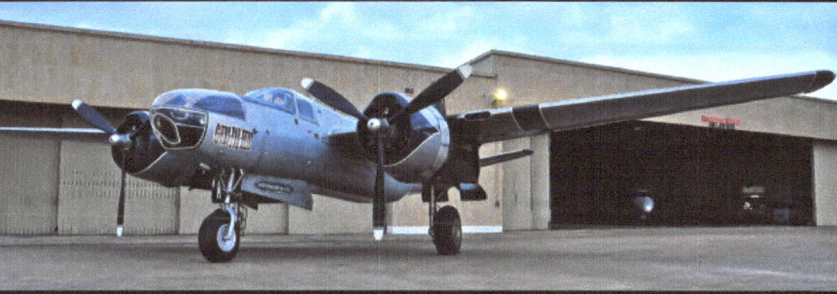

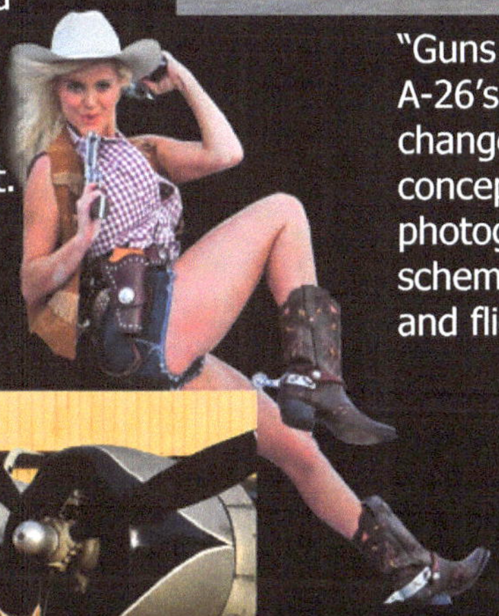

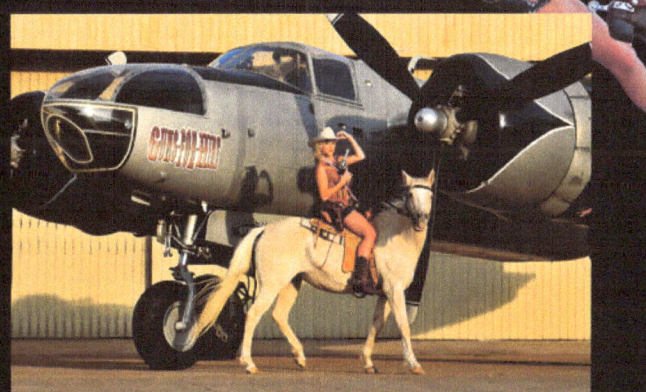

"Guns for Hire" is one of the remaining flight worthy A-26's in the country. She has since had her name changed and a new paint scheme so I got her when my concept was still fresh and was one of the last photographers to shoot her with the original paint scheme. "Guns for Hire" is now the "Miss Million Airess" and flies out of Houston Texas.

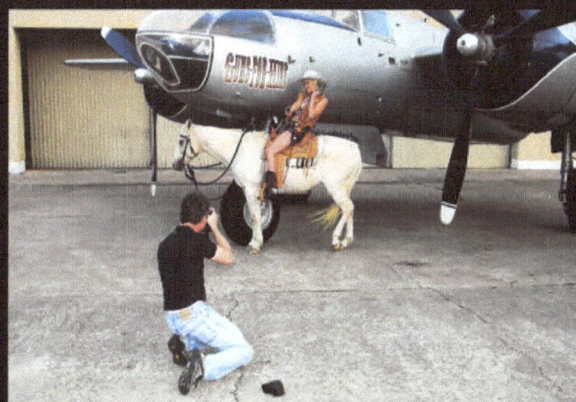

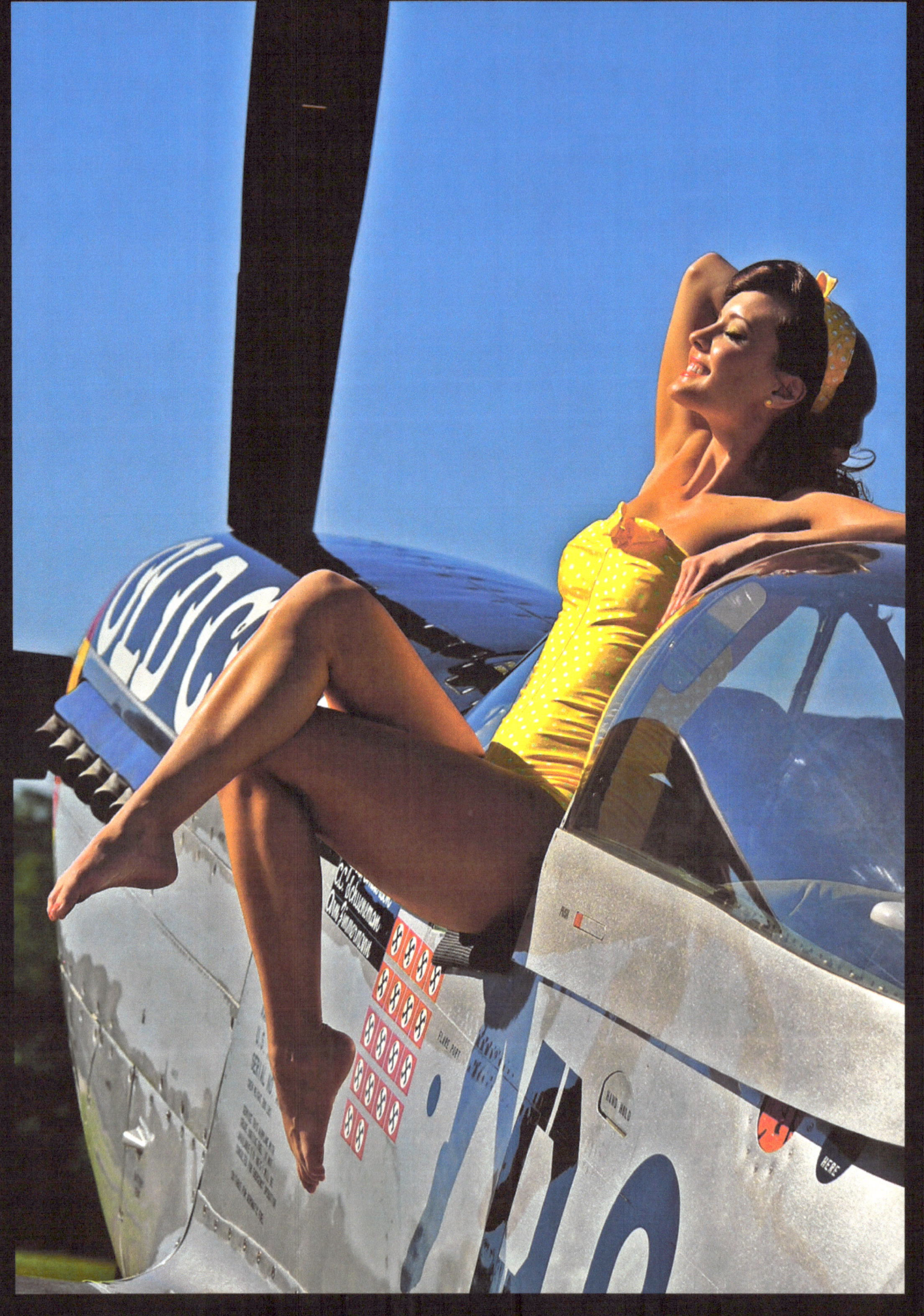

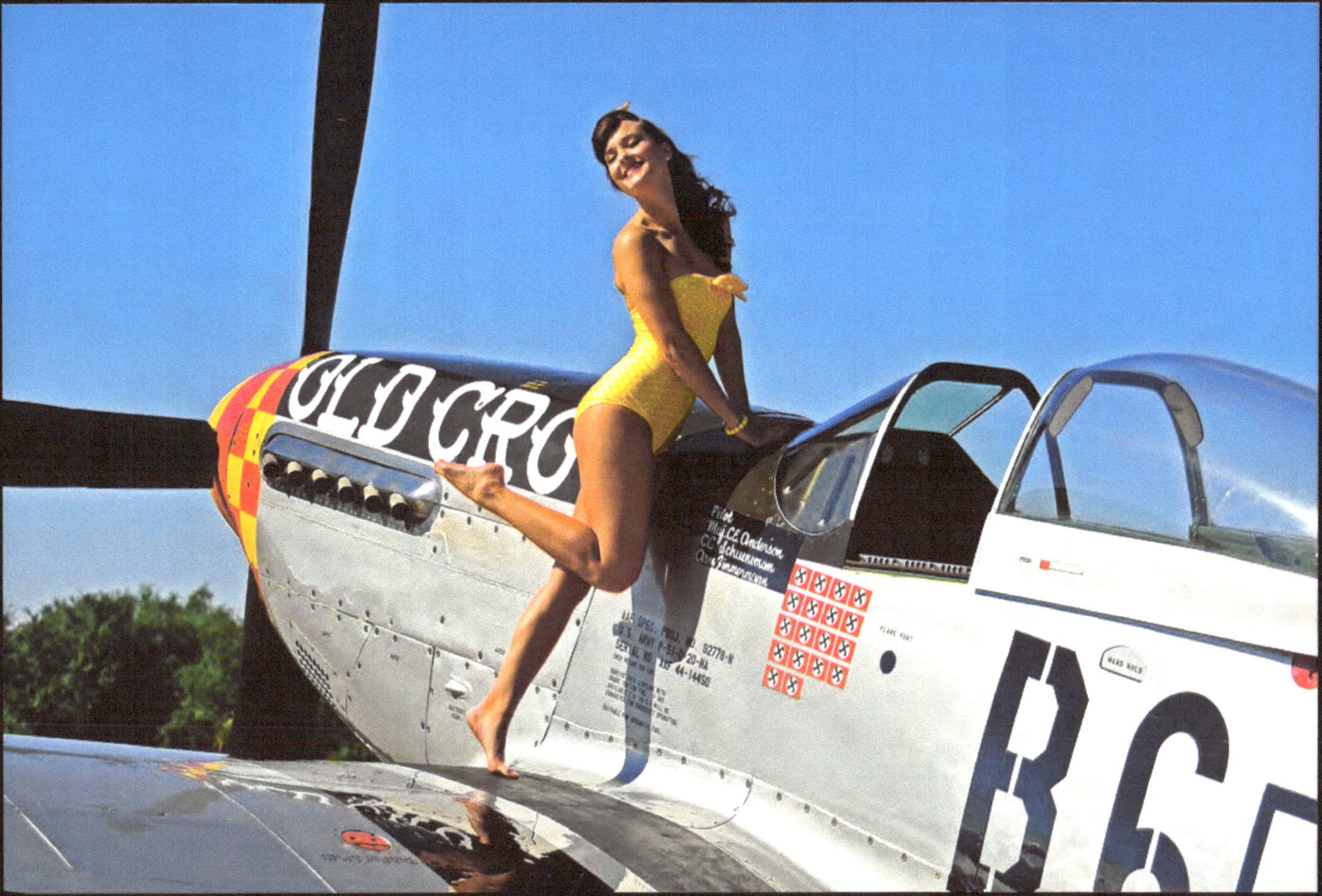

Brooke

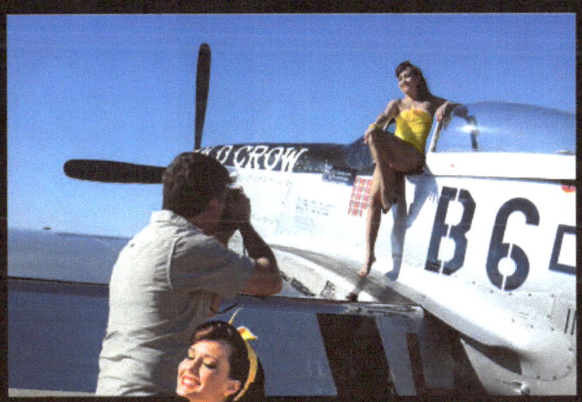

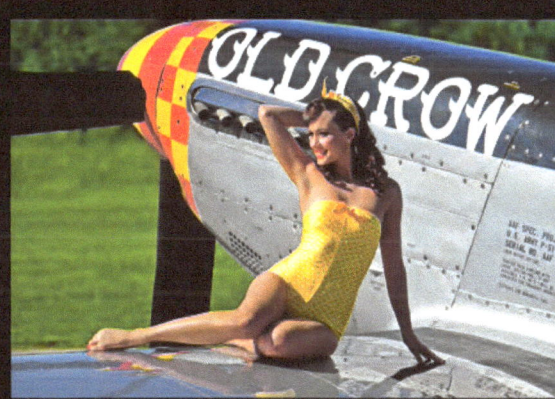

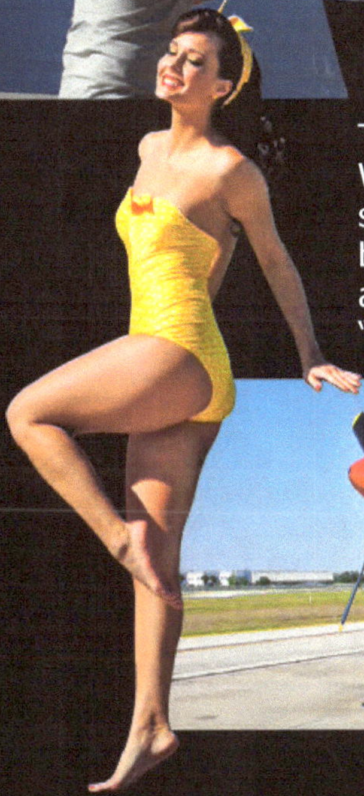

The famed "Old Crow" paint scheme P-51 was flown by triple ace Bud Anderson in WWII. Bud was one of America's top fighter pilots from the war. This fighter was the subject for our pinup shoot. It was an honor to have one of our girls pose with the beautiful P-51 of such legendary prowess. Bud Anderson has dropped by our booth and signed a copy of my work which I will hold dearly. We happened to catch the "Old Crow" during her annual maintenance in Florida.

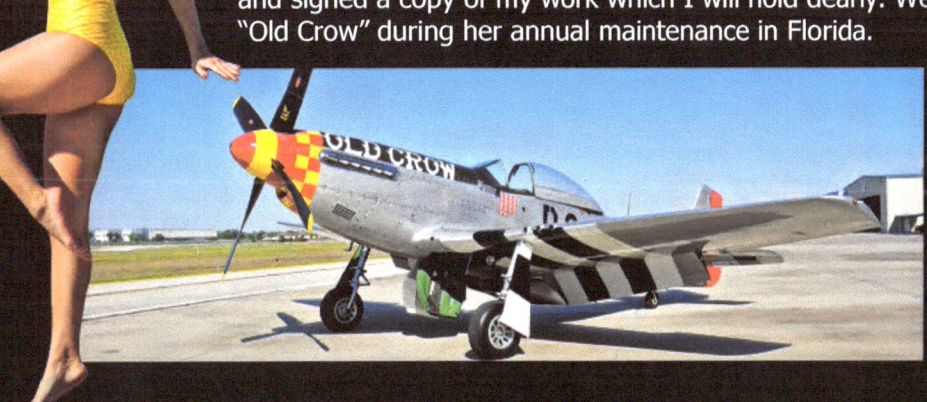

Seen here in this classic 1940's bathing suit, May/June 2013 pinup girl Brooke in her first photo shoot with the Warbird Pinup Girls has become an instant classic.

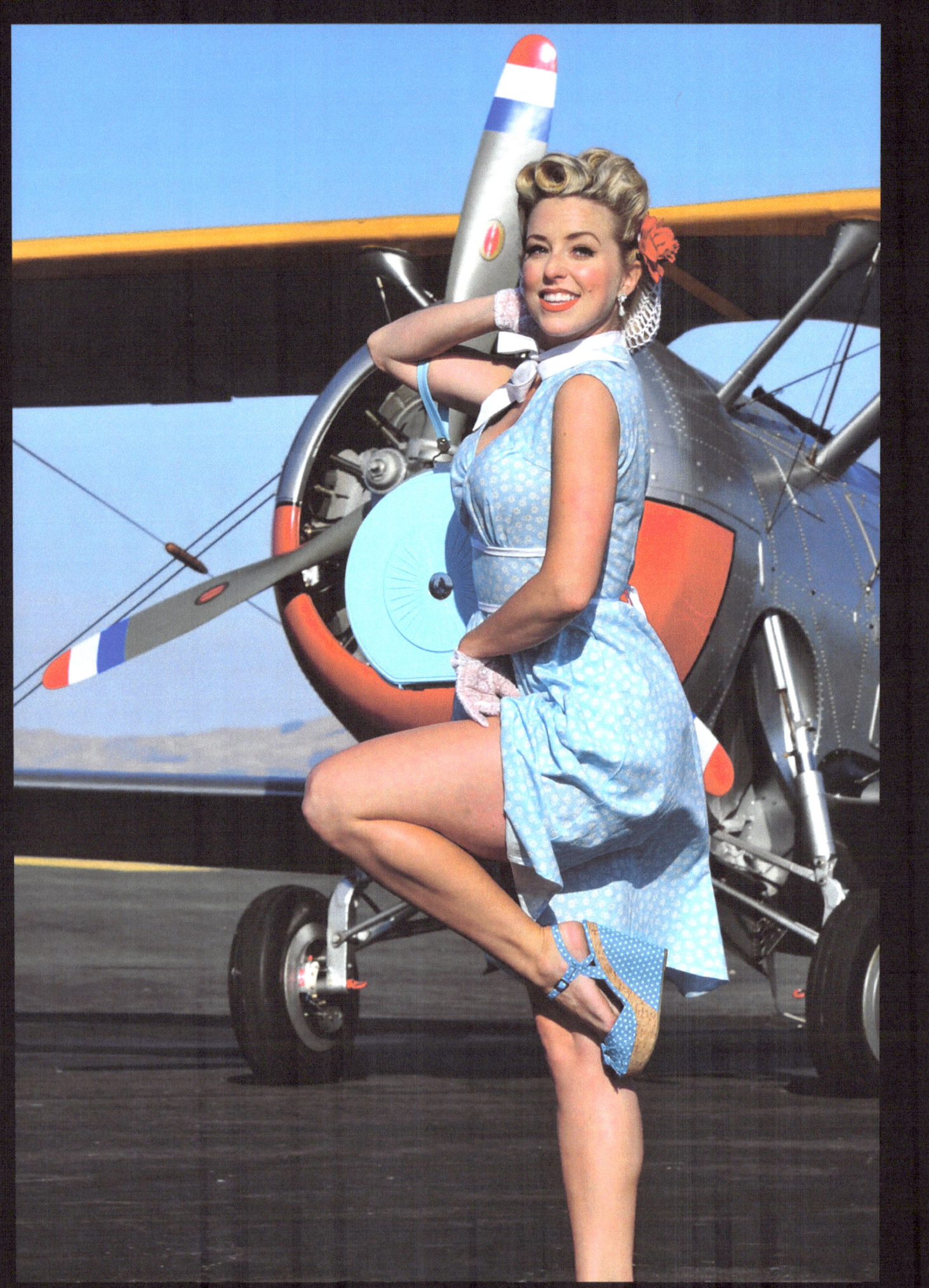

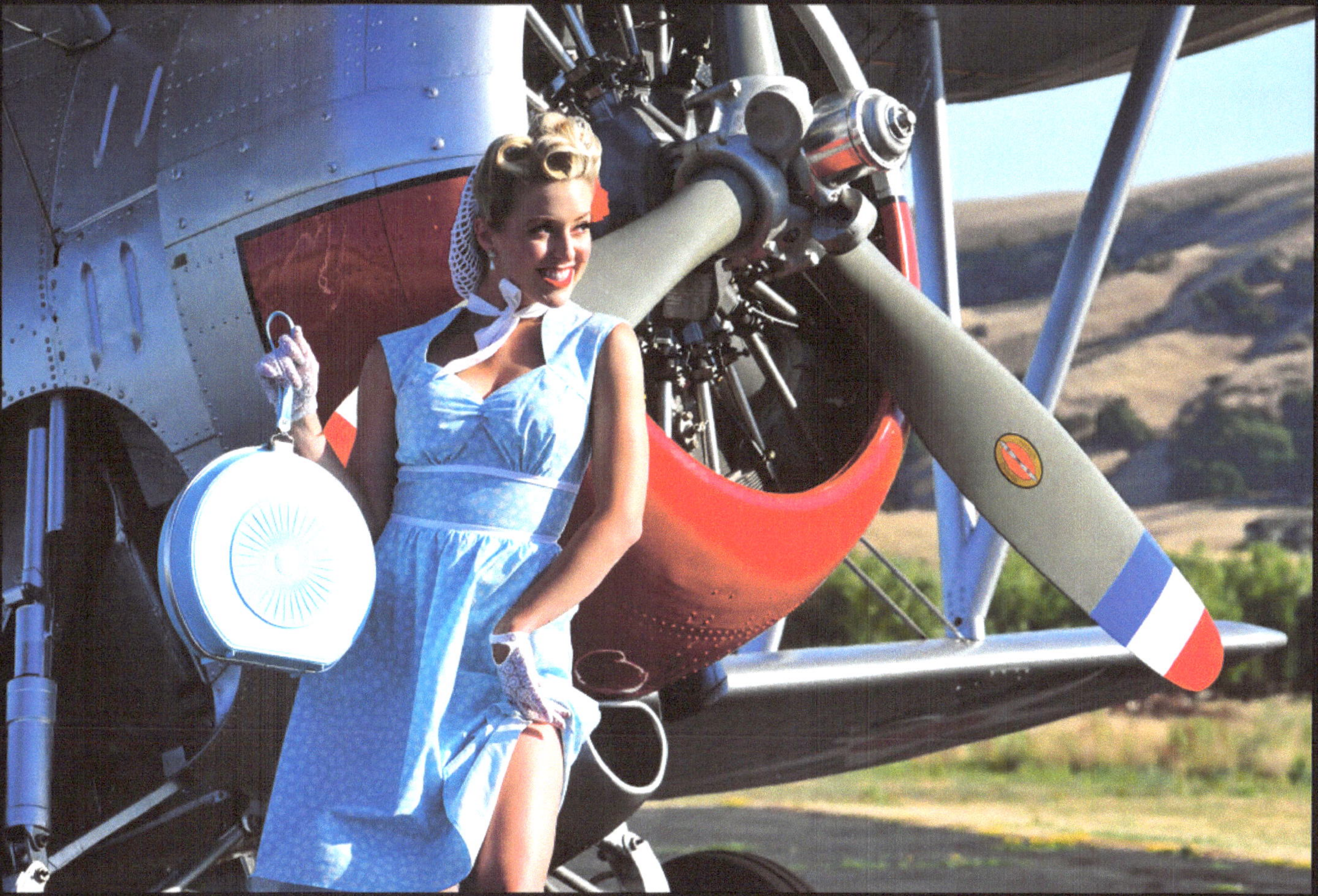

BAILEY

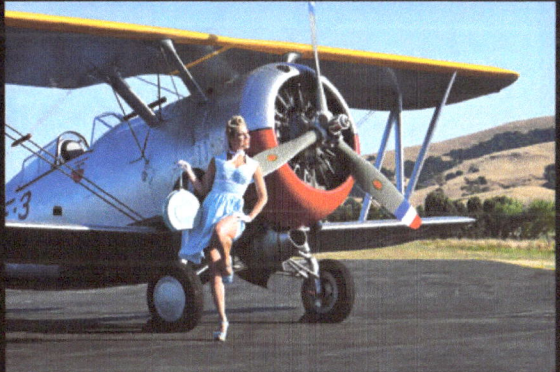

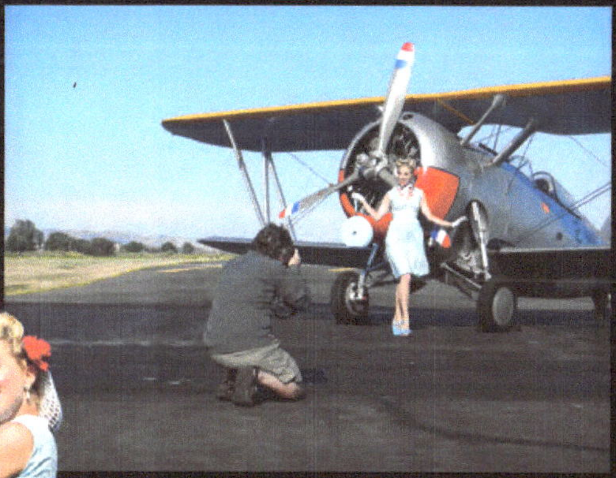

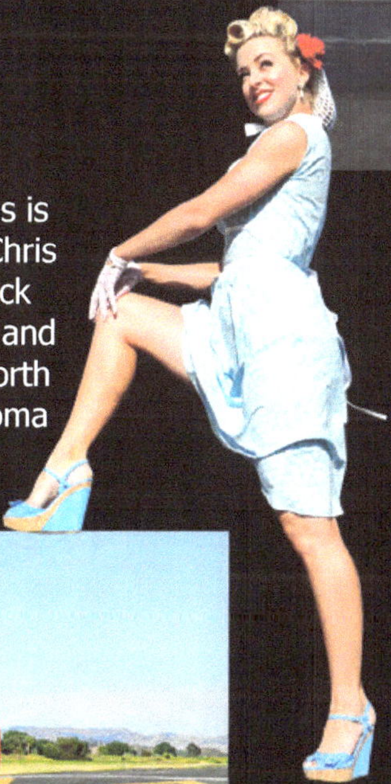

The Grummam F3F-2 is a very rare bird indeed and this is one of the most beautiful restorations we have seen. Chris Prevost from Vintage Aircraft Company brought her back to her original glory from salvaged parts out of Hawaii and was restored in Texas. She can now be seen at the North Bay Air Museum and Vintage Aircraft Company in Sonoma California, where our photo shoot took place.

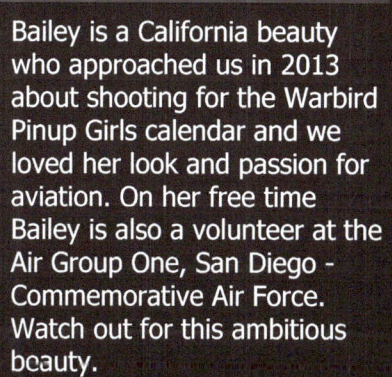

Bailey is a California beauty who approached us in 2013 about shooting for the Warbird Pinup Girls calendar and we loved her look and passion for aviation. On her free time Bailey is also a volunteer at the Air Group One, San Diego - Commemorative Air Force. Watch out for this ambitious beauty.

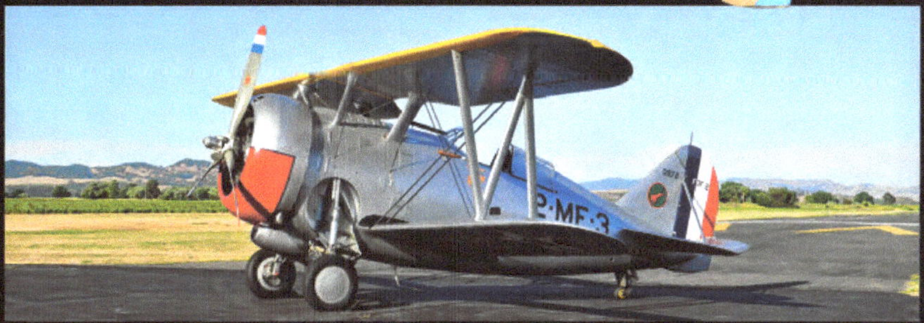

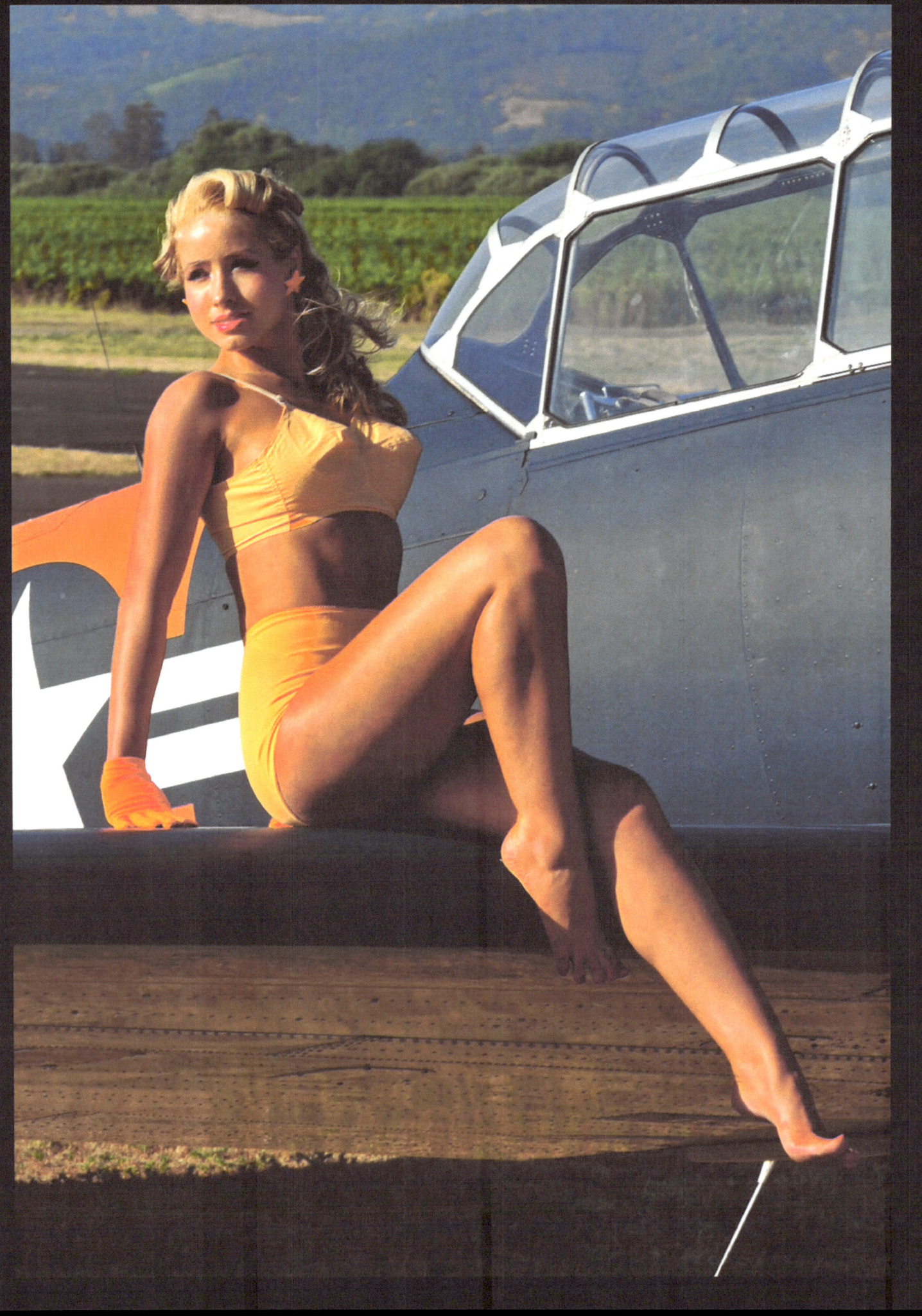

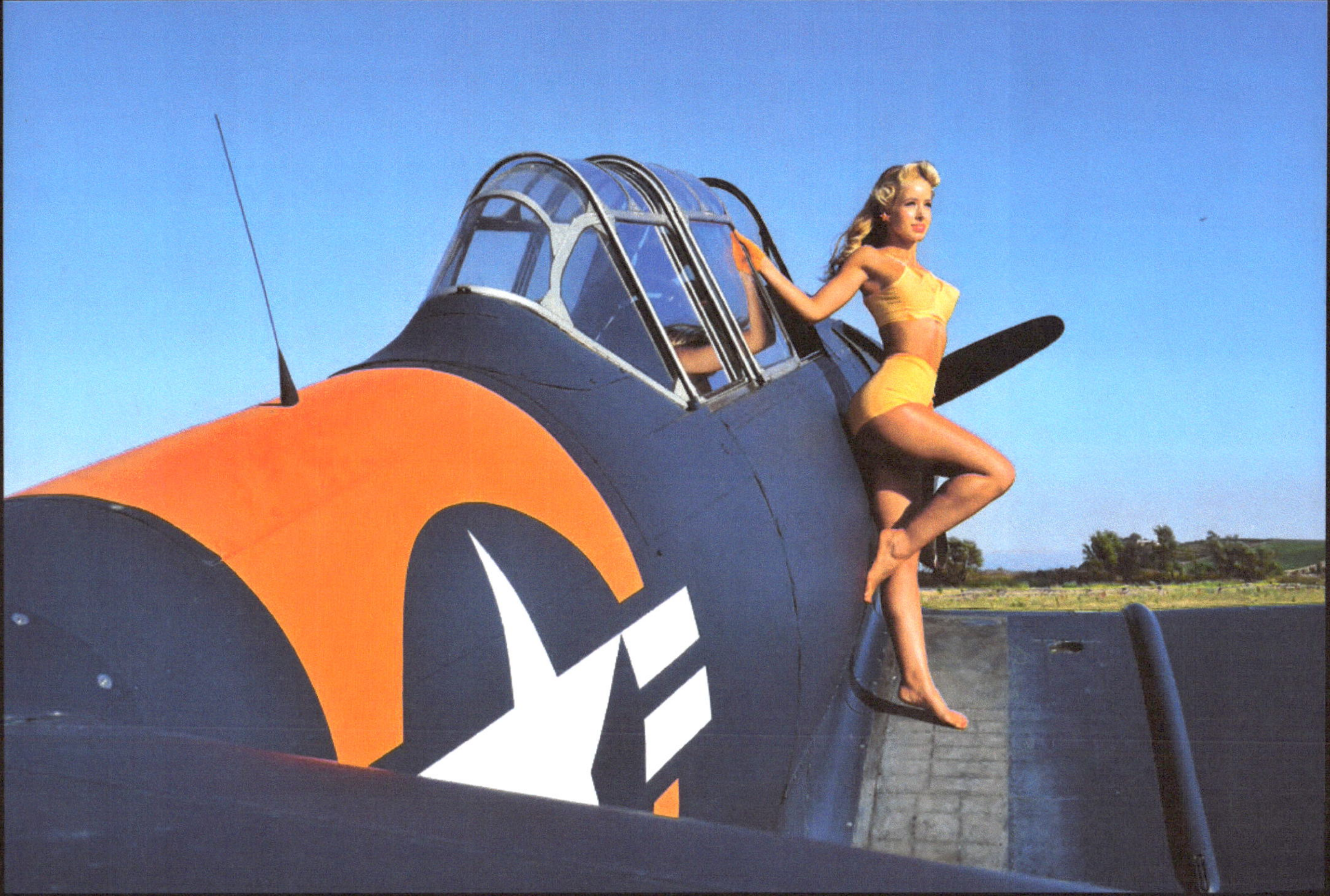

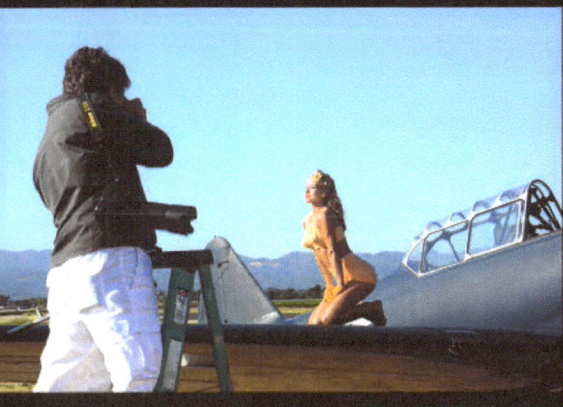

PAMELA

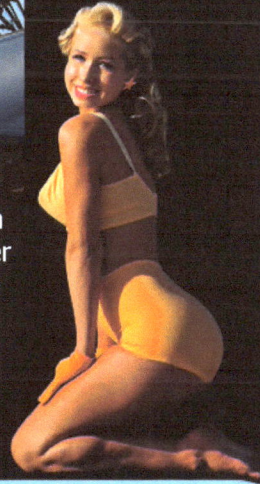

2015 pinup model Pamela comes to us from the Bay area and is a true California girl. Her classic wardrobe is an original vintage piece we found at VMale, one of Detroit's best retro shops. As soon as we saw this classic lingerie we knew it would match the unique paint scheme on our T-6.

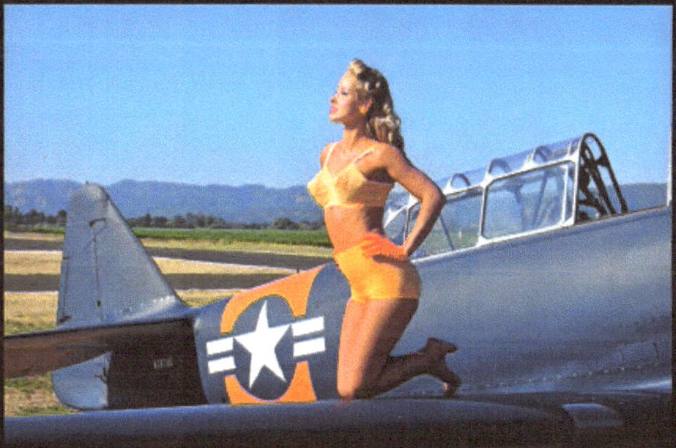

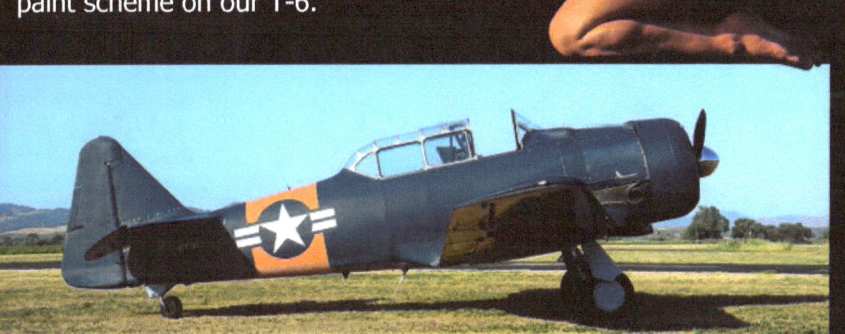

Another example of the great collection at Vintage Aircraft Company in Sonoma California. This unique SNJ-4 spends her days cruising over the wine country and doing fly-bys on the Golden Gate Bridge. The T6 "Texan" or in this case the naval version SNJ model was an advanced trainer used by cadets just before taking control of a real fighter plane.

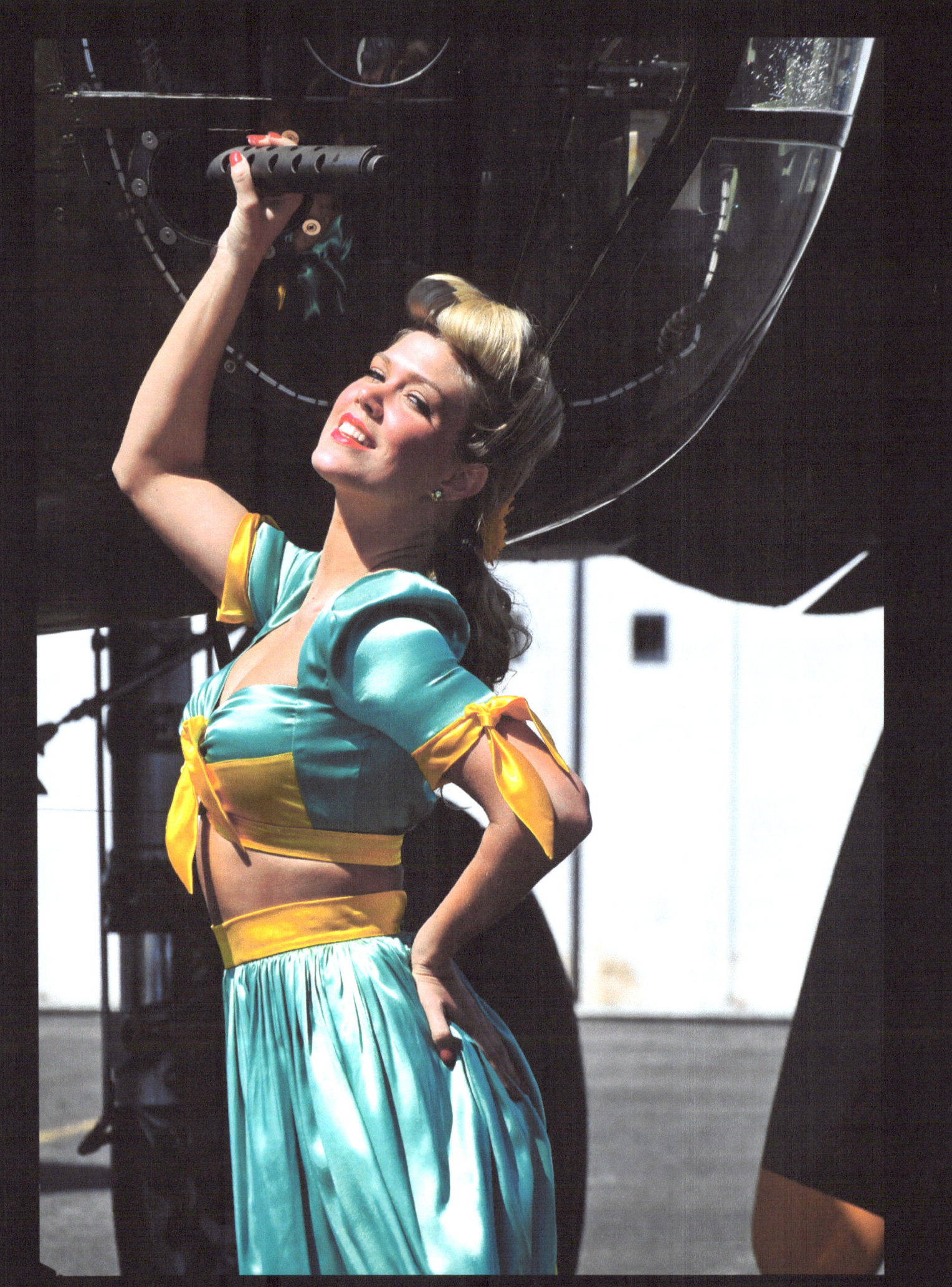

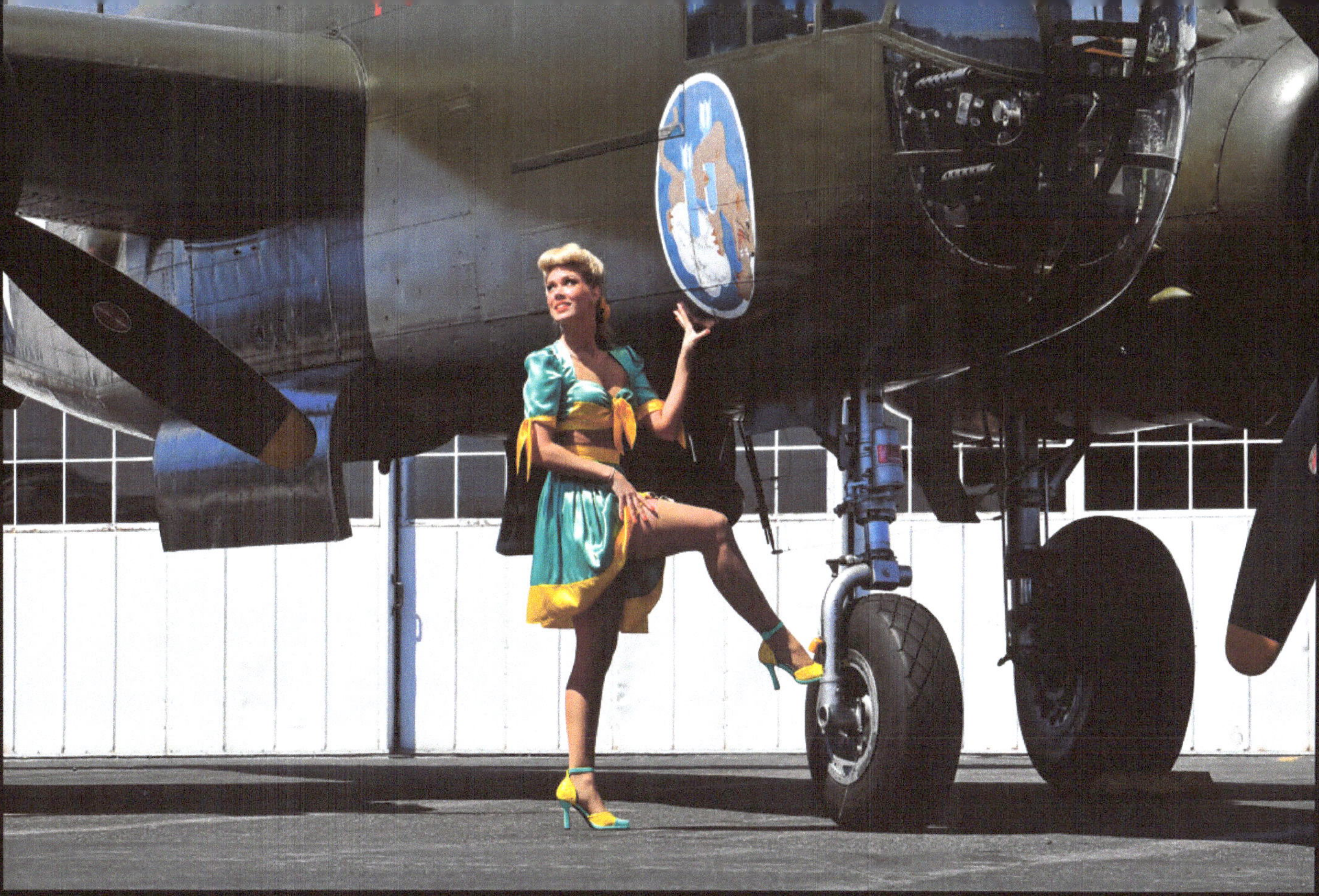

JESSICA

The B-25J Mitchell "Briefing Time" came to us from the Mid-Atlantic Air Museum in Reading Pennsylvania. This bird is a real ham as she has appeared in many Hollywood movies. She appears as tail #6C in the movie Catch 22 as well as six other Hollywood classics.

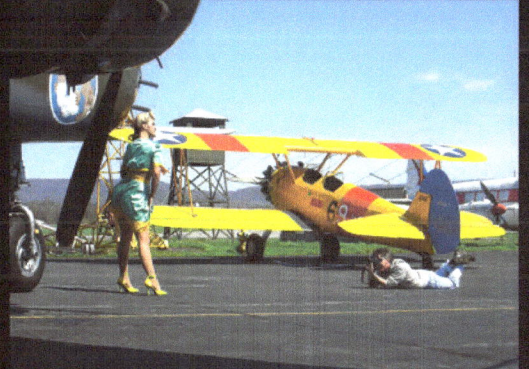

February 2012 pinup girl Jessica is a natural in front of the camera. Seen here in her custom made wardrobe, based on a famous Gil Elvgren painting, Jessica brings a true sense of the traditional pinup girls of WWII. Being a dancer, Jessica was a natural, giving us classic pinup poses with very little direction.

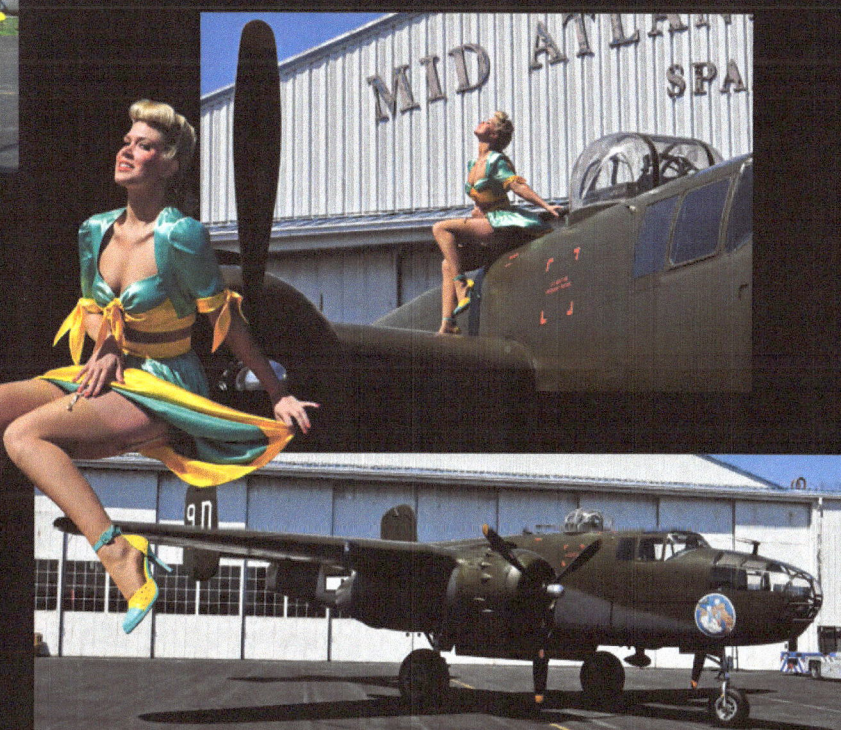

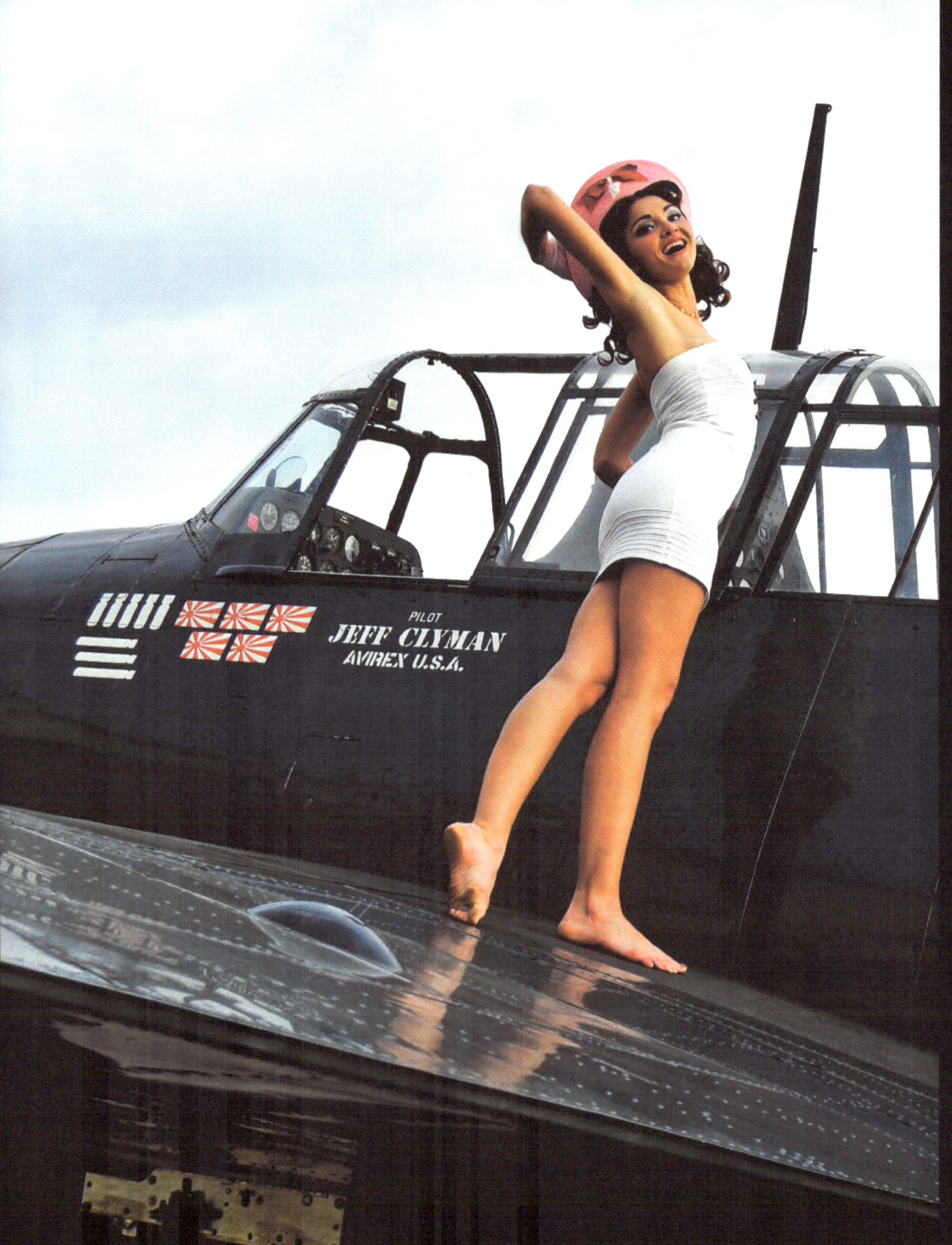

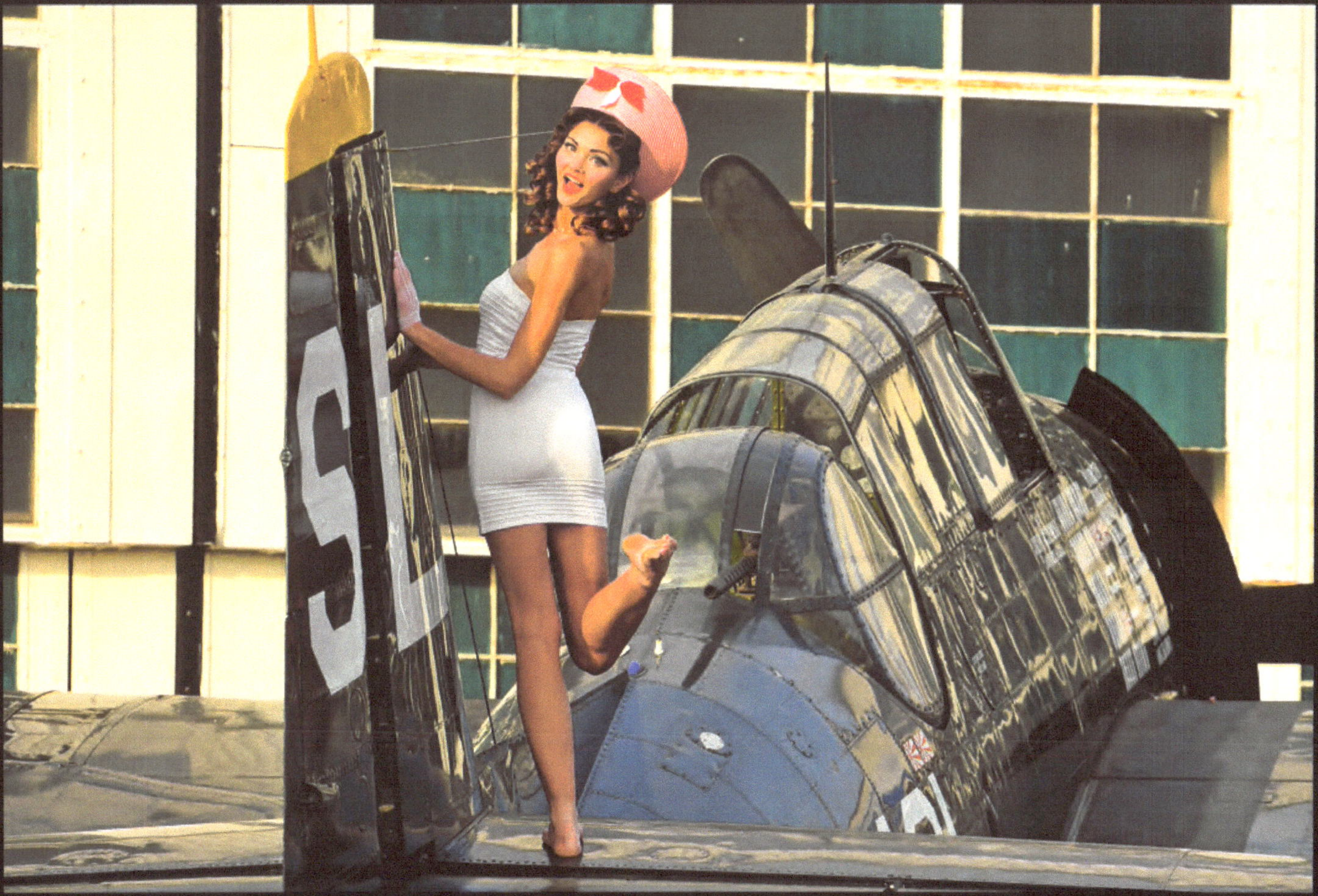

JENNY

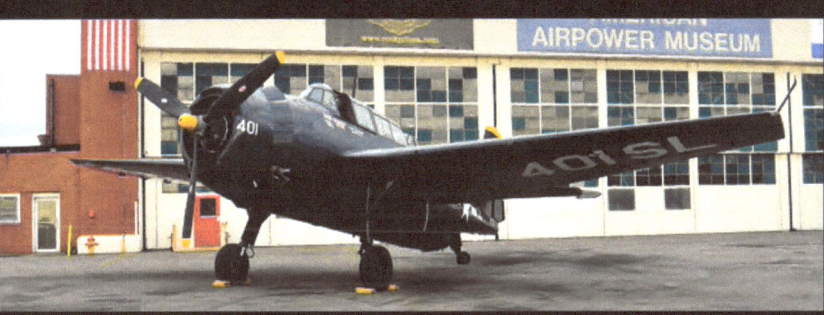

Jenny is a local model with little pinup experience that we test-shot with and decided to try her out for our bombers 2012 calendar "The Bomb". Jenny was brave to pose in her Navy themed dress on a very cold November day on Long Island. Jenny's shot was our January in the 2012 calendar.

The TBM Avenger made presidential history when George H. Bush was shot down and recovered in the South Seas during WWII. The TBM saw tremendous action in the war and was one of the most sturdy carrier based aircraft ever made. With a three man crew - two wing guns, one turret gun and one ventral gun, the Avenger was a force to be reckoned with. Seen here in her Pacific Navy paint scheme, this flight worthy TBM flies out of the American Airpower Museum on Long Island.

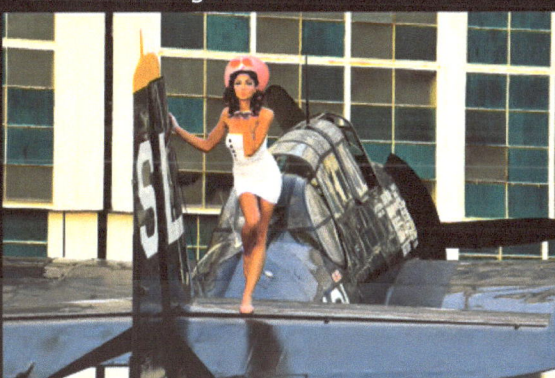

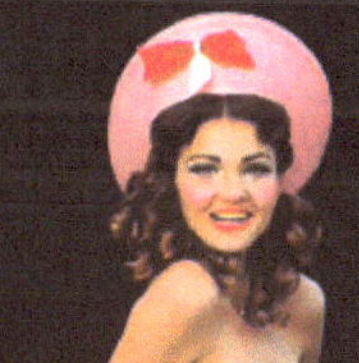

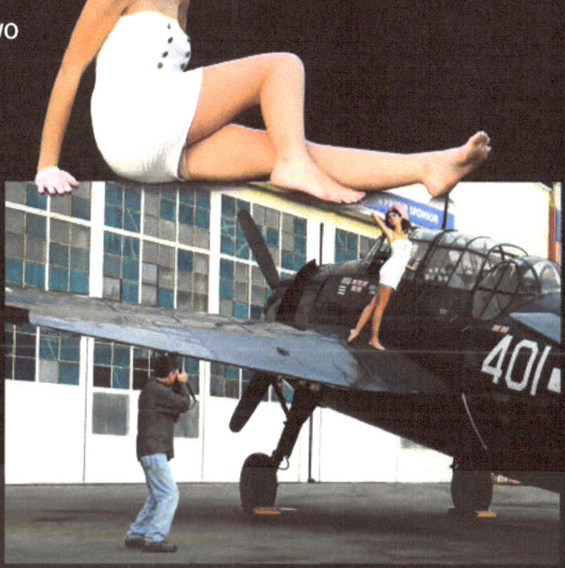

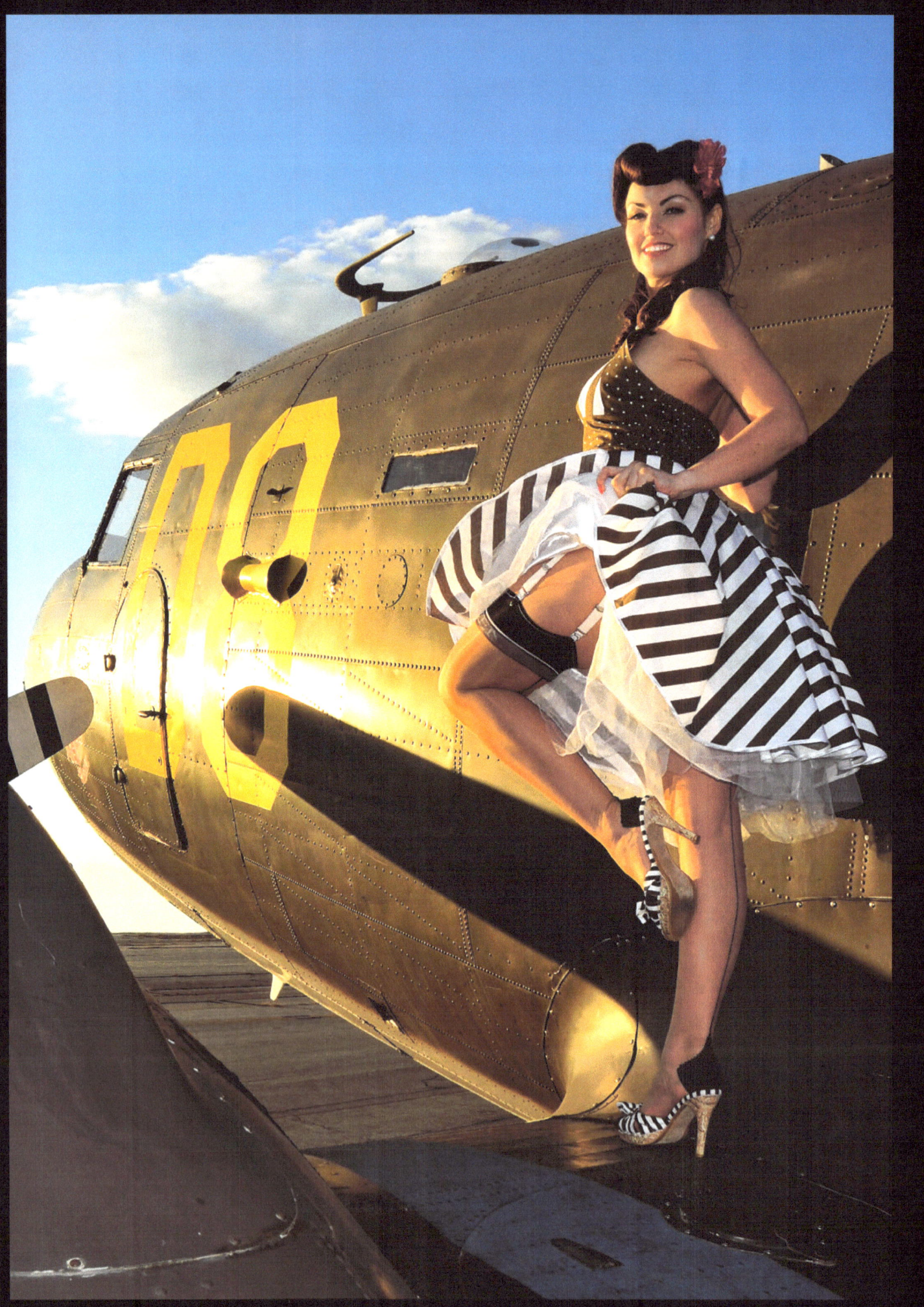

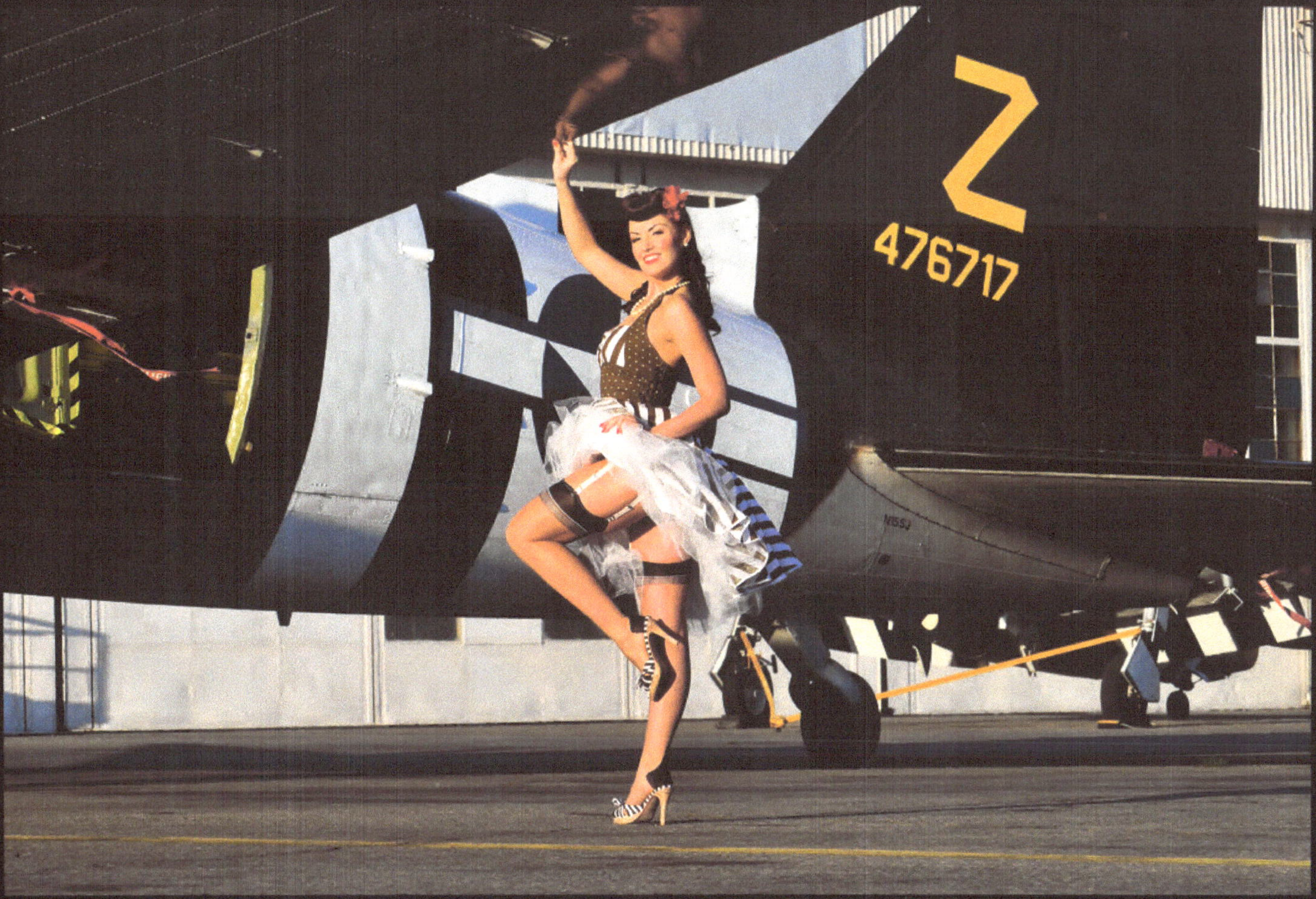

YULIA

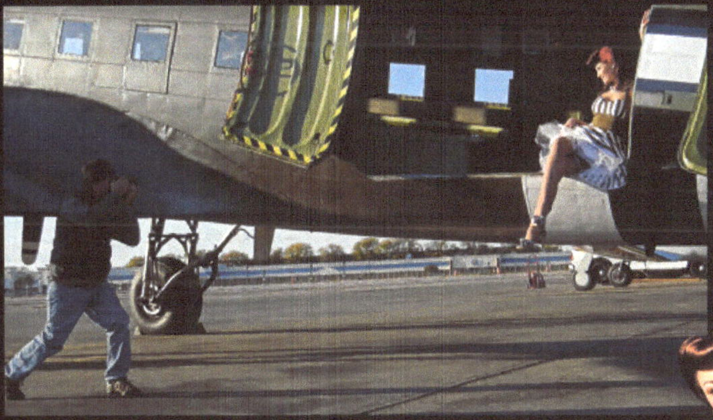

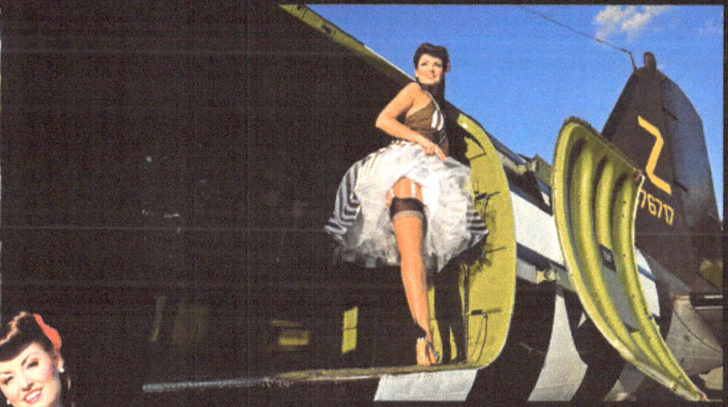

The C-47 Skytrain was the true work horse of the Second World War. Carrying out almost any job you can imagine, they are most famous for dropping our airborne troops behind enemy lines. This beautiful C-47 belongs to the American Airpower Museum on Long Island.

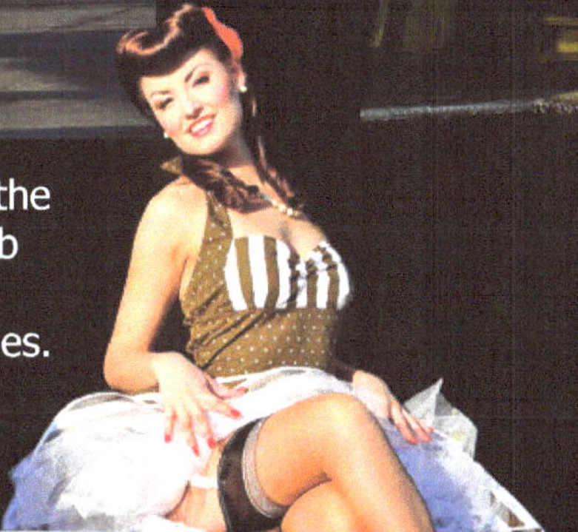

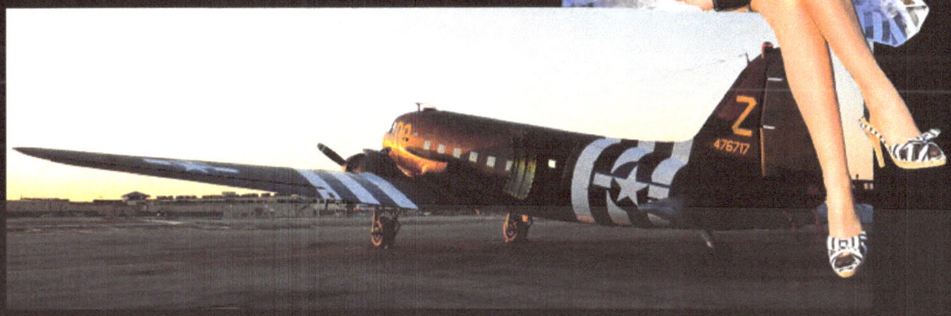

Working with Yulia was a charm. Yulia is a new immigrant from Belaruss and had no pinup experience, but she sure had what it took and after only a short time of working together we pulled off a truly classic 1940's pinup girl that the troops would have been proud of. Yulia appears as our September 2014 pinup girl.

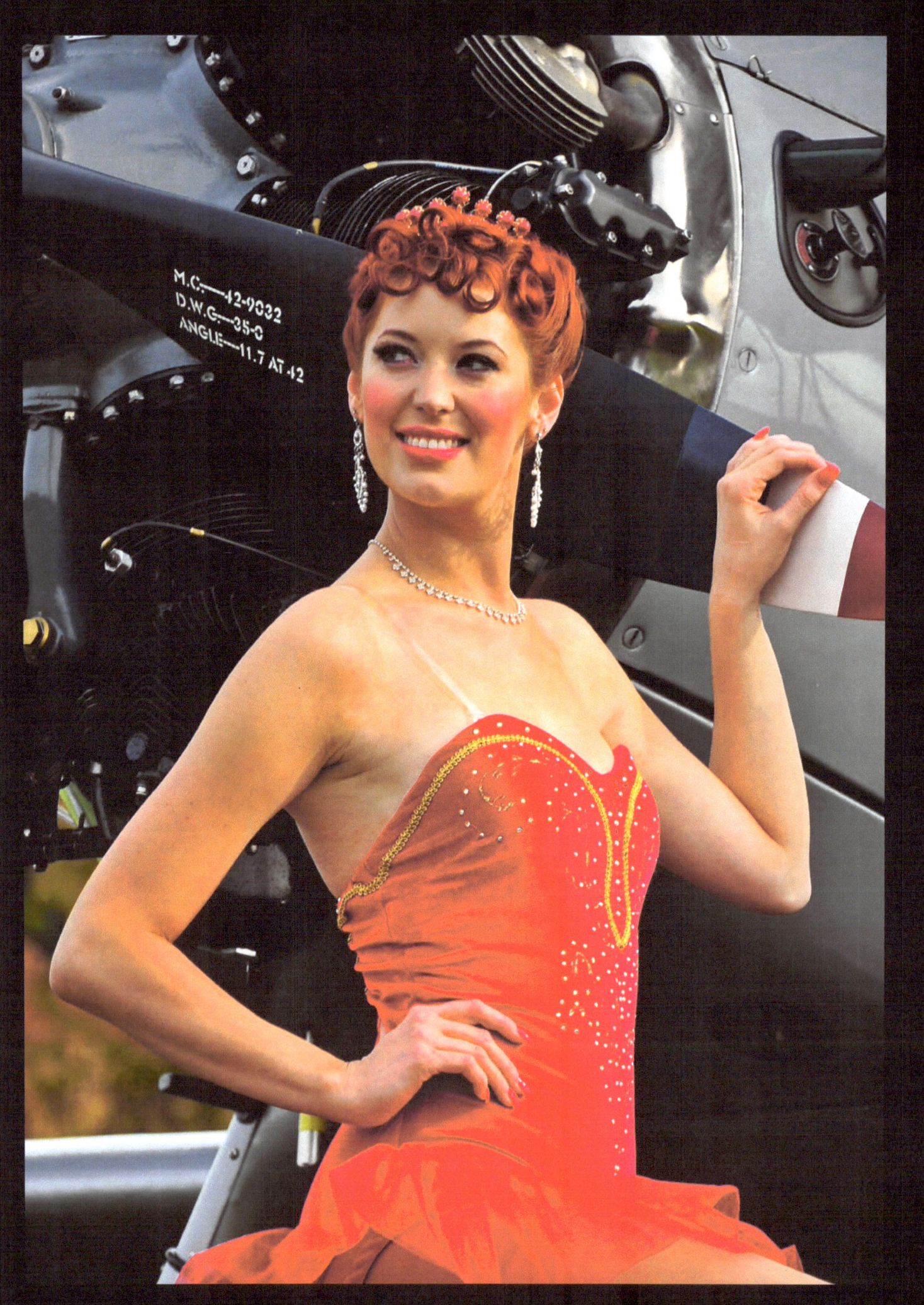

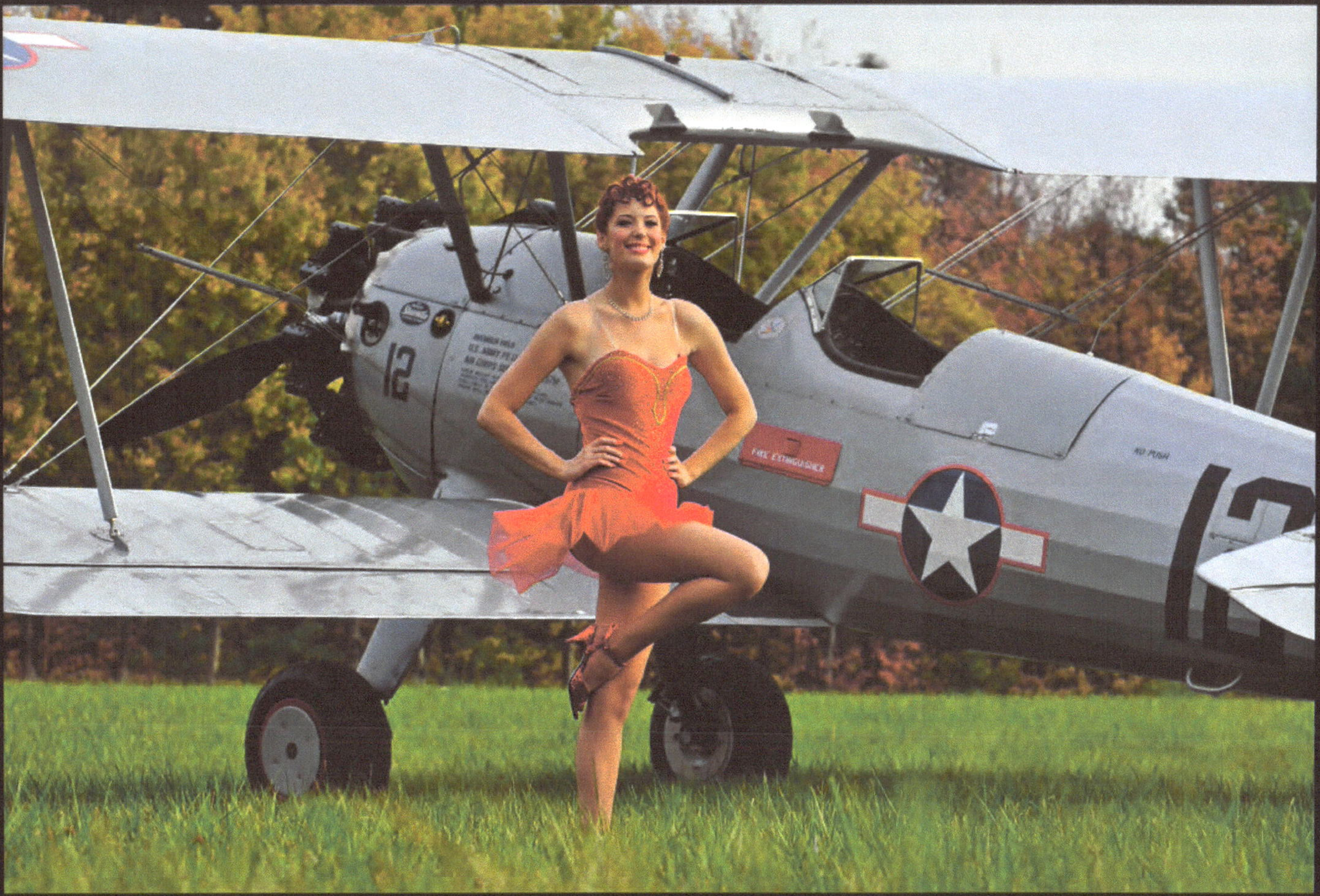

KELLY

Competing for attention in this Warbird Pinup Girls calendar shoot is the award winning PT-17 Stearman owned and operated by Mike Porter in Ohio. This is one of the finest restorations we have seen, simply an exquisite example of this flight worthy classic.

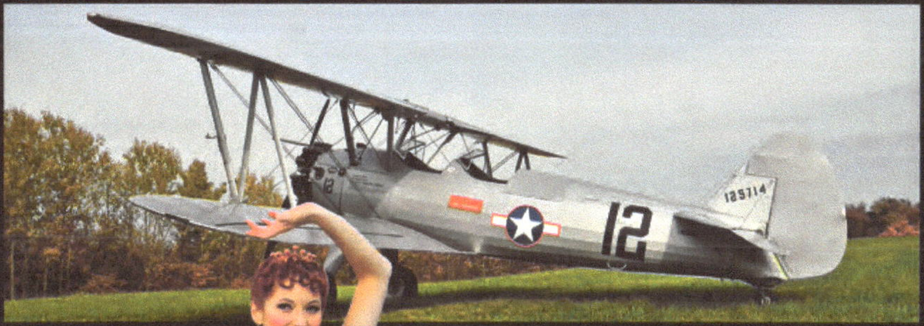

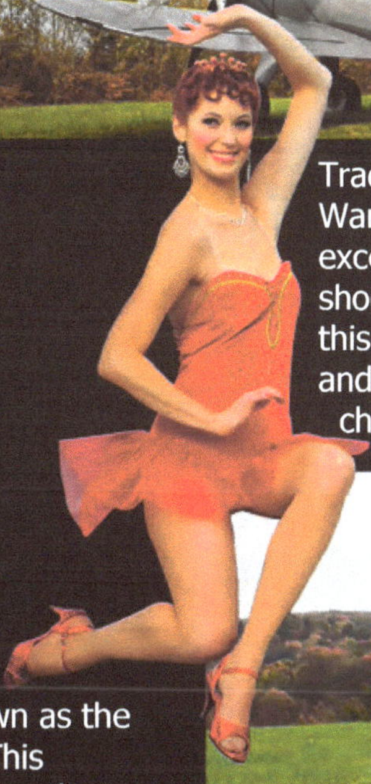

Tradition and authenticity is our goal at Warbird Pinup Girls. This is exceptionally true at this 2014 calendar shoot with pinup girl Kelly as she sports this custom made Vargas inspired attire and works on her classic poses with choreographer Tammy Jean.

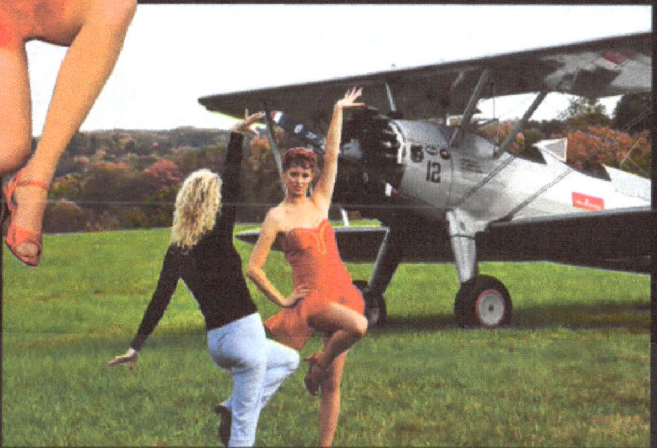

This amazing airplane participated in what was known as the WASP Program, "Women's Airforce Service Pilots". This pioneering group of female aviators employed by the military under the direction of the US Army Air Forces, was trained for none-combat duties including training and the transport of military aircraft to new locations.

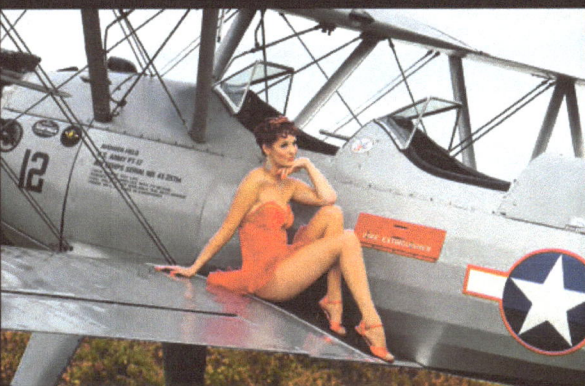

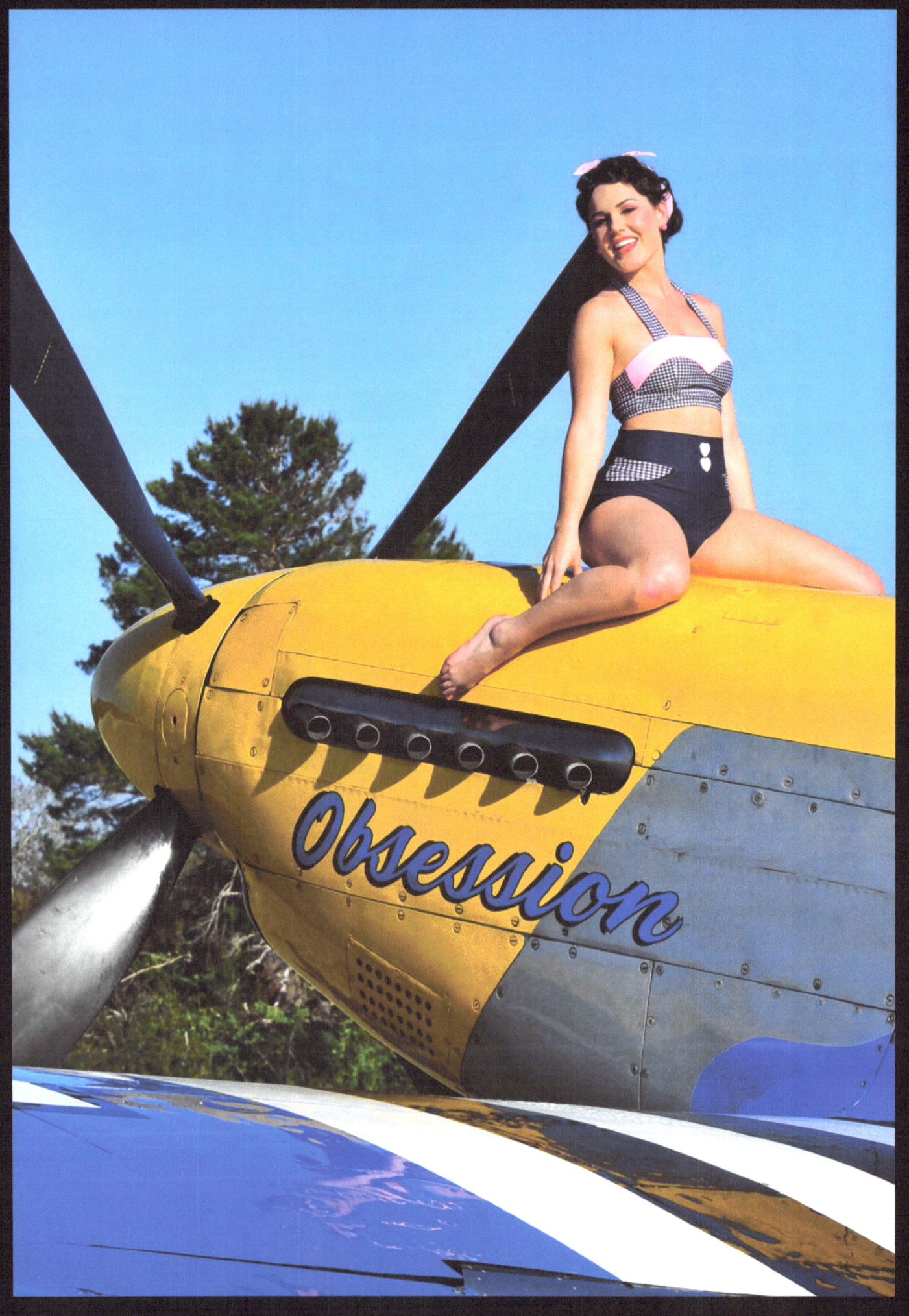

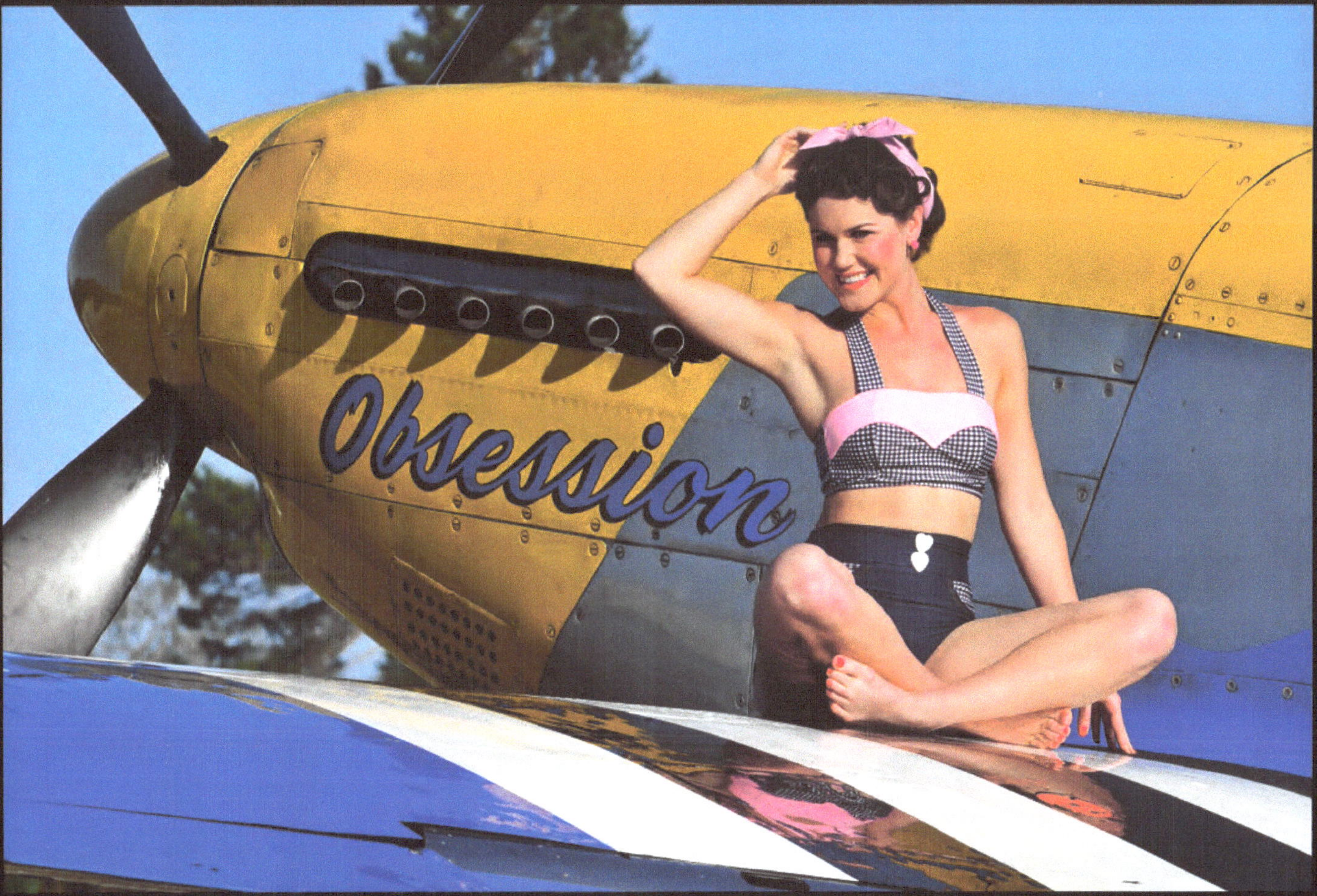

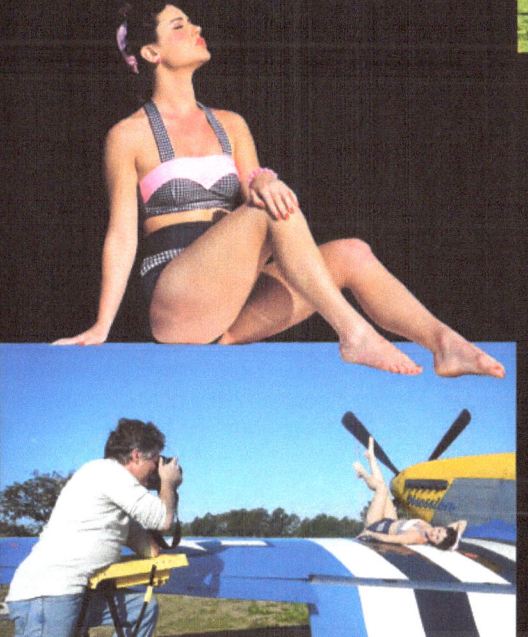

LEXI

Returning 2013 pinup girl Lexi is an adorable model we pulled right from Walt Disney's Magic Kingdom where she works as a Princess. Sporting a classic two piece bathing suit, Lexi has all the classic qualities of a true pinup girl.

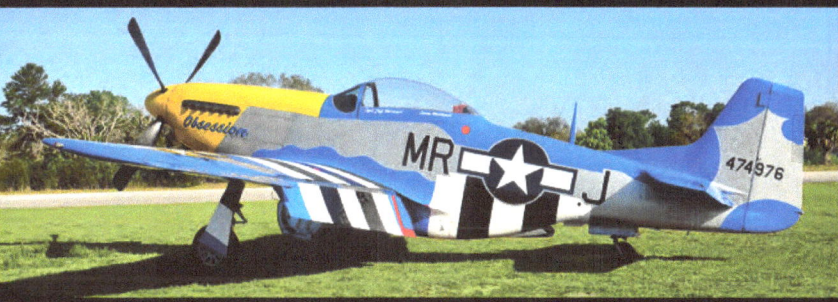

"Obsession" is right, just have a look at this beautifully maintained P-51 owned and operated by airline pilot Jeff Michaels. Sporting the D-Day invasion stripes, this classic WWII fighter couldn't look better in the early morning Florida sunshine. Appearing in our 2014 calendar as our June warbird.

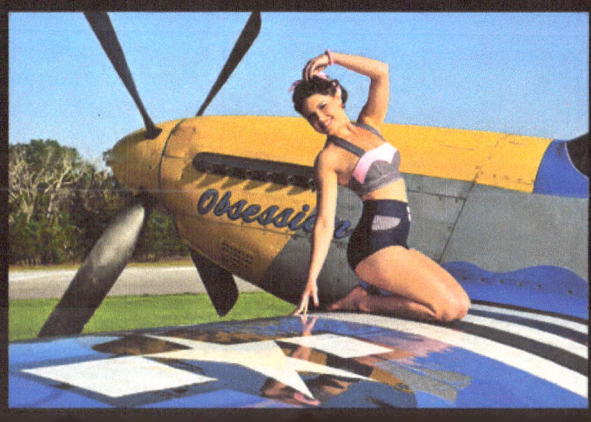

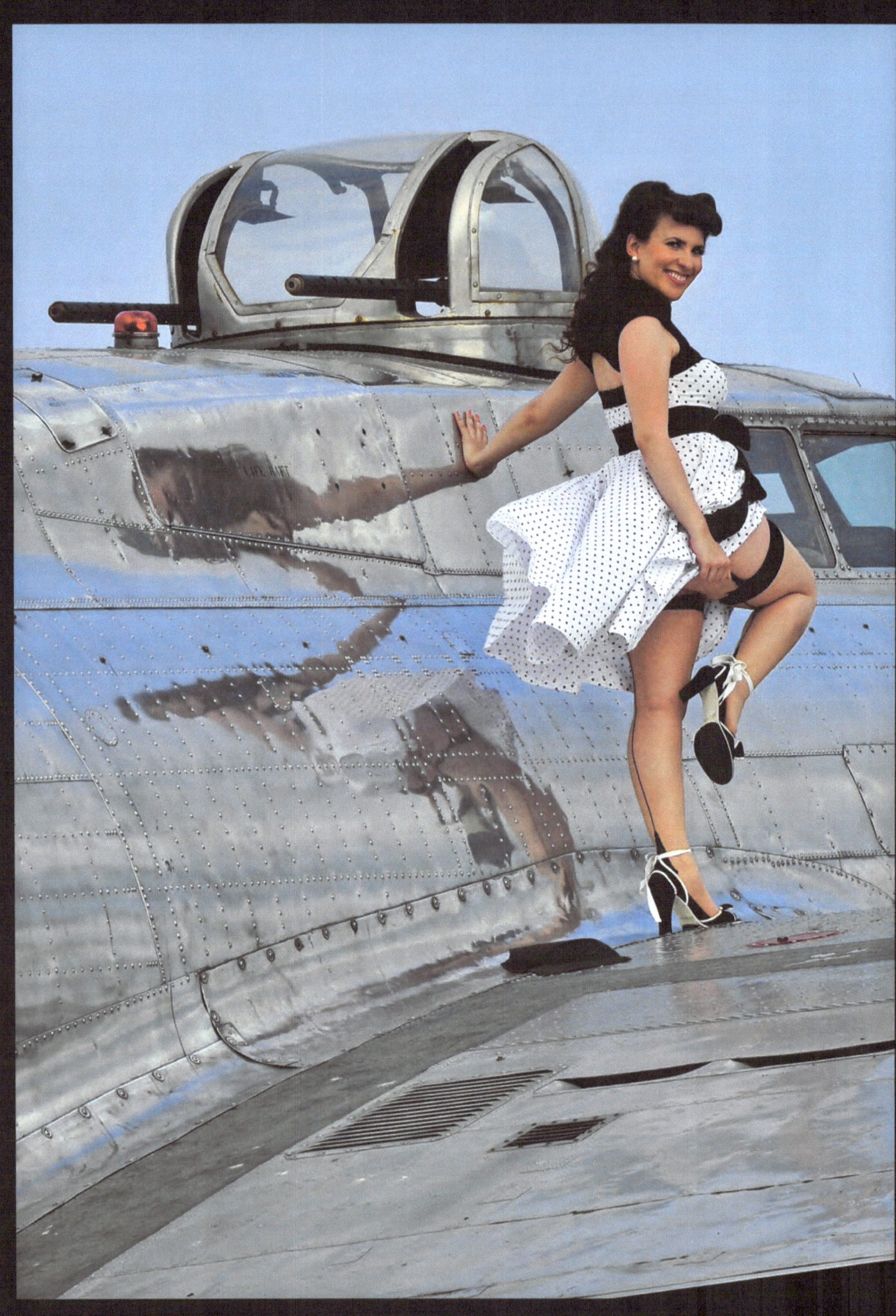

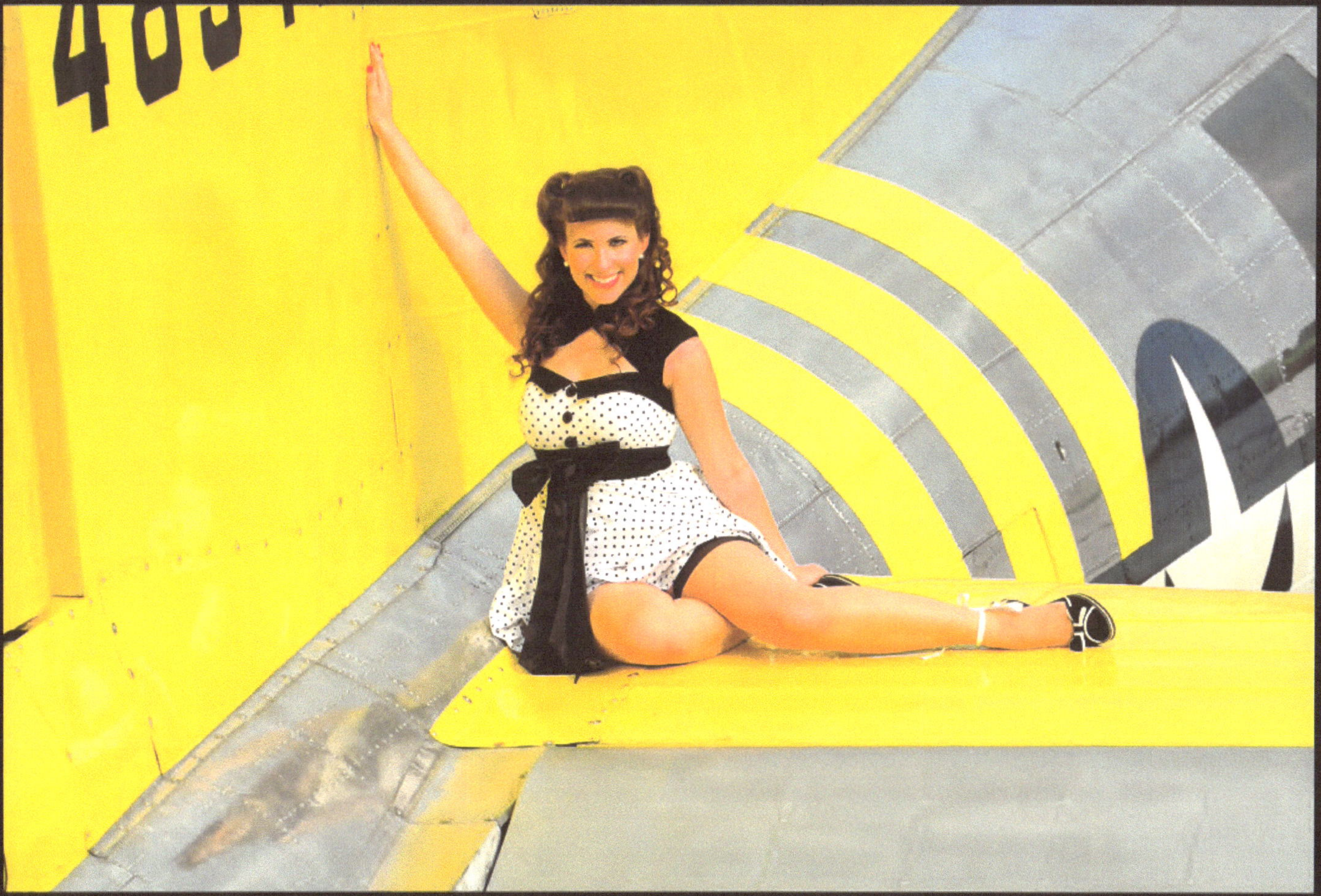

ALEXIS

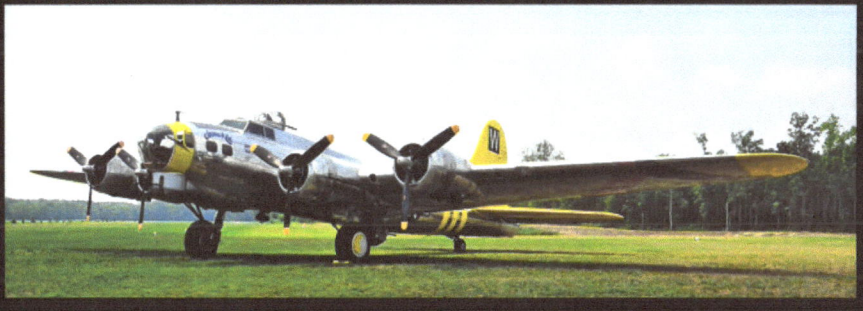

One of our most ambitious models, Alexis, pursued the Warbird Pinup Girls until we finally gave her a chance to audition. We cast her and she met us in Virginia for our 2-day shoot and gave Chuckie a pinup girl to remember.

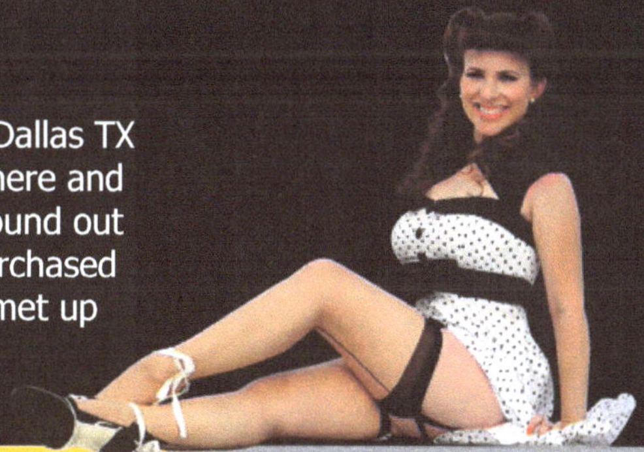

We first saw the B-17G "Chuckie" stashed in the back of a hangar near Dallas TX while shooting the "Pacific Prowler" B-25. She looked very lonely back there and I thought she might not even be flight worthy. A few months later we found out that Jerry Yagen from the Military Aviation Museum in Virginia Beach purchased her and brought her out of the mothballs and had her flying again. We met up with her in Virginia and paired her up with the fresh faced Alexis.

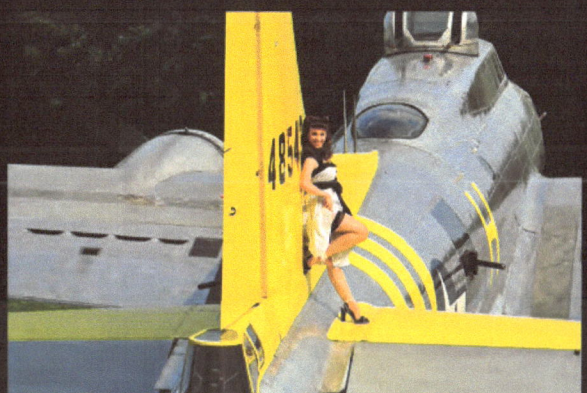

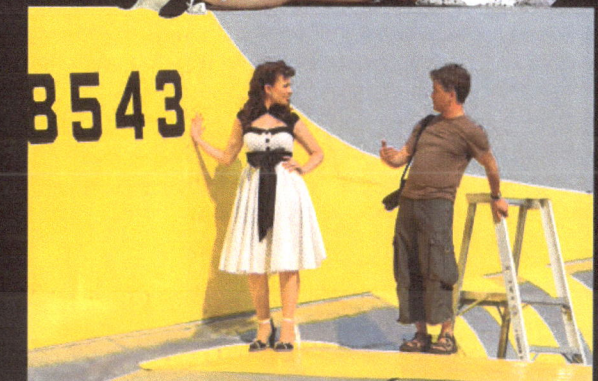

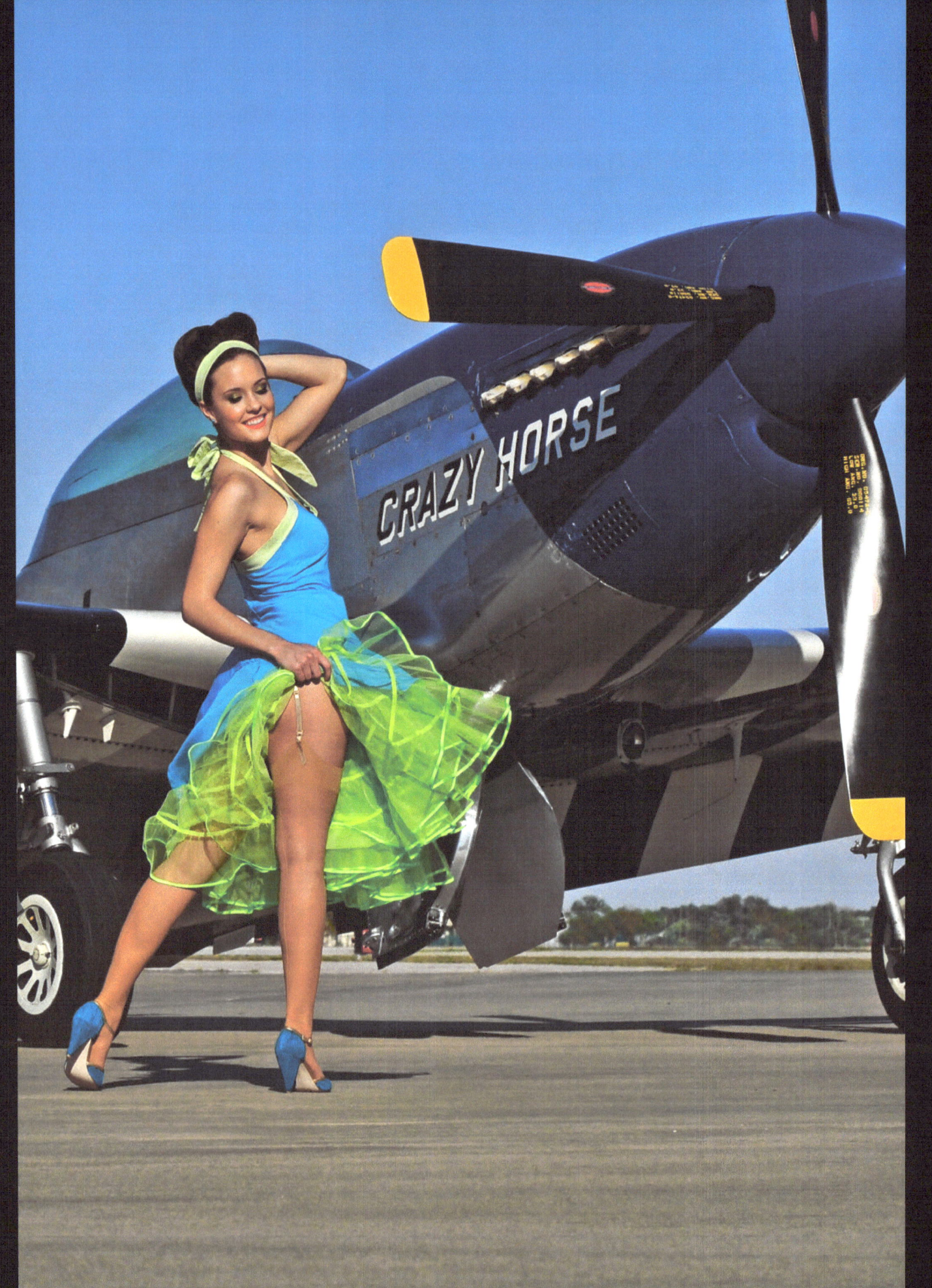

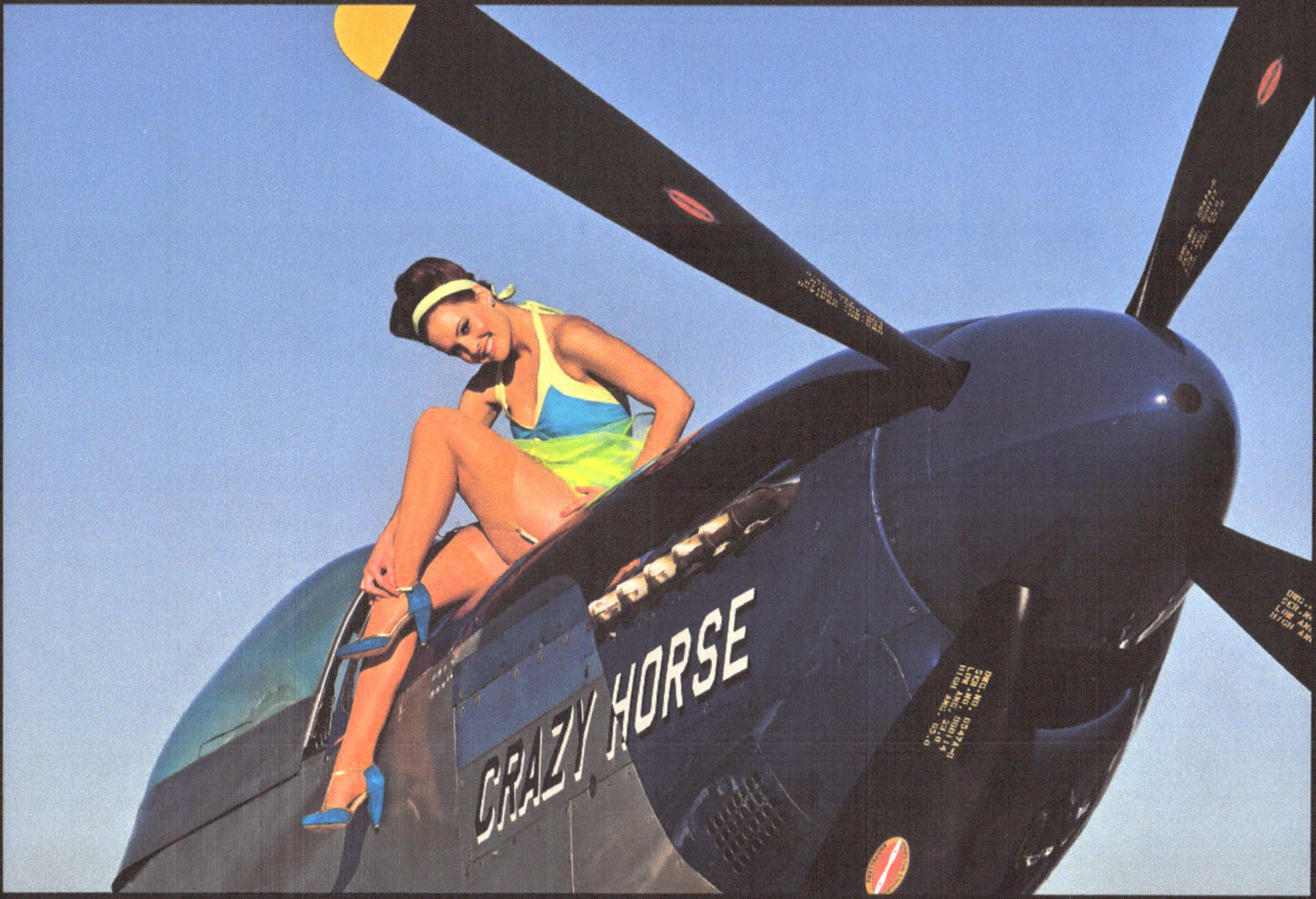

BROOKE

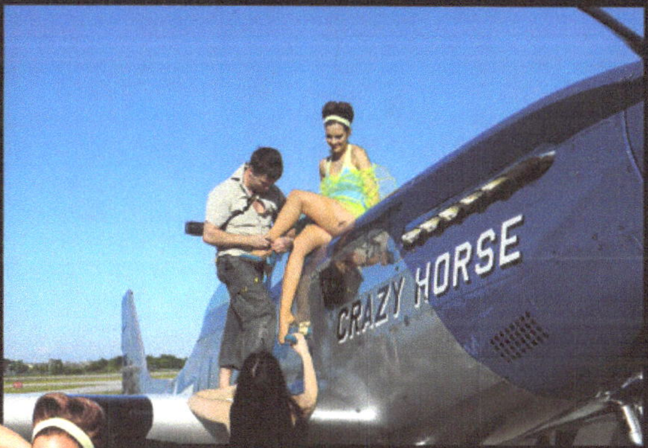

One of the most famous P-51 Mustangs on the circuit today, "Crazy Horse" is the sister ship of the Crazy Horse twins 1 & 2 from Stallion 51 Flight Ops in Kissimmee Florida. Both Mustangs are dual control TF-51 configurations and are used to train pilots in this legendary fighter plane. These aircraft can be seen throughout the country at air shows and special events. If you're interested in taming these wild horses, drop by Kissimmee Florida at Stallion

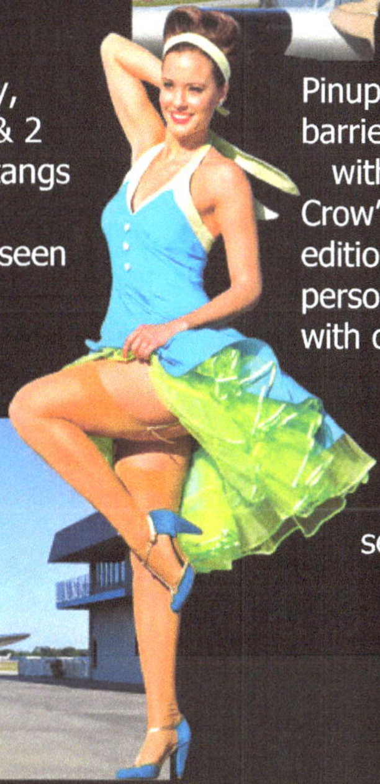

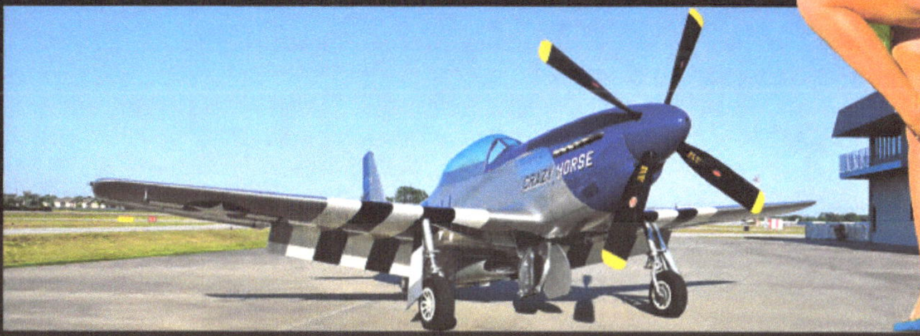

Pinup girl Brooke, broke all the barriers when she first appeared with the P-51 Mustang "Old Crow" in our 2013 all Mustangs edition. Sexy, intelligent and personable, Brooke is a huge hit with our fans on the circuit.

We brought Brook back for our 2014 edition where she appears with the P-51 Mustang "Crazy Horse" seen here.

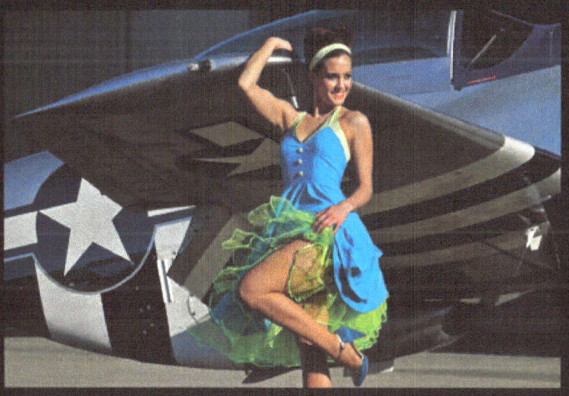

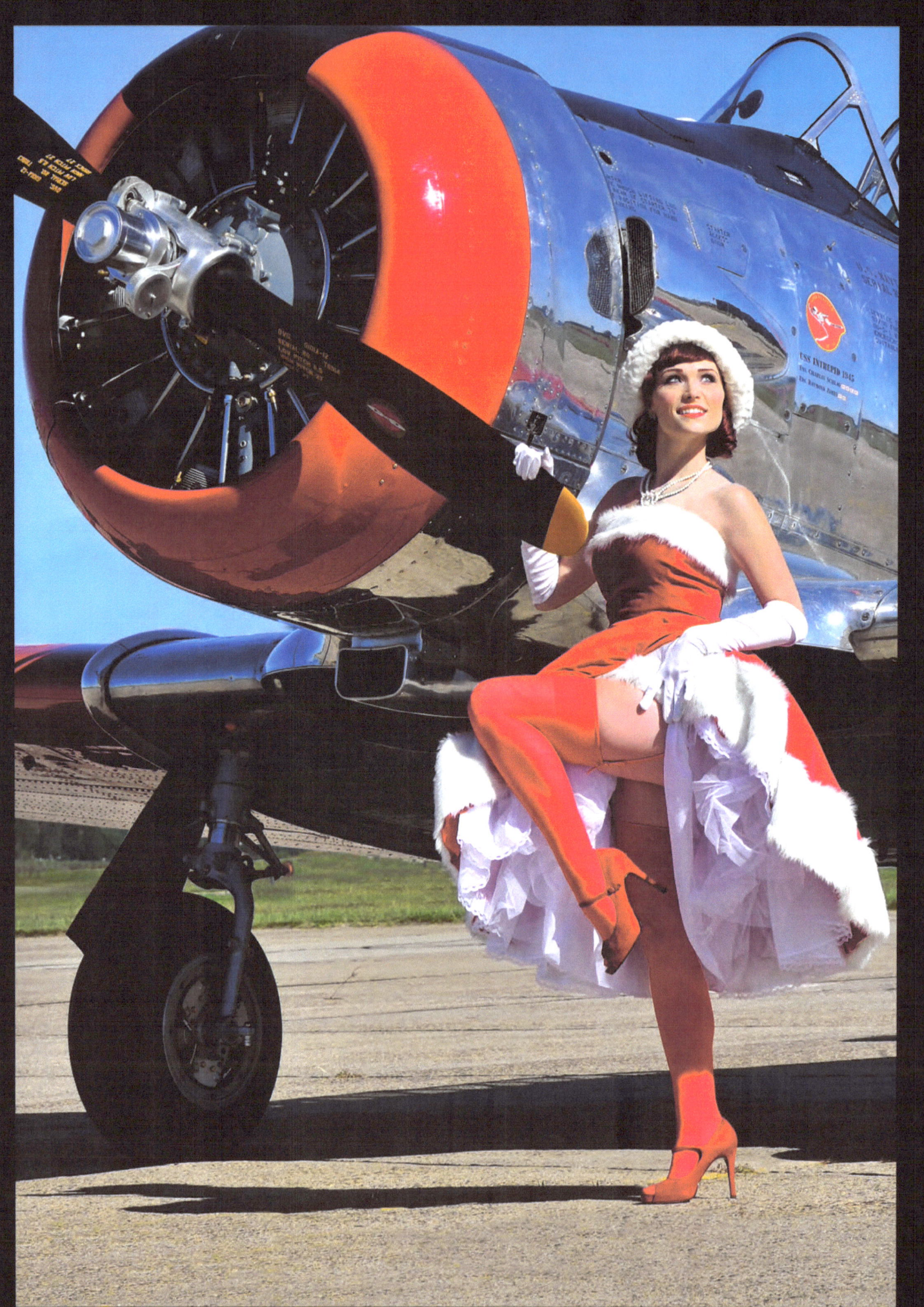

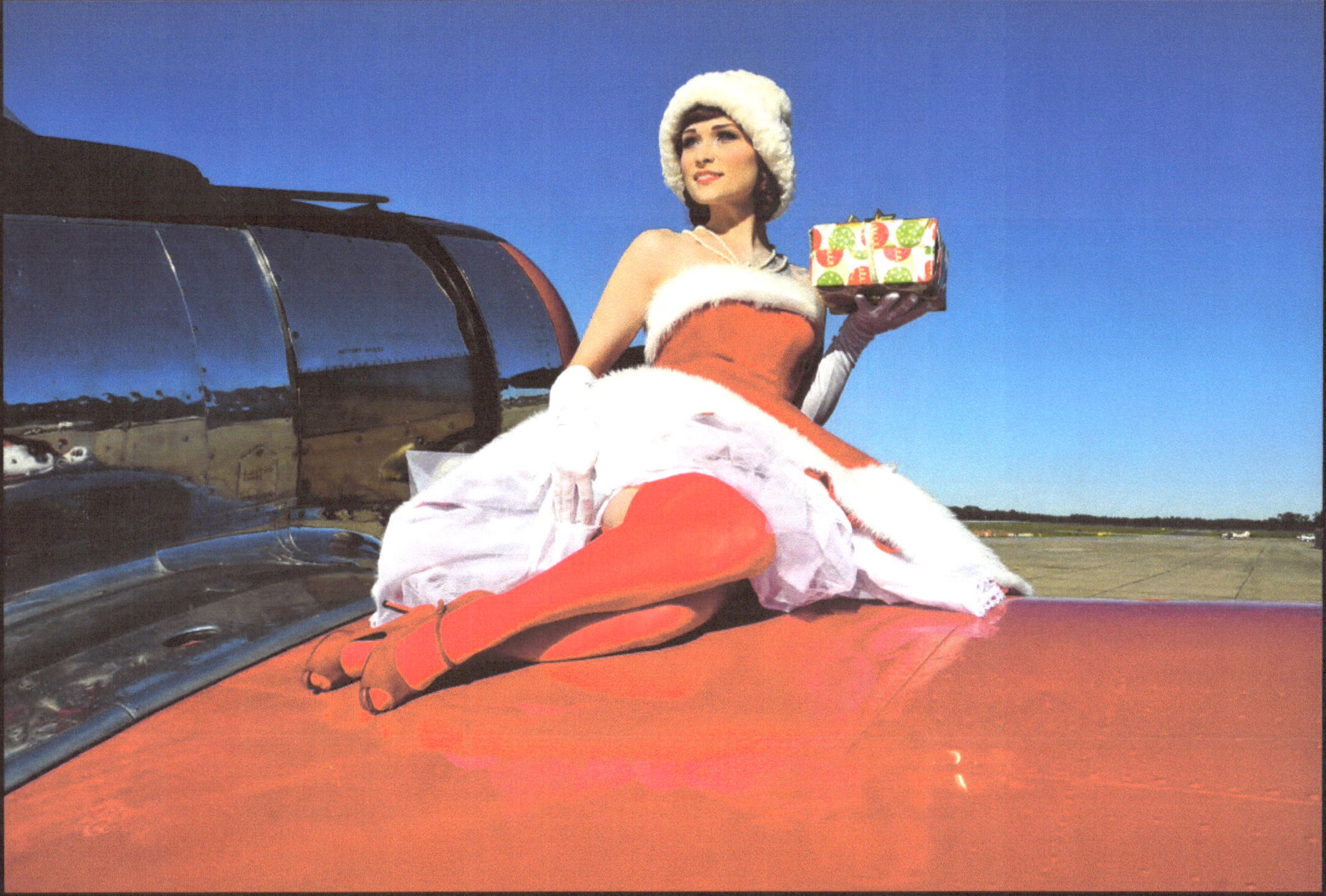

PAIGE

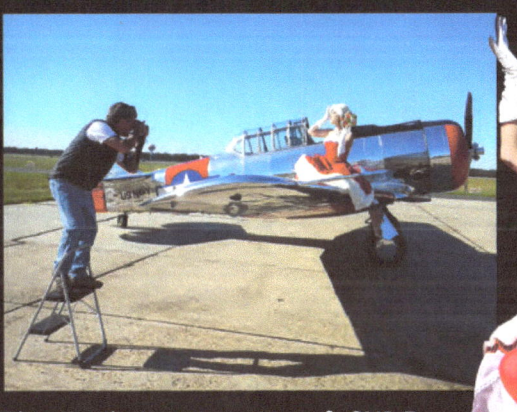

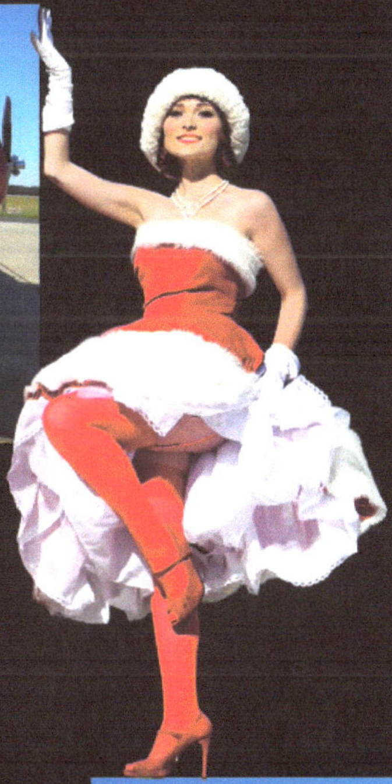

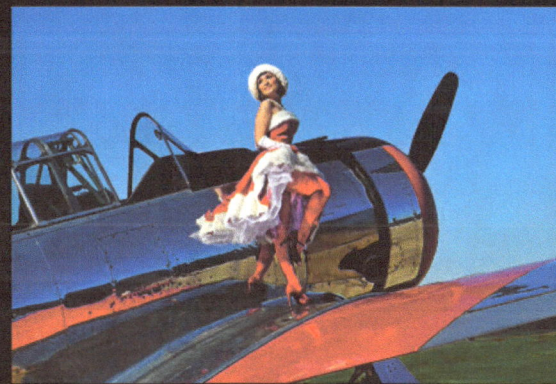

This North American Aircraft SNJ-5 first saw the light of day in 1944. She spent most of her service at NAS Pensacola then had a short stint at NAS North Island in San Diego before being placed in storage in 1958. She was given over to the civilian world and has brought private owners a great deal of joy ever since. The current owner keeps her tuned and shining in New Jersey. Perfect for our holiday color scheme.

Returning 2012 cover model Paige is back in 2014 as our lovely holiday pinup girl in this custom made Christmas dress. Paige is a true throw back to the 1940's with her amazing retro look.

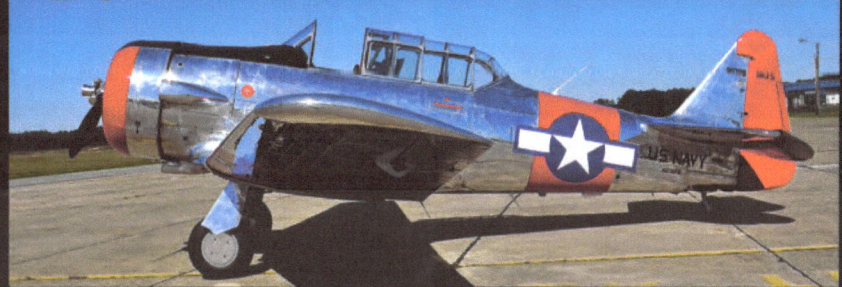

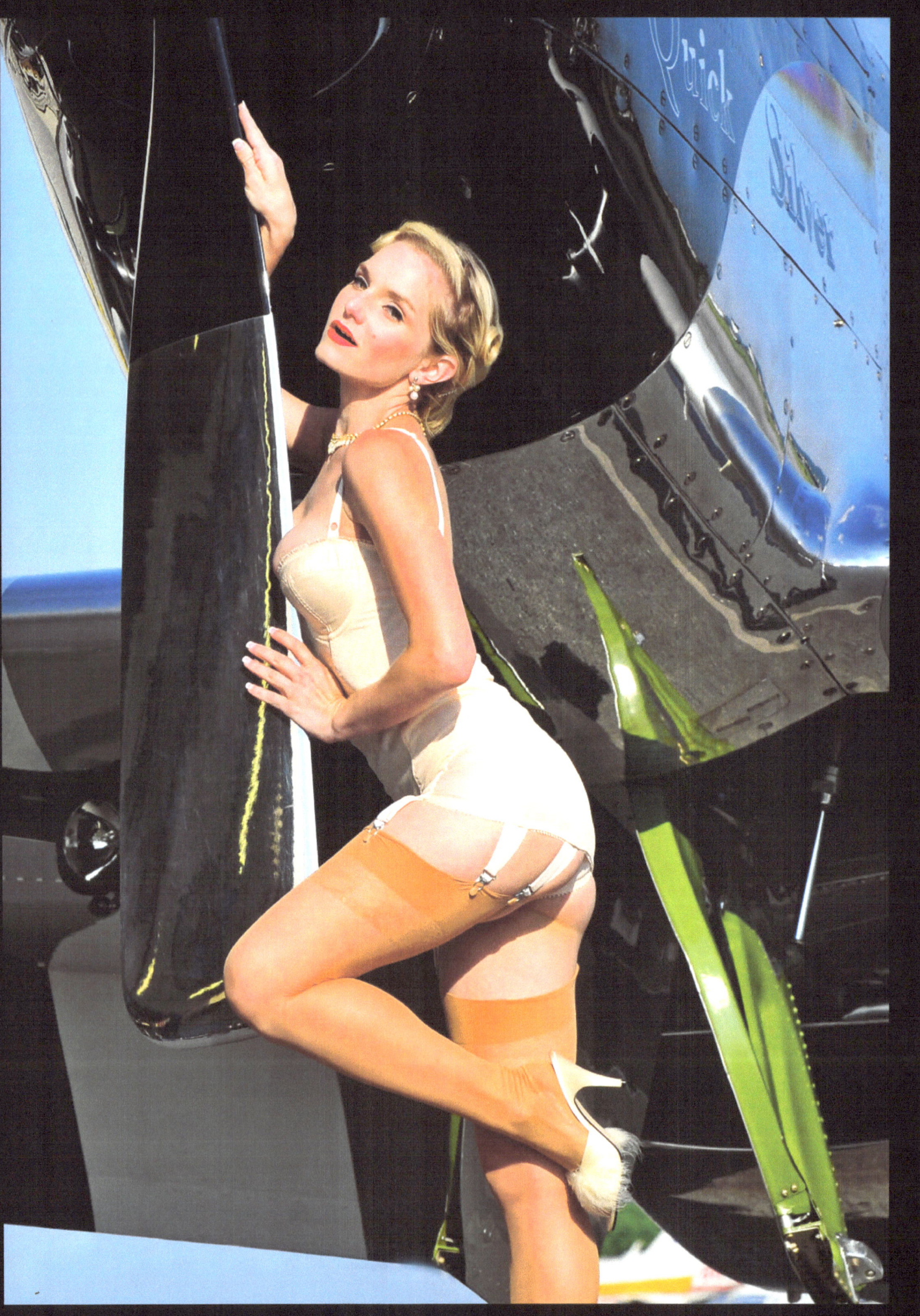

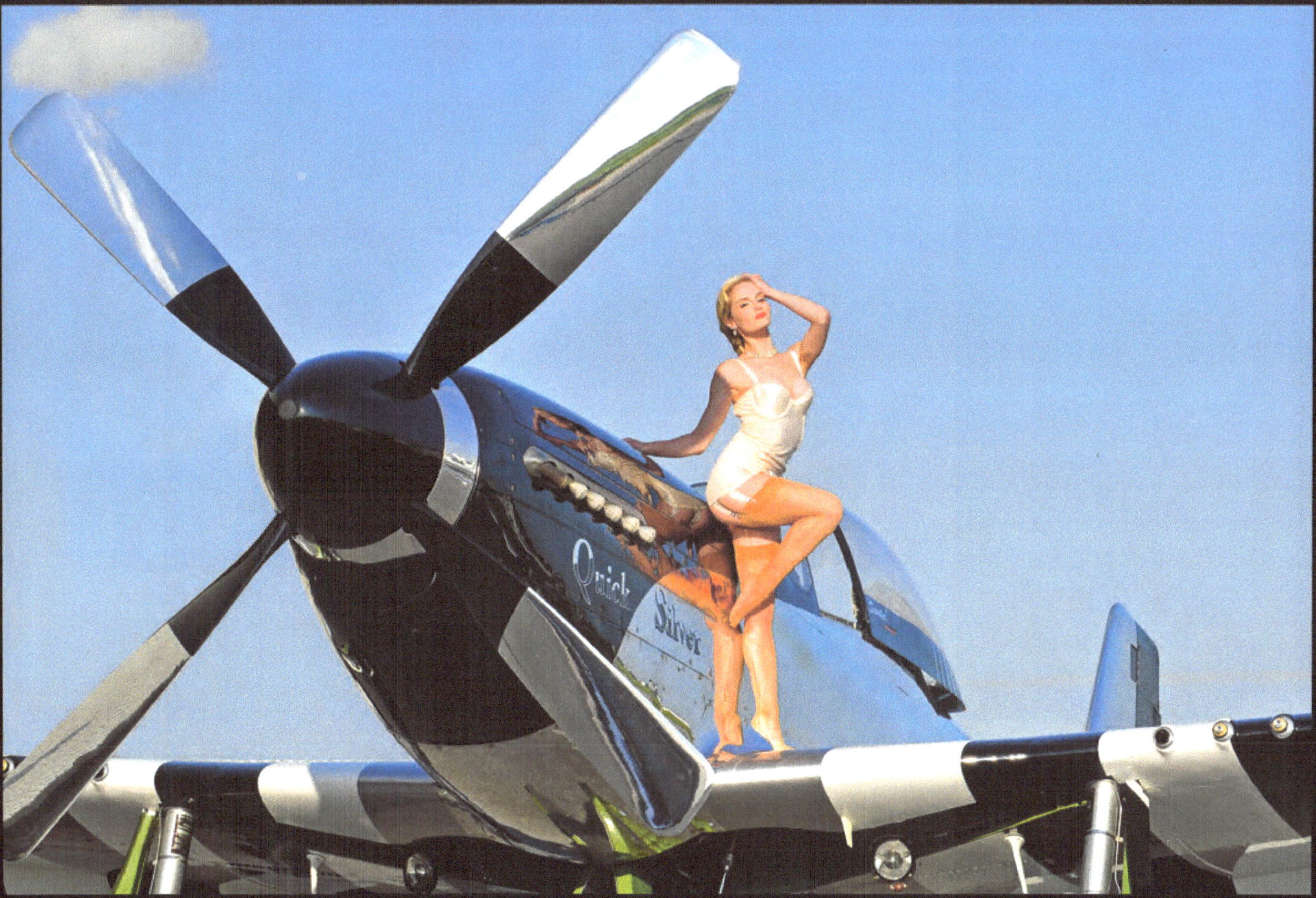

LIZ

2013 cover model Liz brought the house down with this edgy yet classic pinup to help celebrate the "Cadillac of the Sky", the P-51 Mustang. The 2013 edition was a huge hit and Liz will forever be remembered for this epic cover.

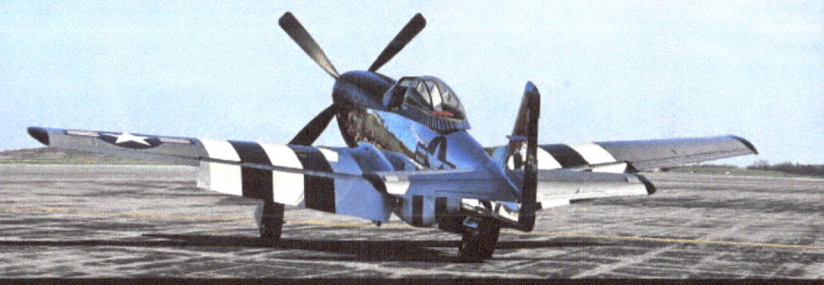

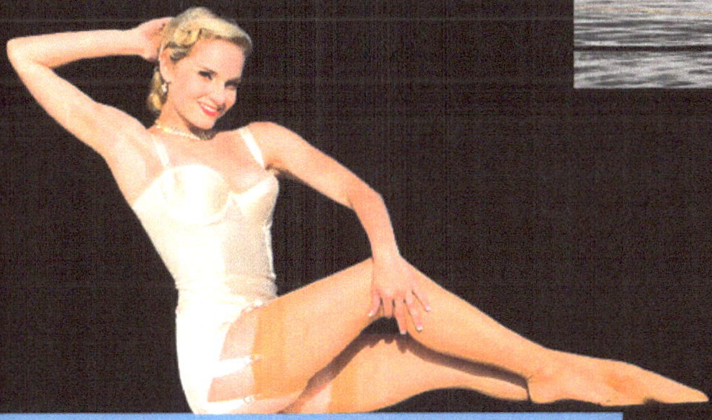

"Quick Silver" is unlike any other P-51 I have seen. She is a true labor of love, built by the father and son team of Bill and Scott Yoak from Virginia. Constructed from over a 100 different Mustangs and restored to perfection, this Mustang stands out among all P-51's. We were proud to feature "Quick Silver" as our cover aircraft in 2013.

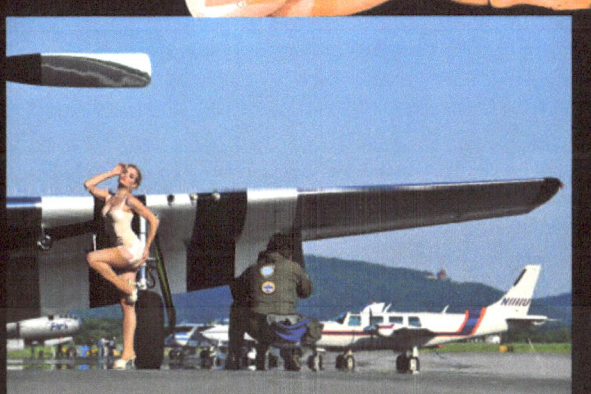

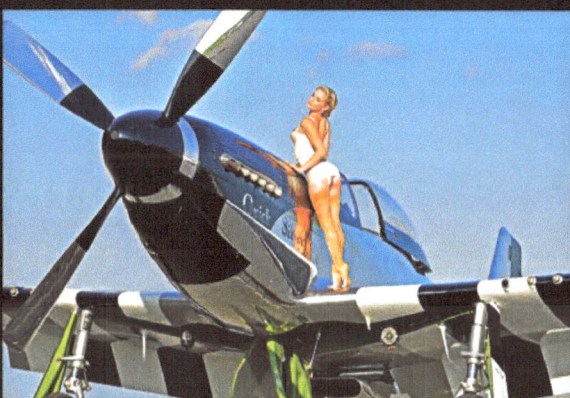

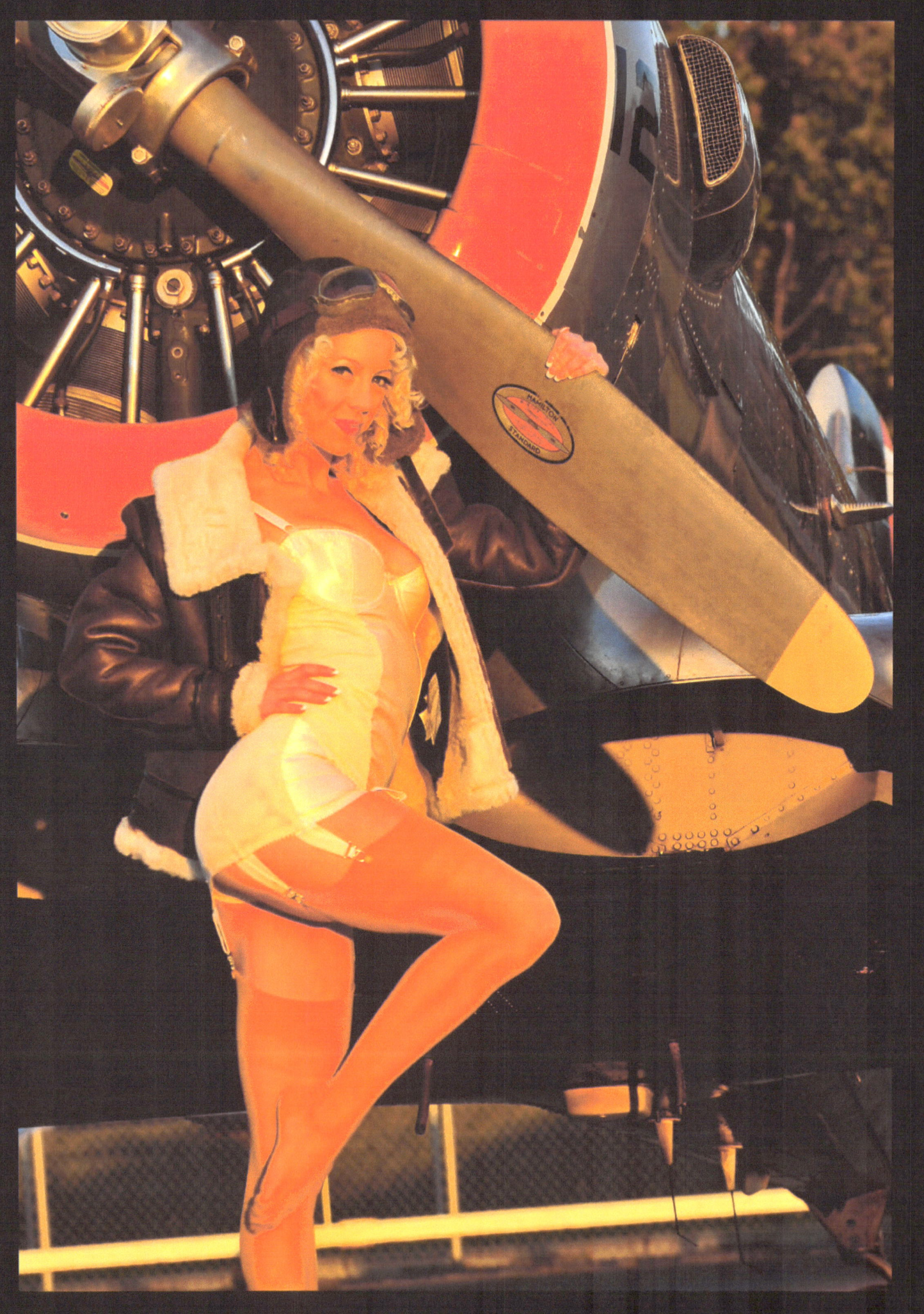

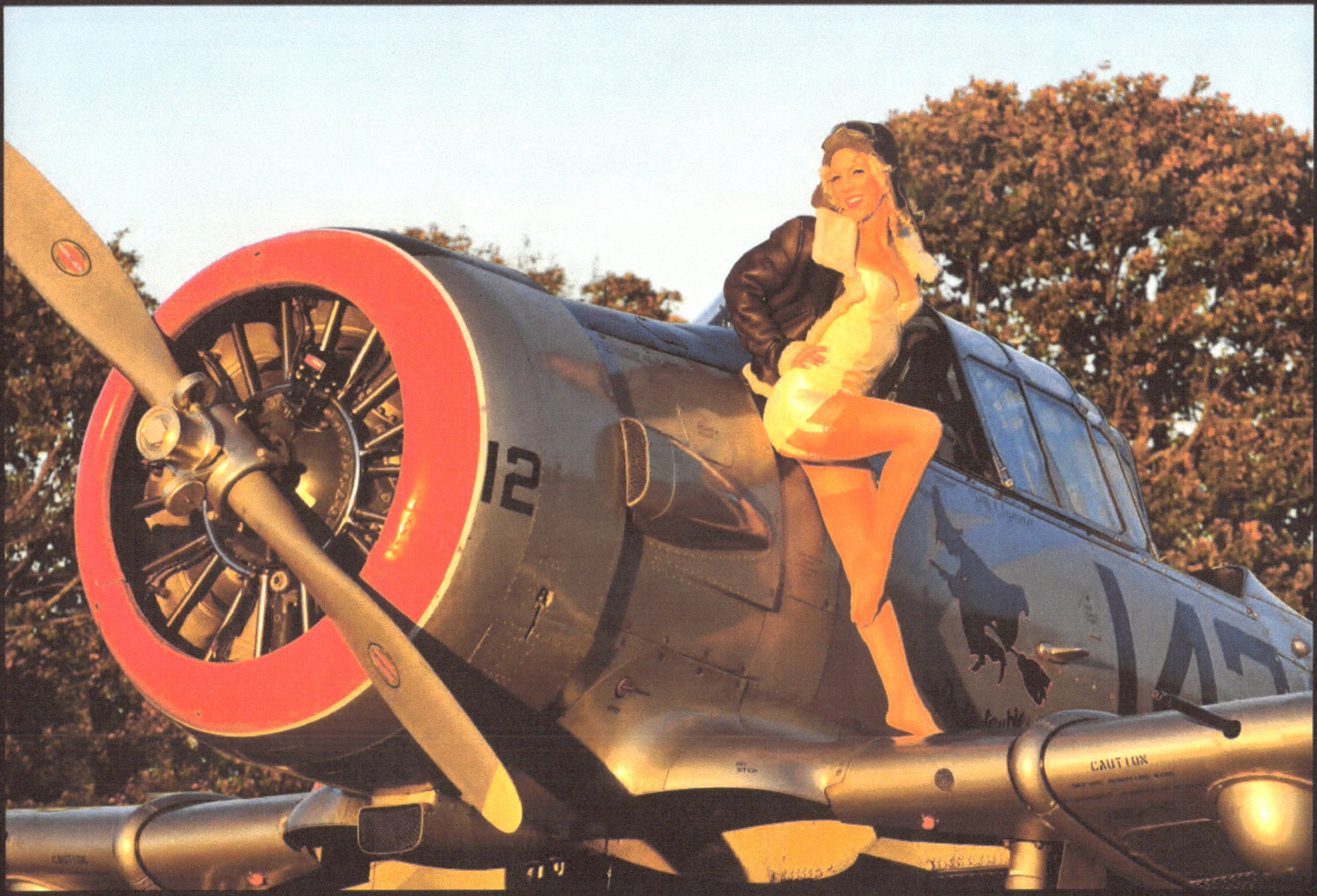

Tammy

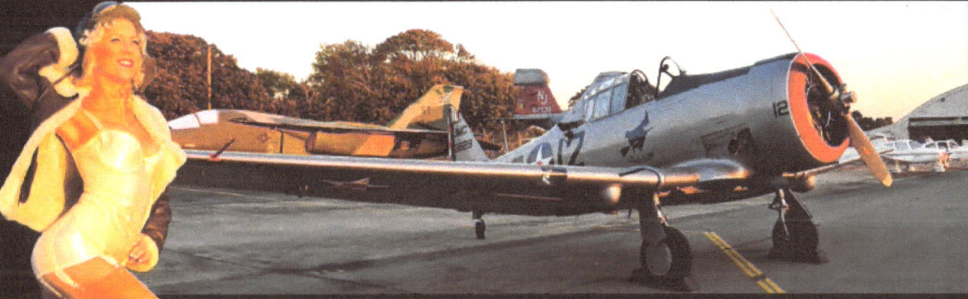

Brought back by popular demand, October 2014 pinup girl Tammy has made quite a following after her first appearance in our 2012 all bombers calendar. Tammy works closely with us and travels regularly to our events and shows.

The advanced trainer AT-6 has one of the longest service records of any military aircraft ever made. It also has a reputation of being one of the most sturdy and well-built airplanes of its era. Although a trainer, the AT-6 did manage to see combat in WWII and Korea. This beautiful "Texan" resides at the American Airpower Museum on Long Island.

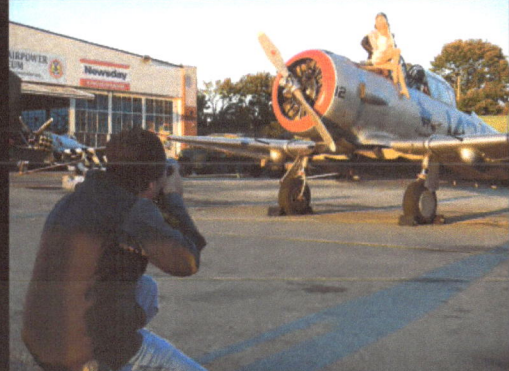

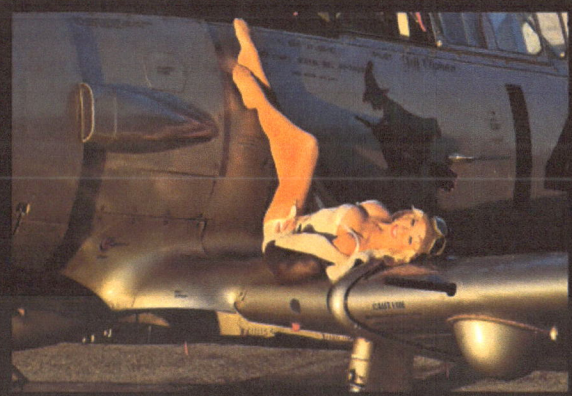

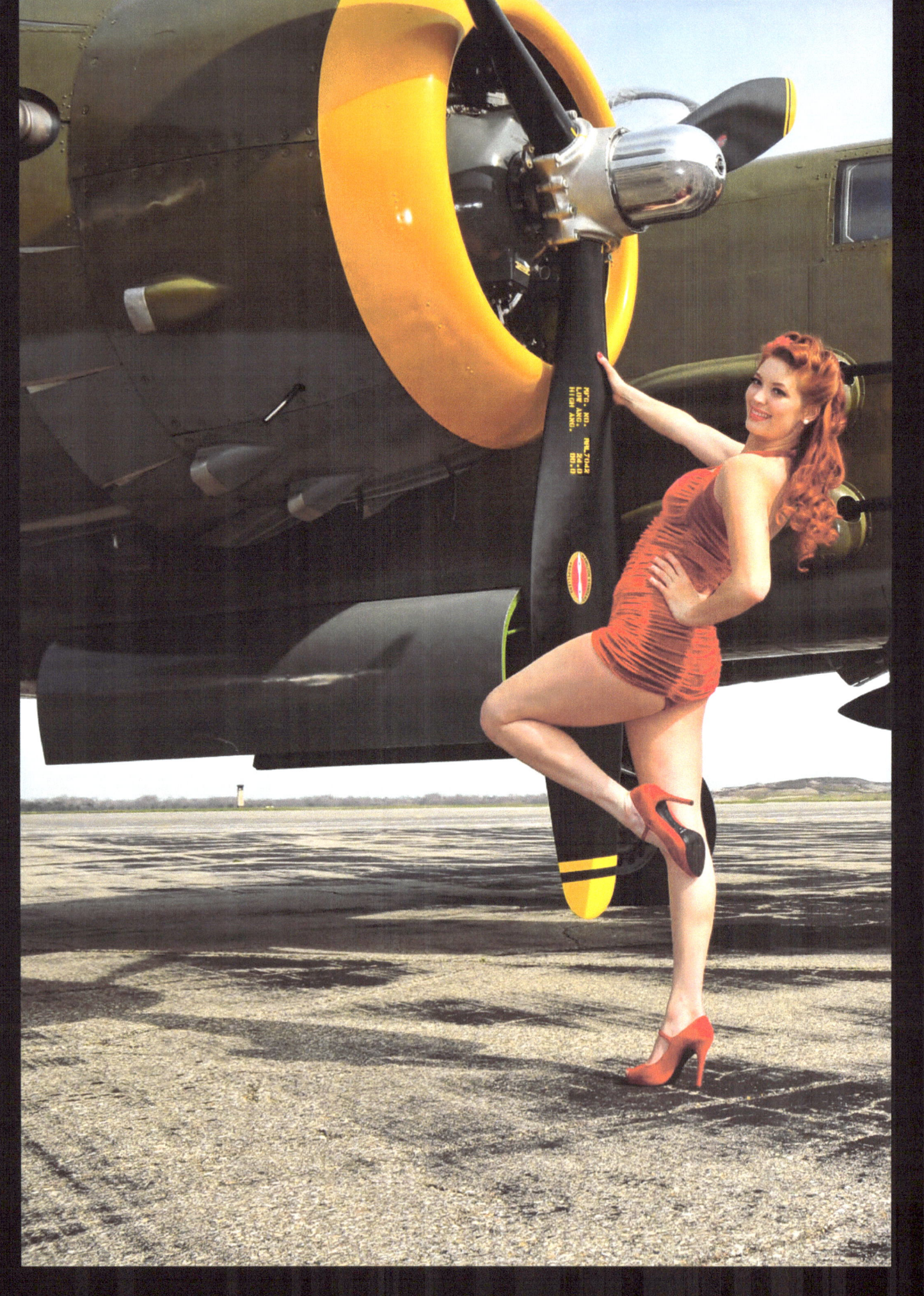

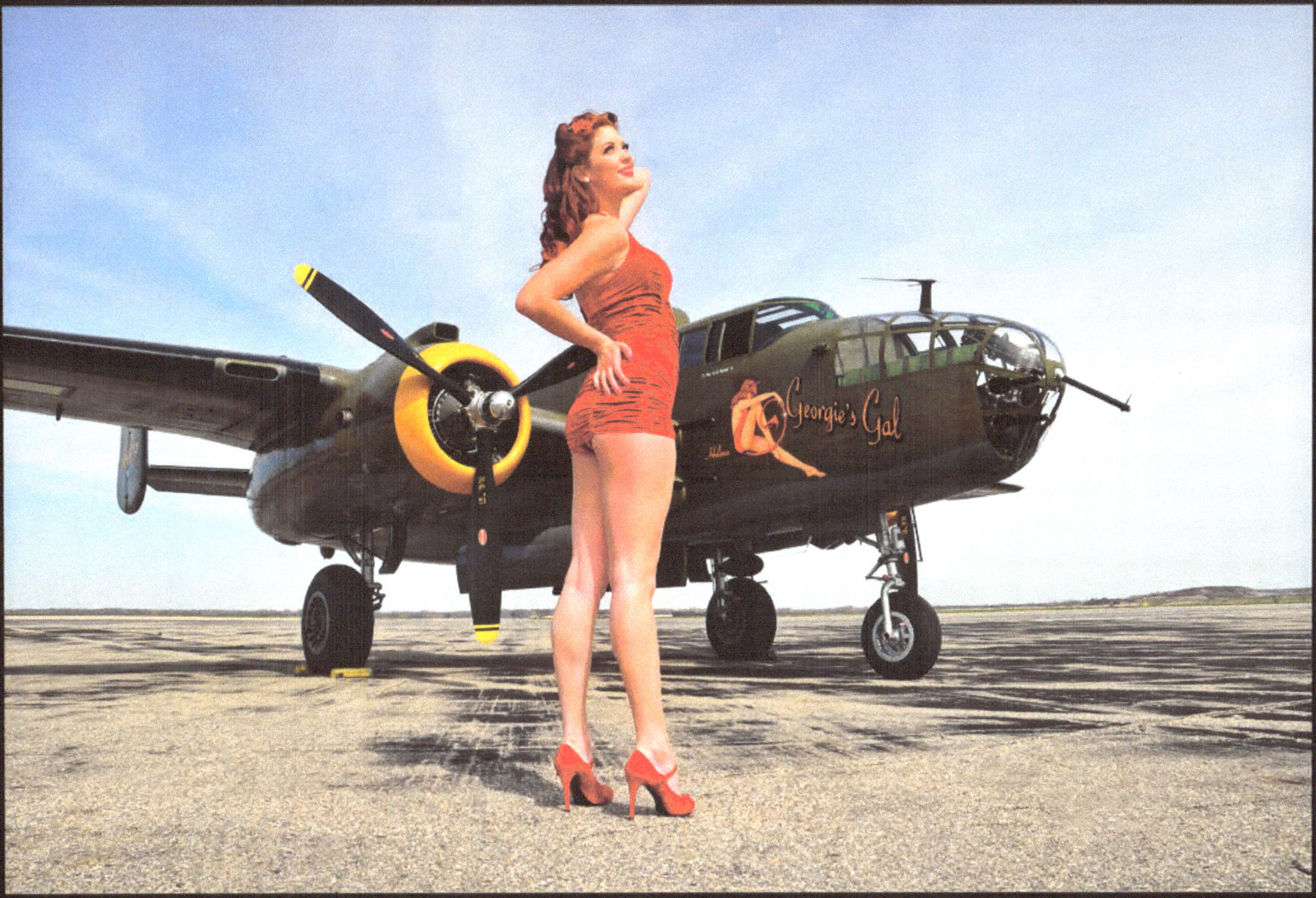

KELLY

Kelly is a returning model also seen before in our 2014 calendar. This never before seen shot will be featured in the upcoming 2015 Warbird Pinup Girls calendar. Kelly is a beauty queen from Michigan and the right stuff is an understatement.

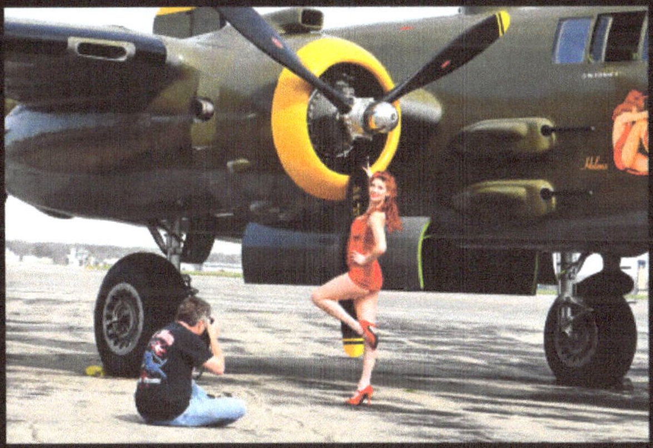

The B-25 was a major player in all the bombing campaigns of WWII. Named "The Mitchell" in honor of General Billy Mitchell, one of America's pioneering aviators. This B-25J has changed hands many times over the years and dons many different names including "The Devil Made Me Do It", "A Man of War" and "Martha Jean" just to name a few. now "Georgie's Gal" resides at the Liberty Aviation Museum in Port Clinton, Ohio.

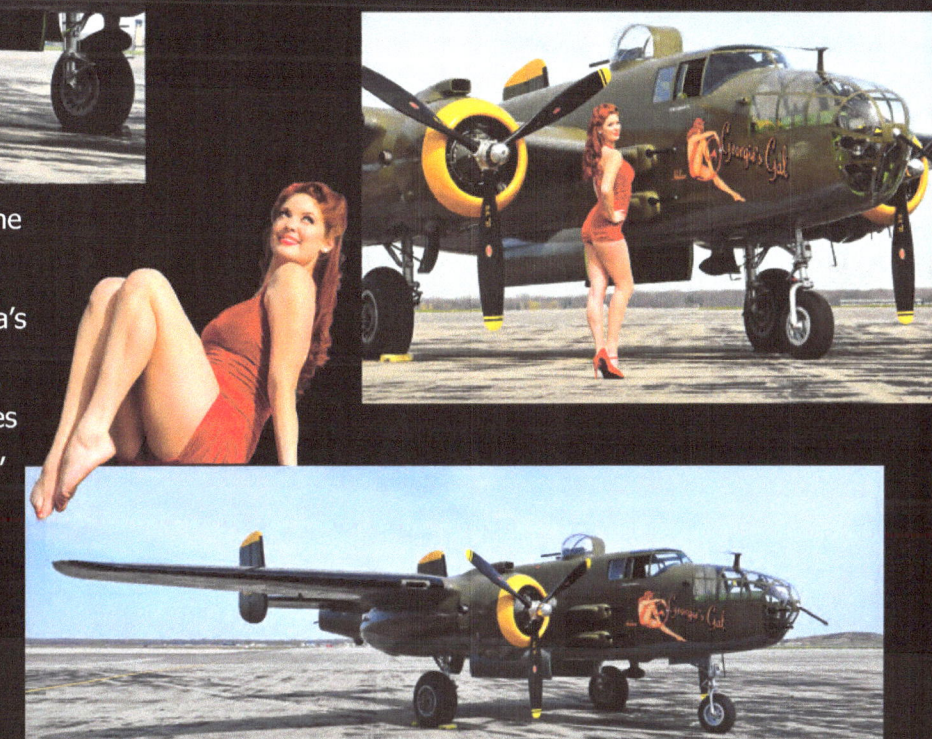

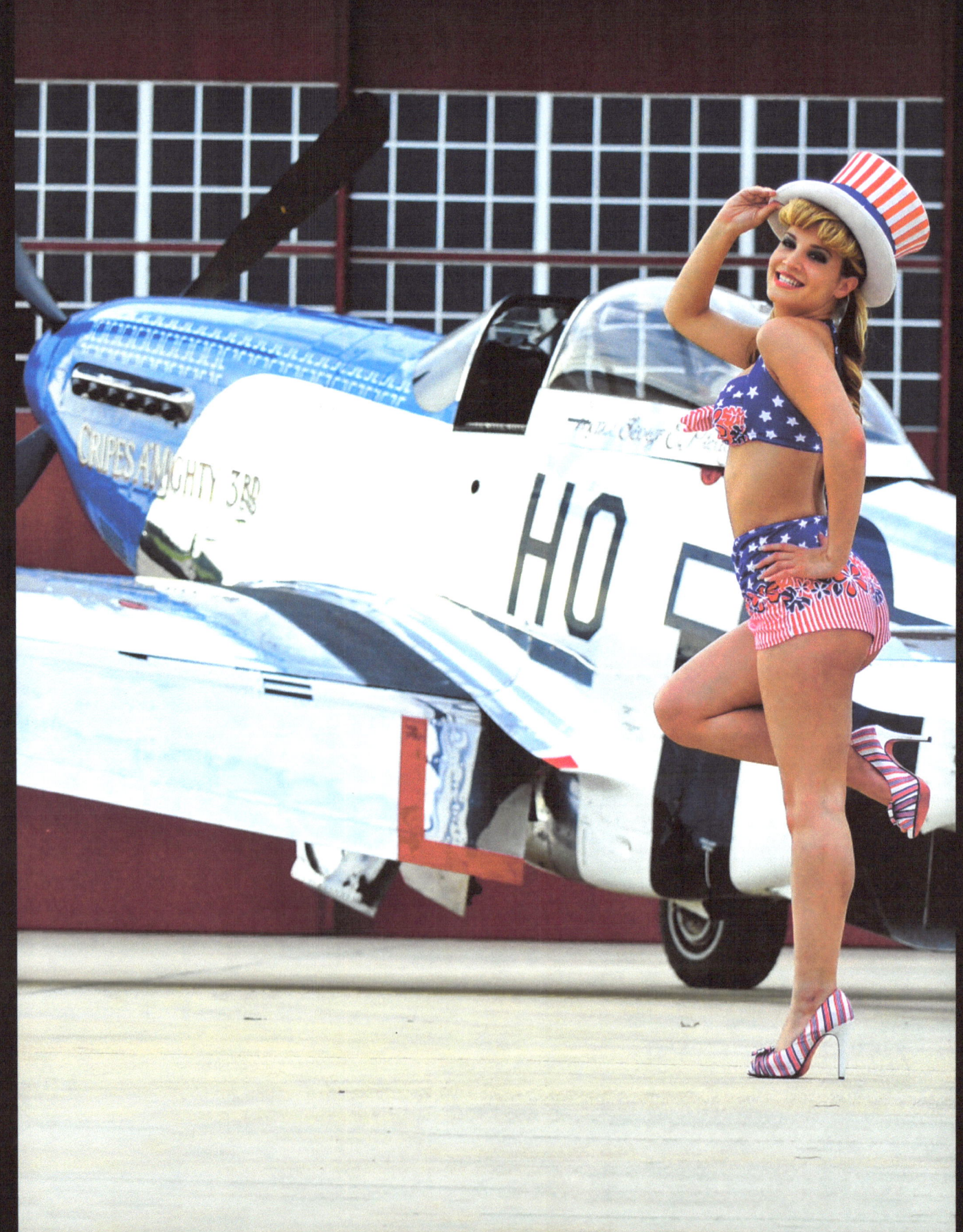

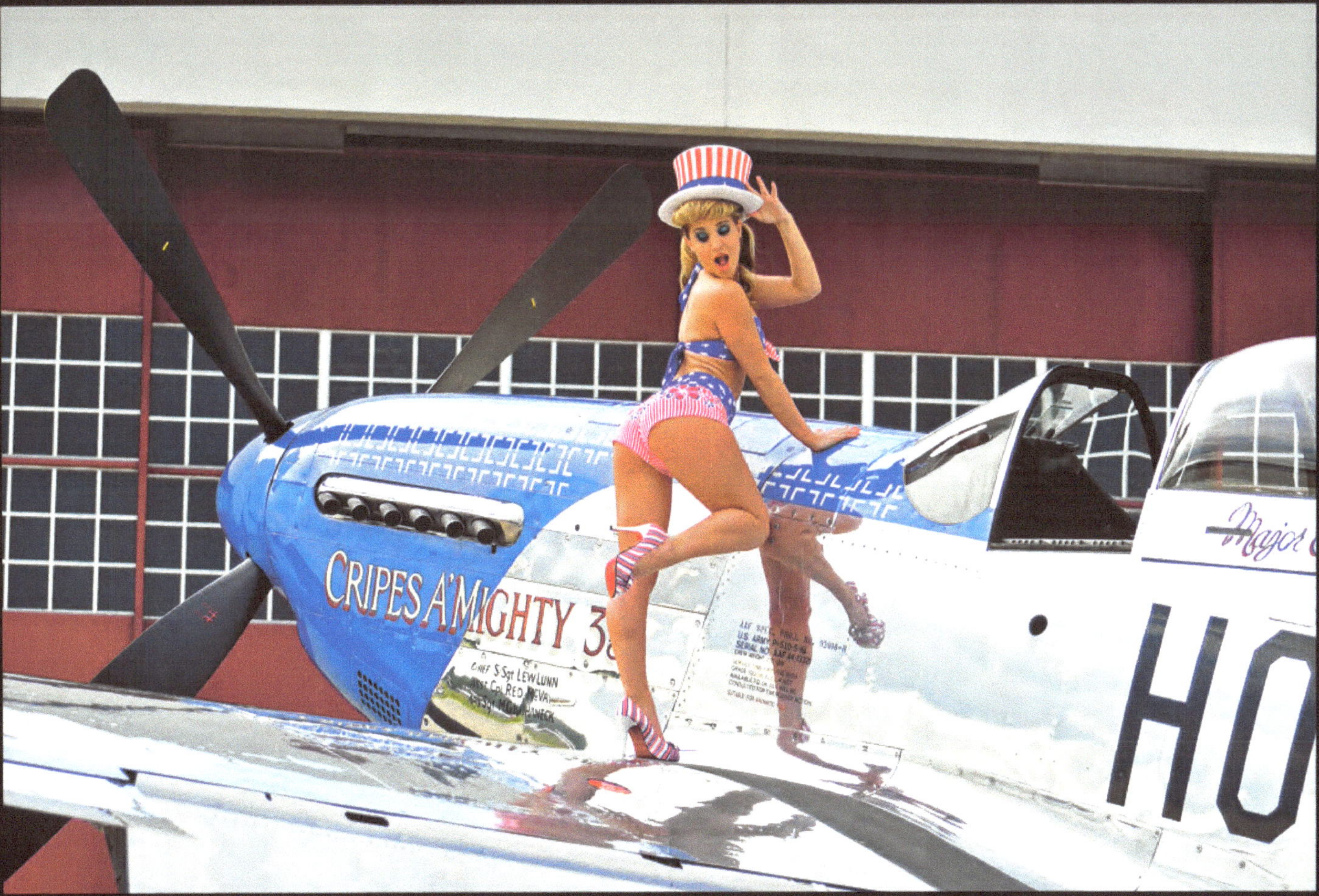

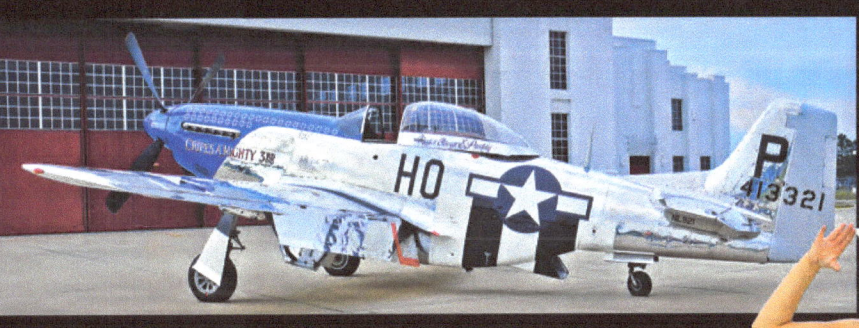

NICOLE

July/August 2013 pinup girl Nicole seen here in our traditional patriotic 4th of July look. Nicole's unique 1940's inspired bathing suit was custom made for us especially for this photo shoot and is one of a kind. Nicole, originally from Philadelphia now lives in Florida where this shoot took place.

The red hangar doors at Fantasy of Flight made a great addition to the patriotic color scheme in this photo.

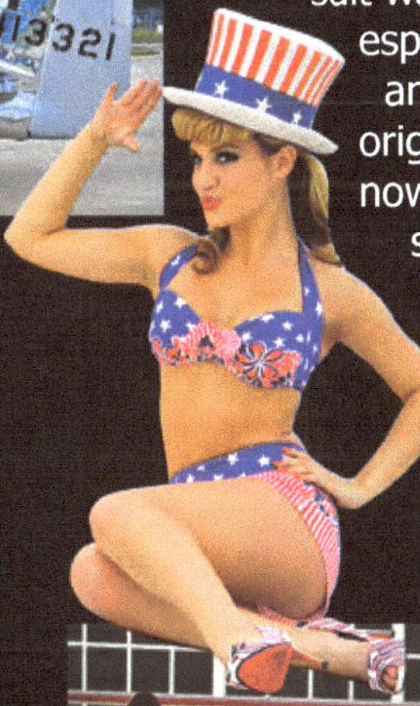

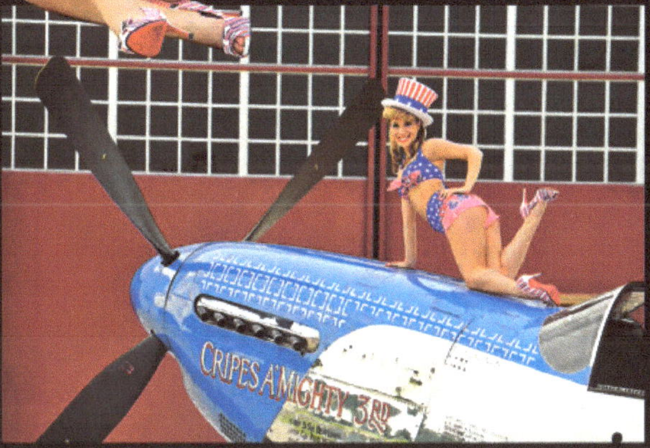

Originally delivered to the RNZAF in 1945, this P-51D Mustang was put directly into storage. In 1952 she was activated for a short time, then put back in storage in 1955. In 1974 she was shipped to the USA and painted with the "Cripes A'Mighty 3RD". In 1983 she was picked up by Fantasy of Flight in Polk City Florida where she lives today and is flown regularly.

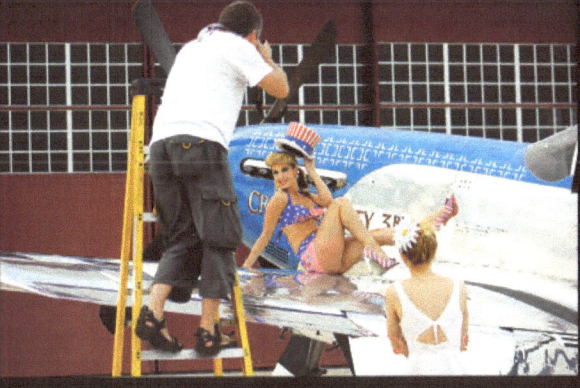

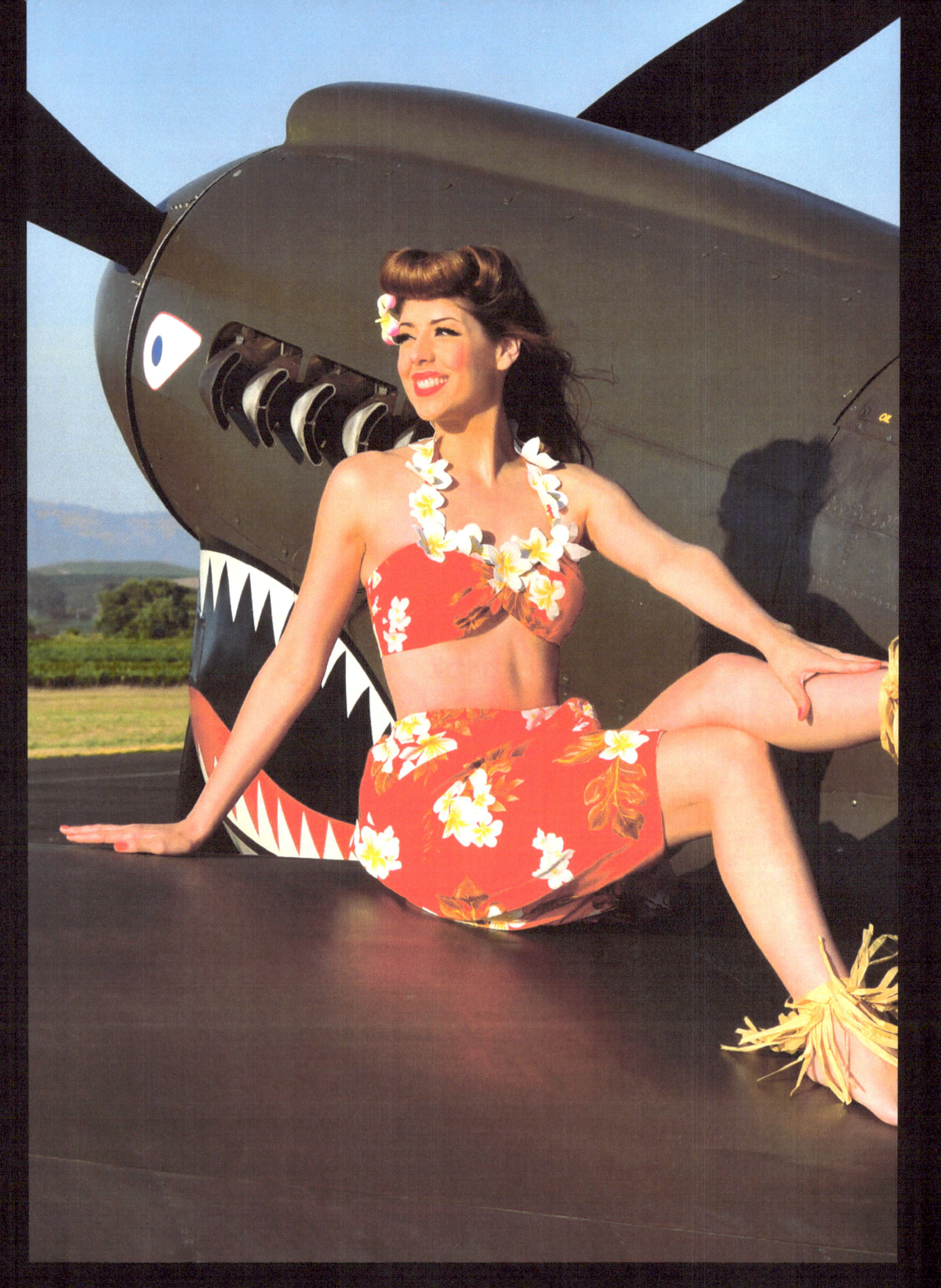

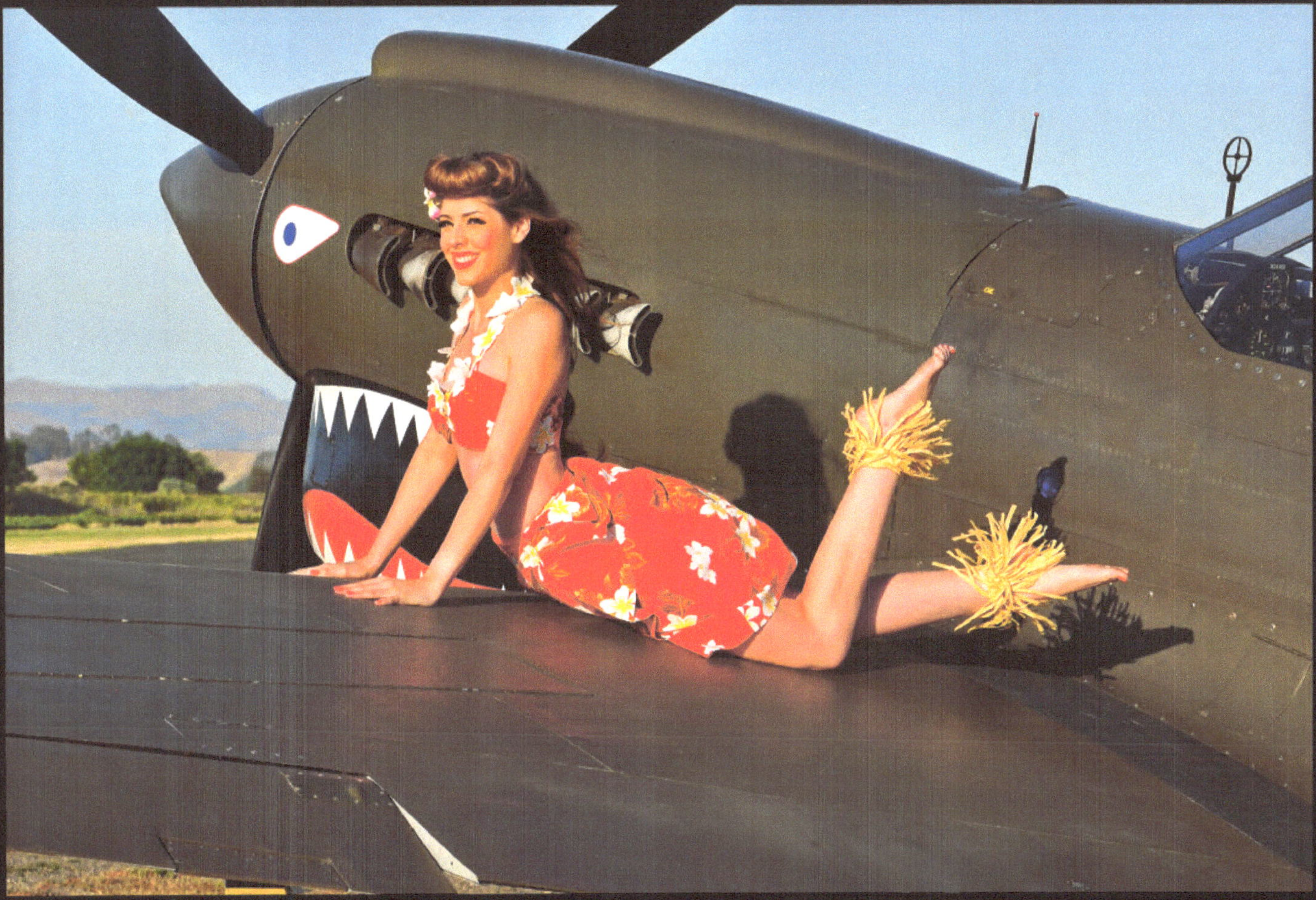

Jen

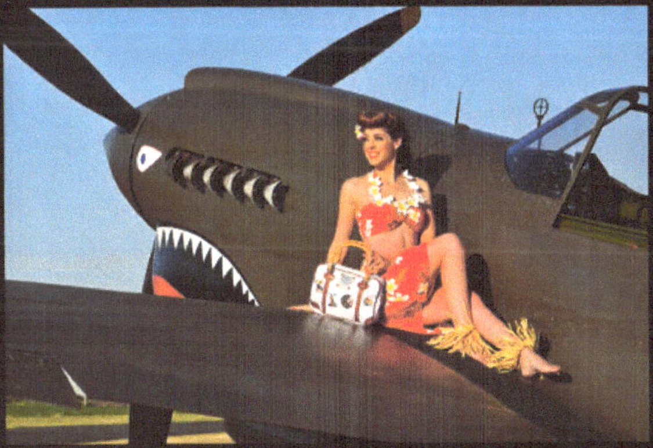

2015 pinup girl Jen seen here in a never released 1940's South Pacific inspired photo. Jen is a California beauty we selected to be featured in our 2015 calendar. She did remarkably well considering the chilly breeze of the Northern California evening, and fit the Hawaiian long-haired look we were after perfectly in this custom made floral sarong and top.

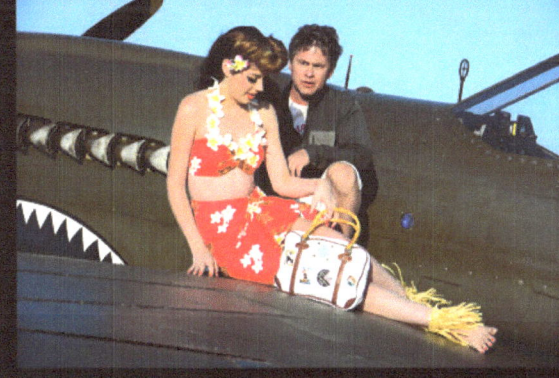

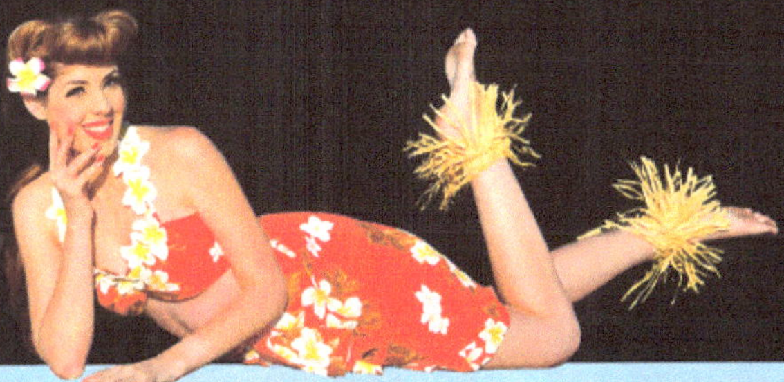

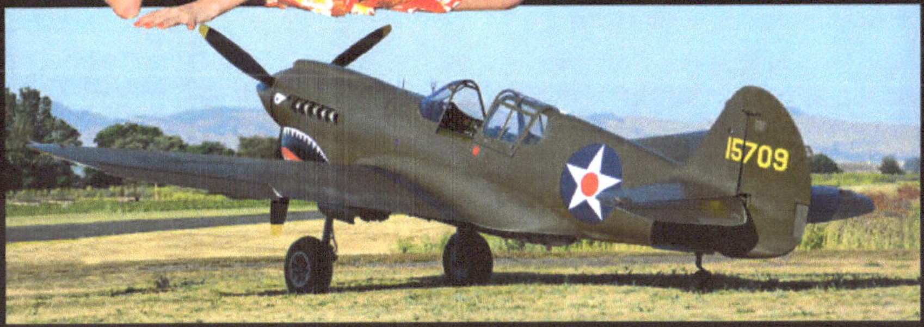

This beautiful flight worthy P-40 sports the traditional Army Aircorp star along with the shark mouth nose art used by the "Flying Tigers" and the 23rd fighter group. This dual seat P-40 lives at the Vintage Aircraft Company in Sonoma California.

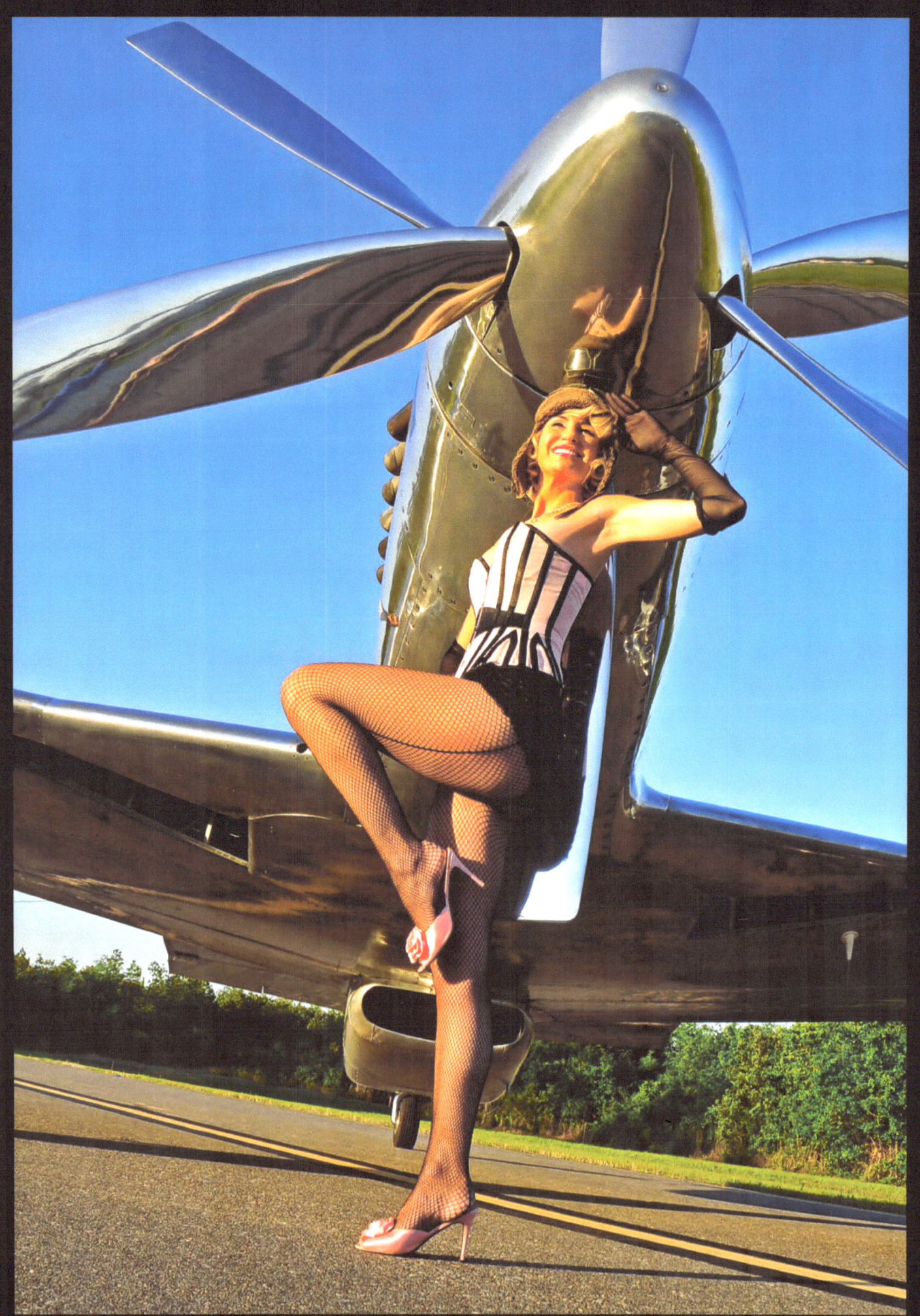

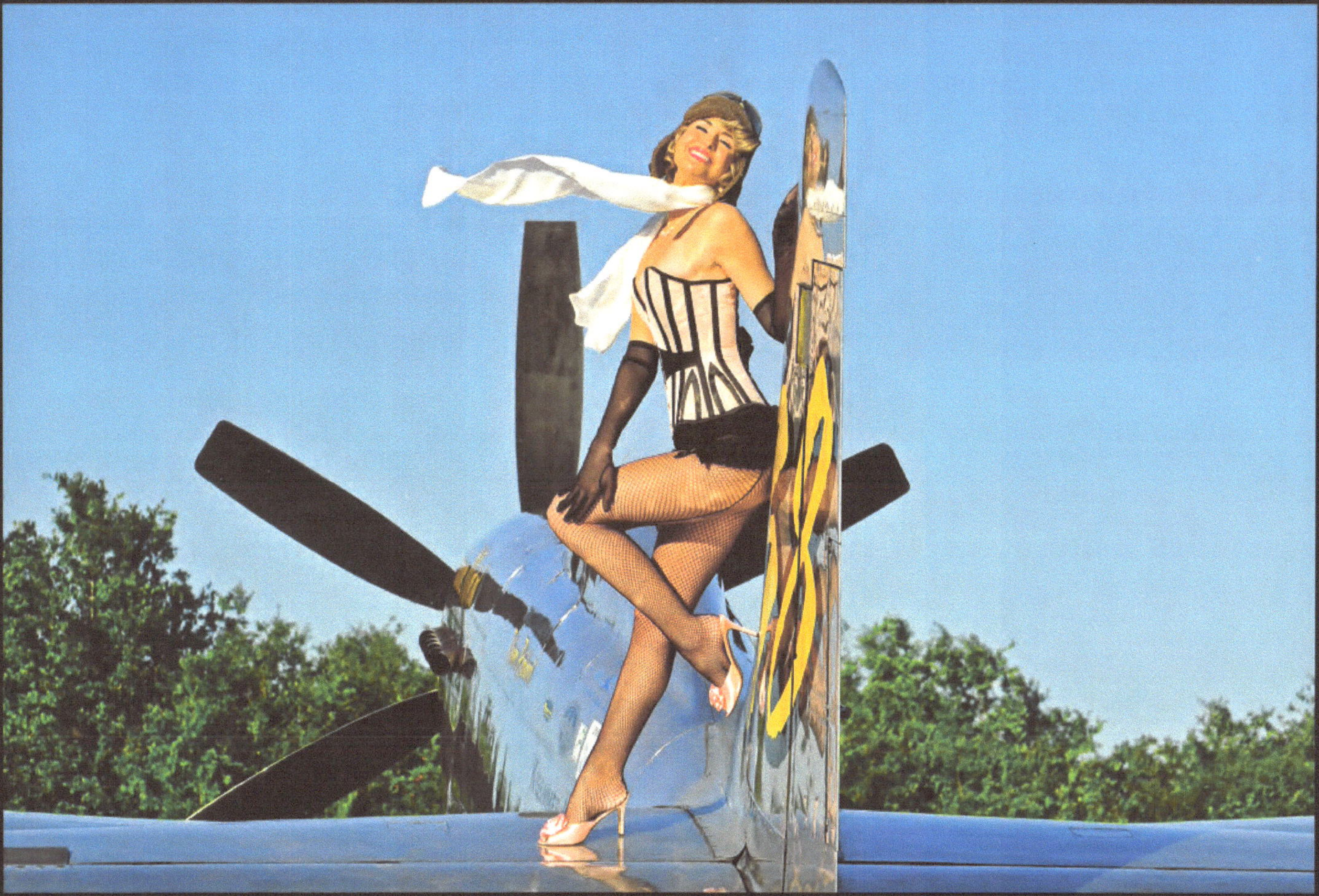

MEREDITH

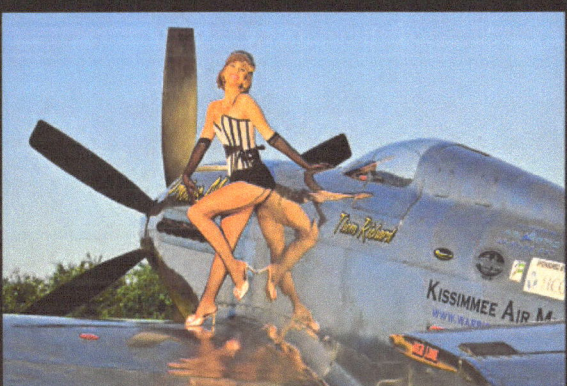

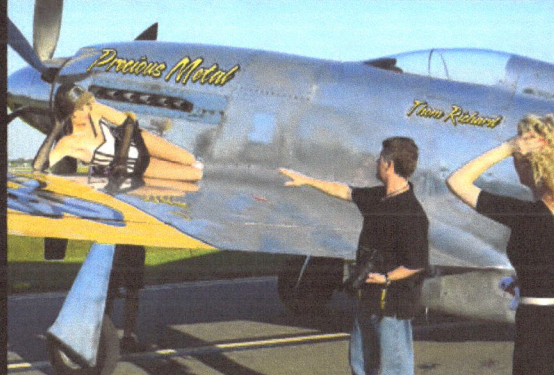

One of the most unique aircraft in our collection, "Precious Metal" flies only in the unlimited class at the Reno Air Races. This modified P-51D is unlike any other aircraft in the world. Fitted with a Griffon power plant and a twin counter rotating prop system, it has been noted as one of the fastest prop driven aircraft in the world. Maintained and operated by Warbird Adventures in Kissimmee Florida. Watch for a checkered flag on this modified warbird.

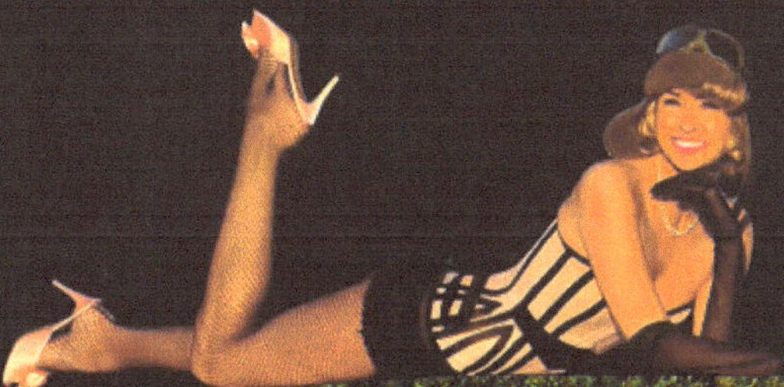

2013 March/April pinup girl Meredith is that all American girl. With a winning smile and a sexy getup she pulled off a classic pinup Aviatrix. Meredith had competition with this unique aircraft but stands out as one of our classic beauties in the 2013 all Mustangs edition.

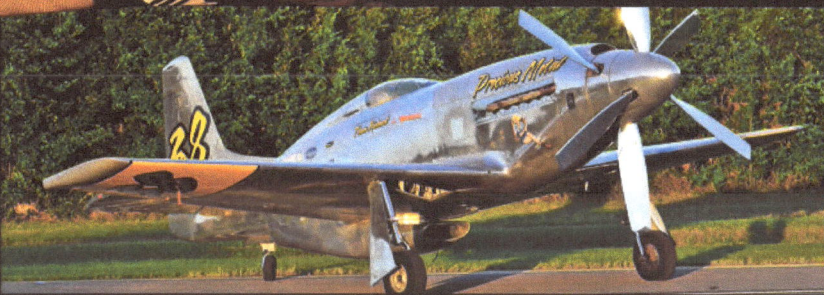

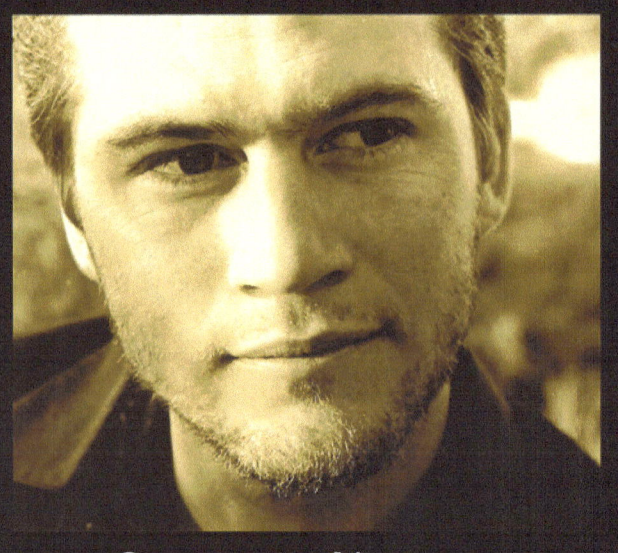

CHRISTIAN KIEFFER

After graduating from the South East Center of Photographic studies in Daytona Beach Florida, I was chosen from 4,000 photographers to intern and eventually staff at Walt Disney Creative Photography department in Orlando Florida. In my time with Disney I was required to handle many large-scale photography shoots including national advertizing campaigns and many film and television projects. I had many photographs published by Disney including much of the opening promotions for the Animal Kingdom theme park.

In 1999 I left Disney and moved west to Los Angeles where I began working in the film industry shortly after arriving. I worked primarily as a location scout for the studios on commercial and film projects.

I have worked on over a hundred productions including Vanilla Sky, Swordfish, AI, BMW films.com projects and many TV commercials. In 2004 I moved to Melbourne Australia where I had an opportunity to live and work on some editorial images as well as some personal photography. I returned in 2006 to the east coast where I am from. Shortly after, I met my wife Gili and we started our own multimedia company called Elysium Multimedia. I was highly motivated to start my own project that I would have total control of, so I reached back to my past to the things that I was inspired by to help form the original concepts for the "Warbird Pinup Girls" calendar. Today we are on our 5 annual edition.

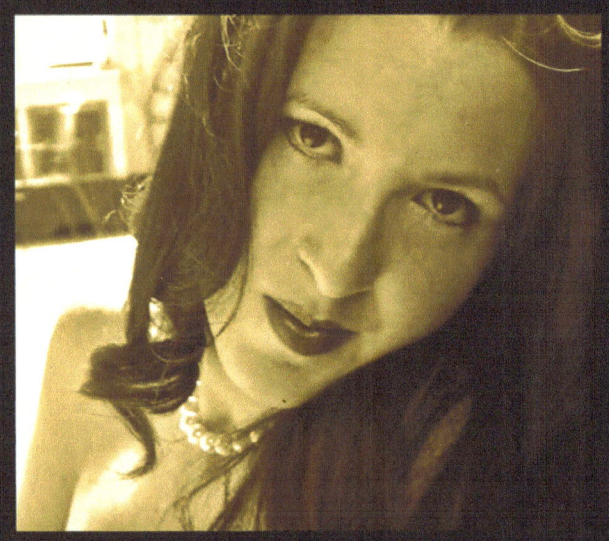

GILI KIEFFER

When I first came to the United States in 2006 I was not familiar with the 1940's pin up girls. Although I always loved Marilyn Monroe and the classics, I never heard of WWII nose-art and the Alberto Vargas famous pinup girls. In 2008 my husband Christian introduced me to the retro style from the 40's and I immediately fell in love with it. Having majored in fashion the Warbird Pinup Girls project felt like a great fit for me and I quickly started getting involved with the styling for Christian's photo shoots. I always thought that the women in the 40's were very classy, elegant and graceful and I enjoyed browsing through the vintage shops for great accessories and accents to our pinup looks. Being a web and graphic designer, I helped Christian design our calendars and marketing materials. When working on the Warbird Pinup Girls I always try to recreate these looks as authenticly and accurately as I can. Many people still look back to those days and love those classic looks and how we recreated them in our modern images.

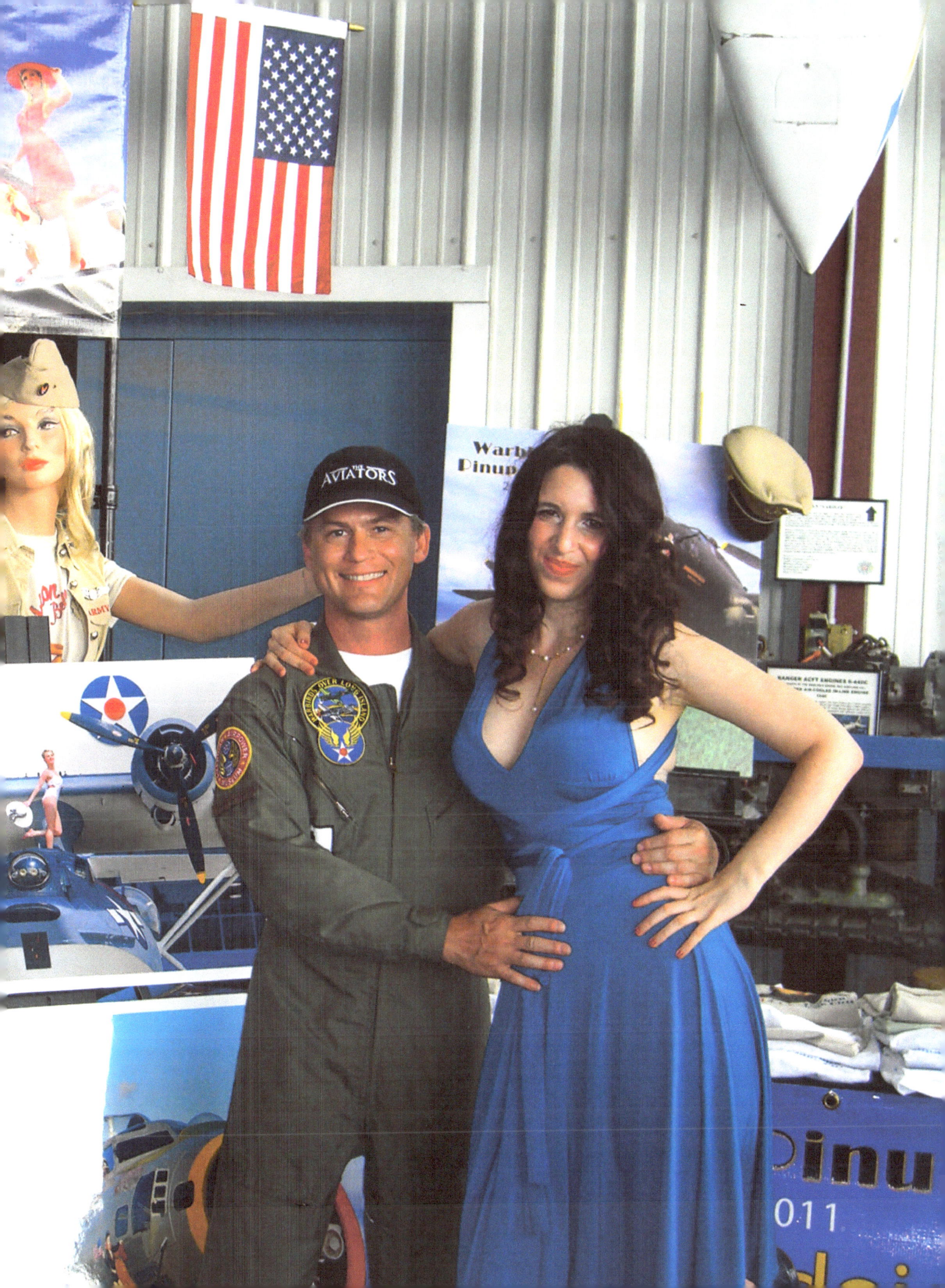

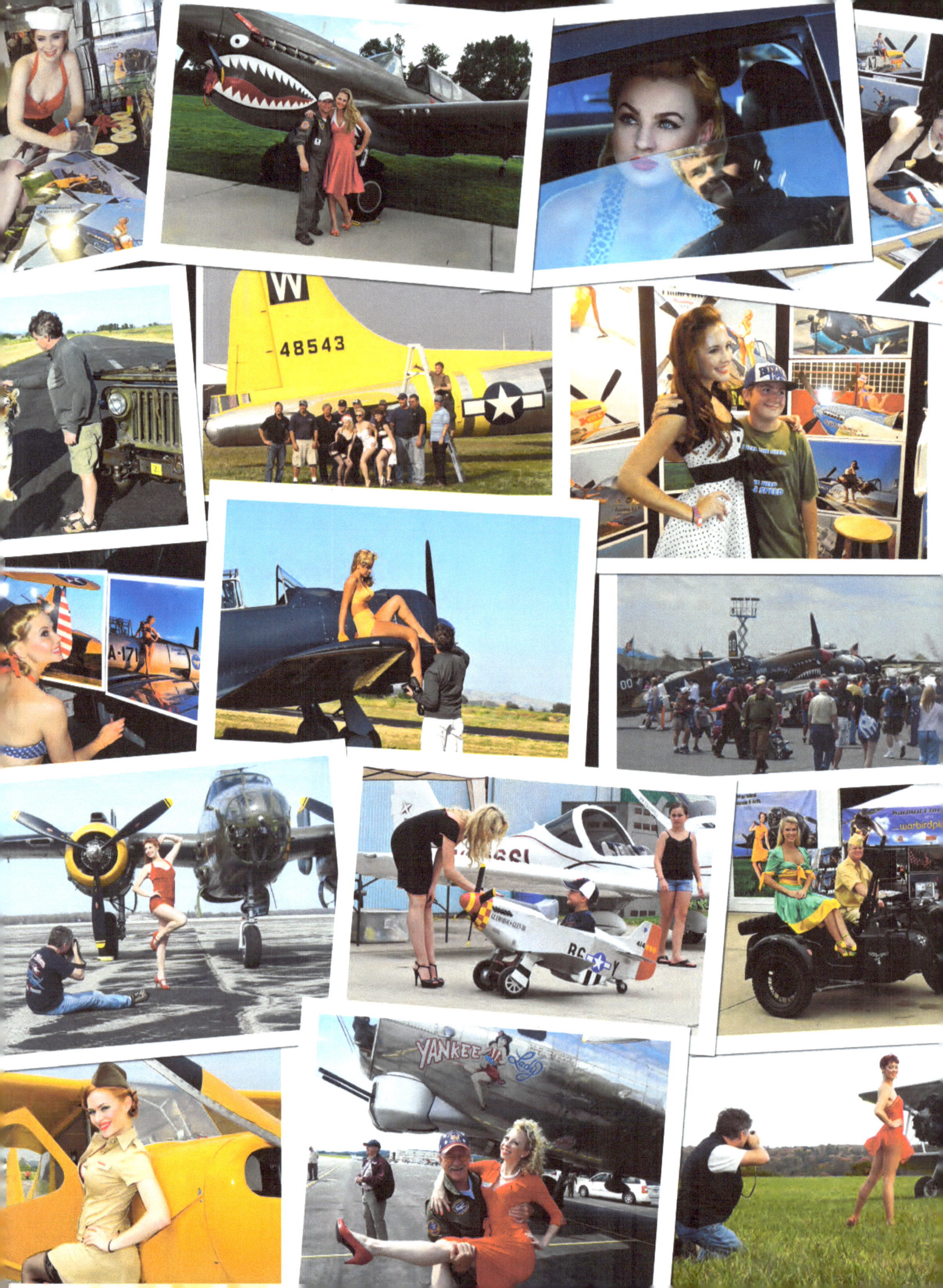

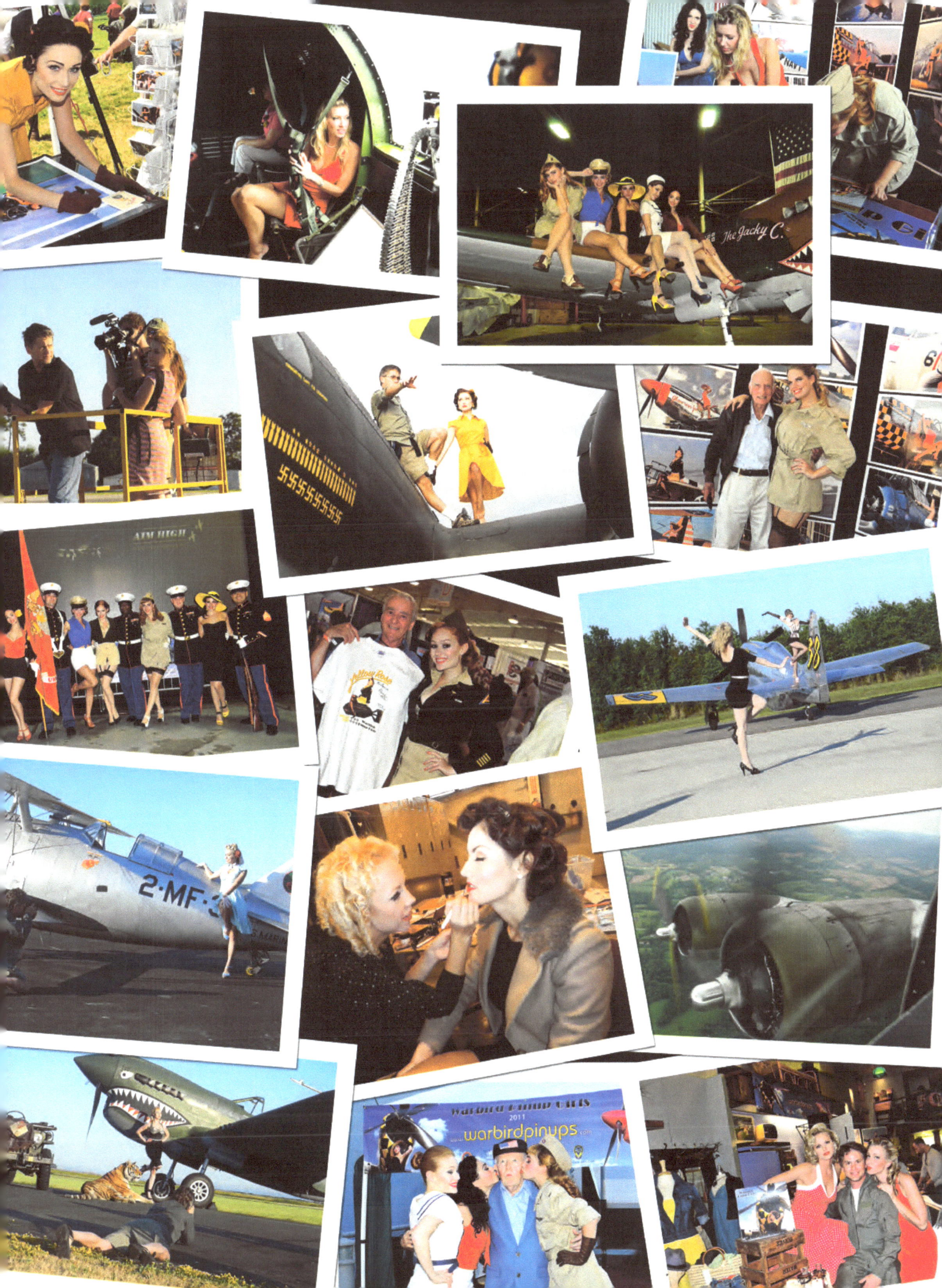

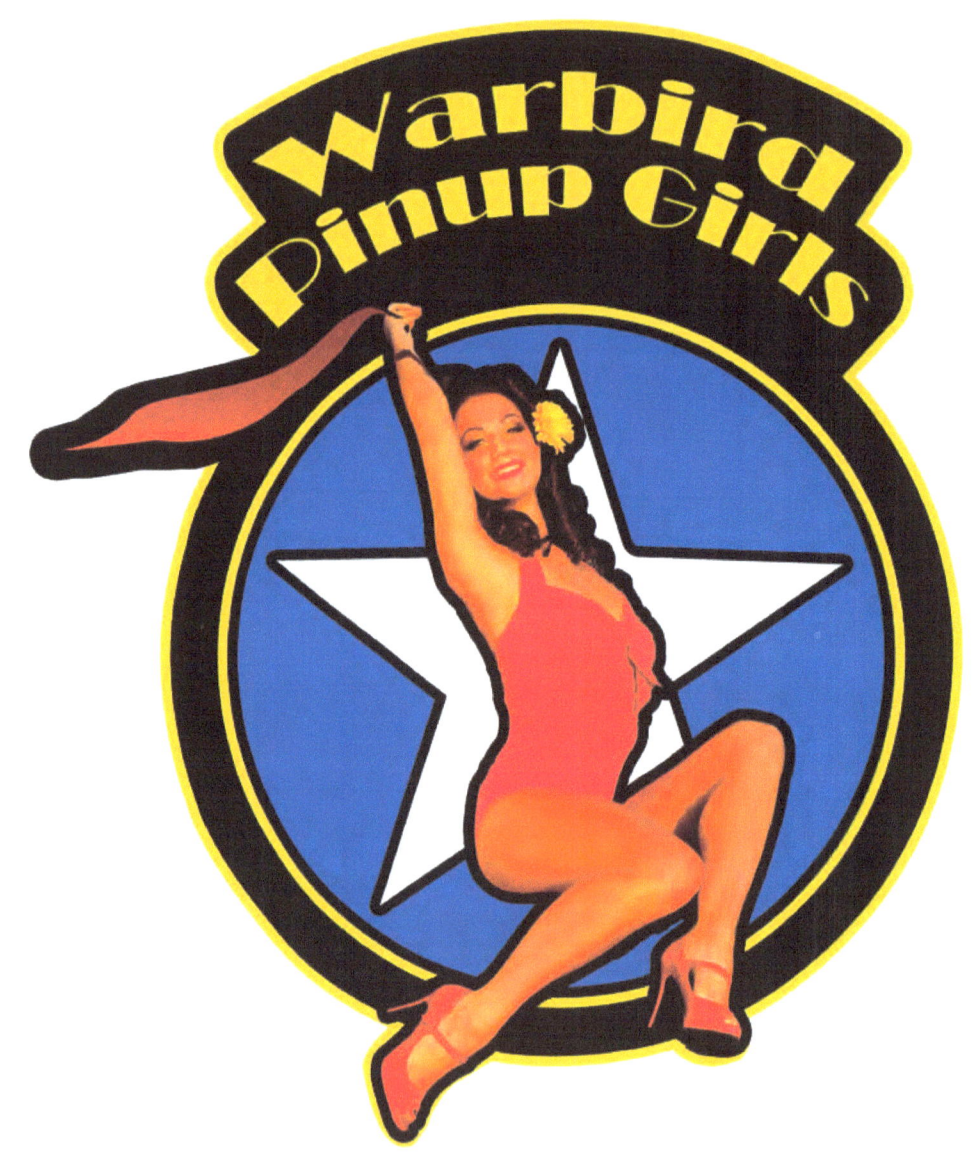

www.warbirdpinups.com

www.ingramcontent.com/pod-product-compliance
Lightning Source LLC
Chambersburg PA
CBHW050727180526
45159CB00003B/1150